537-8585 Emergency
- none

732-4441

O9-AIE-474

A MAN IN CHRIST

A MAN IN CHRIST

THE VITAL ELEMENTS
OF ST. PAUL'S RELIGION

BY

JAMES S. STEWART, M.A., B.D.

BAKER BOOK HOUSE
Grand Rapids, Michigan

Reprinted 1975 by
Baker Book House
by arrangement with
Harper & Row, Publishers, Inc.
ISBN: 0-8010-8045-2

First printing, March 1975
Second printing, December 1977
Third printing, October 1980

PHOTOLITHOPRINTED BY CUSHING - MALLOY, INC.
ANN ARBOR, MICHIGAN, UNITED STATES OF AMERICA

TO
MY MOTHER

PREFACE

THIS book is based upon a course of lectures which I delivered recently in Edinburgh at the invitation of the Cunningham Trustees. It aims at disentangling Paul's personal religion from the schemes and scholasticisms beneath which later generations have buried it. The conviction has grown steadily upon me that union with Christ, rather than justification or election or eschatology, or indeed any of the other great apostolic themes, is the real clue to an understanding of Paul's thought and experience; and I have followed this newer line of approach throughout. It is my hope that the pages which follow may have something to say, not only to Pauline students, but also to the general reader, and particularly to those who to-day are seeking —by a fresh study of the New Testament—a surer grip of the centralities of the faith and a deepening of their own spiritual life.

My thanks are due to the Cunningham Council, whose generous invitation supplied the initial impetus for this study; to the Professors and students of New College, Edinburgh, for the cordiality with which they received the lectures; to my friends, the Rev. Professor W. R. Forrester, M.C., B.D., St. Mary's College, St. Andrews, and the Rev. William Hamilton, M.A., Aberdeen, who have read the proofs; and to my wife, without whose constant encouragement the task could hardly have been seen through to an end. The preparation of the lectures and the actual writing of the book have gone on amid the absorbing and incessant claims of congregational work in a busy parish. But I would fain believe that, for one who seeks to interpret the vital religion of Paul (a religion, it should never be forgotten, hammered out in the turmoil of the mission-field), the daily pressure of the demands of the active ministry may not be altogether a disadvantage.

J. S. STEWART

CONTENTS

CHAPTER I

PAUL OR PAULINISM ?

CHAPTER II

HERITAGE AND ENVIRONMENT

CHAPTER III

DISILLUSIONMENT AND DISCOVERY

CONTENTS

xi

A MAN IN CHRIST

CHAPTER IV

MYSTICISM AND MORALITY

CONTENTS

CHAPTER V

RECONCILIATION AND JUSTIFICATION

CHAPTER VI

HISTORIC JESUS AND EXALTED CHRIST

CONTENTS

ABBREVIATIONS

EGT = Expositor's Greek Testament.
HBNT = Handbuch zum Neuen Testament.
HDAC = Hastings' Dictionary of the Apostolic Church.
HDCG = Hastings' Dictionary of Christ and the Gospels.
ICC = International Critical Commentary.
MNTC = The Moffatt New Testament Commentary.
RGG = Die Religion in Geschichte und Gegenwart.

CHAPTER I

PAUL OR PAULINISM?

WHEN St. Paul composed his great Hymn of
Praise to Love, he began by distinguishing
between the vital religion of Jesus Christ, as
it had gripped his own experience, and certain more or
less imperfect and unbalanced forms of religion, which
from that day to this have sheltered themselves under
the name of Christianity.[1] Gifts and graces which God
intended to be the adornment of the Christian community may cease to be its adornment, and become its
snare. " Though I speak with the tongues of men and
of angels "—that is religion as ecstatic emotionalism.
" Though I have the gift of prophecy, and understand
all mysteries, and all knowledge "—that is religion as
gnosis, intellectualism, speculation. " Though I have
all faith, so that I could remove mountains "—that is
religion as working energy.[2] " Though I bestow all my
goods to feed the poor "—that is religion as humanitarianism. " Though I give my body to be burned "
—that is religion as asceticism. All these one-sided and
patently inadequate representations of the Gospel, Paul
expressly repudiates. Yet history, which has been
unjust to many of its greatest men, has given us from
time to time, by a strange irony of fate, a Paul who is

---

[1] I Cor. 13[1-3].

[2] No doubt " faith," as here used, bears the specifically Pauline
meaning of self-surrender to God in Christ ; but at the moment
Paul is thinking rather of the gift of overcoming obstacles and
achieving practical results. Cf. Denney, *The Way Everlasting*, 159.

I

himself the type and the embodiment of the very things against which he strove with might and main. We have had Paul the ecstatic visionary, Paul the speculative theologian, Paul the organiser and ecclesiastic, Paul the humanitarian moralist, Paul the ascetic. Of these portraits which have appeared at different times in the course of Pauline study, by far the most unfortunate in its results has been the second—Paul the dogmatist, the doctrinaire thinker, the creator of a philosophy of religion, the constructor of a system. This is history's greatest injustice to its greatest saint. It is the blunder which has ruined Paul for thousands.

Sometimes a man's worst enemy is himself; unconsciously he damages his own influence. But Paul's worst enemy down the centuries has not been Paul: it has been Paulinism. How much this great lover of Christ has suffered by the elaborate speculative systems into which his successors have forced his glowing message, how much his influence has been harmed and his popular appeal reduced by the forbidding structure of theory and dogma beneath which his interpreters have so often buried his words of flame, it would be hard to tell. Most of the nineteenth century reconstructions of Paul's teaching, from Baur down to Wrede, sinned in this respect; and although to-day there is a new insistence on the fact that Paul's theology is first and last the theology of a converted man,[1] and that everything runs back to the day when in response to Christ's arresting hand upon his soul he had made his personal surrender, yet the shadow of Paulinism still lingers with us, and not until that shadow has been cleared away will the man come fully into his own. Like a

---

[1] Wernle, *Jesus und Paulus*, 41 : " Sein ganzes Denken ist Bekehrungsdenken."

certain famous painting of Dante, which was hidden
for centuries behind the whitewash of a common wall,
and then at last was recovered and shone out and made
the room splendid and glorious, so the vital religion of
Paul, overlaid with the systems and theologies of later
generations, has to be recaptured in our day. The great
thing is that that vital religion is still there, for anyone
who cares to seek.

I

It seems unlikely that the efforts to force Paul's
teaching into a rigid system could ever have been so
long and strenuously continued if due weight had been
given to three considerations.

The first is *the subject-matter of the teaching itself.*
What are Paul's leading themes ? The righteousness
of God, the death of Jesus on Calvary, the reconciliation
of the world, the eternally living and present Christ.
Paul at least recognised, if some of his commentators
have not, that where themes like these are concerned,
you cannot in the last resort measure and explain : you
can only wonder and adore. We may take it for certain
that any formula or system which claims to gather up
into itself the whole meaning of God's righteousness, or
of Christ's redeeming work, is *ipso facto* wrong. The
only right way to see the cross of Jesus is on your knees.
The apostle himself reminds us of that, when he
declares, immediately after one of his greatest accounts
of his Lord's atoning death, " Before the name of Jesus
every knee should bow." [1] In this world, men kneel
to what they love. And love has a way of breaking
through every carefully articulated system : it sees so
much more than the system-makers. Hence it is a

[1] Phil. 2[10].

3

right instinct that bids us beware of reconstructions of
Paul's doctrine which claim to co-ordinate every aspect
of the apostle's religious thought into a complete and
perfect whole, leaving no loose ends anywhere. It is
one of the great services of the Barthian movement to
our generation that it keeps up an energetic protest
against what it regards as a quite arrogant tendency to
push systems and definitions into that ultimate region
where God alone can speak. Such definitions merely
indicate, as Barth declares, that " man has taken the
divine into his possession ; he has brought it under his
management " ; [1] he has been forgetting that " only
God Himself can speak of God." [2] But Paul never
forgot that ; and therefore at point after point his line
of thought is interrupted by a sudden burst of doxology.
" O the depth of the riches both of the wisdom and
knowledge of God ! How unsearchable are His judgments, and His ways past finding out ! " [3] " Blessed
be God, even the Father of our Lord Jesus Christ ! " [4]
" Thanks be to God, which giveth us the victory." [5]

The second consideration which tells against the
attempt to systematize Paul lies in *the nature of the
situation he was addressing*. It was certainly not to give
a compendium of Christian doctrine that he wrote his
letters. The lines he followed, the themes he dwelt
upon, were largely determined by local circumstances.
The outcropping of a syncretistic heresy at Colossae,
the development of irregularities of practice and discipline at Corinth, the danger occasioned to the peace
of the Church by little personal feuds and rivalries at
Philippi, the Jewish attempt to shackle the free Spirit
of Christ in Galatia—these were the factors which gave

---

[1] *The Word of God and the Word of Man*, 68.   [2] *Ib.* 214.
[3] Rom. 11[33].   [4] II Cor. 1[3].   [5] I Cor. 15[57].

Paul in his epistles his starting-point and his direction. It is surely significant, as Dr. Moffatt has pointed out, that " had it not been for some irreverent behaviour at Corinth, we might never have known what he believed about the Lord's Supper." [1] We shall see later that even the epistle to the Romans, most compendious of all the apostle's writings, is not, as Bernhard Weiss and many others have regarded it, a theological treatise designed to set forth the whole of the Christian faith. But leaving particular points aside for the moment, let us reiterate the fact that Paul's religious position was hammered out, not in the study, but on the mission-field. The difficulties he had to wrestle with were not such as could be removed by abstract disquisition or by any system of soteriology. Glimpses of the stormy background against which he lived and thought and wrote are offered to us in all his epistles ; and though the physical hardships of the great missionary's lot are mentioned only casually and incidentally, we are aware, as we read, of imminent perils and dangerous currents, and of a man continually hazarding his life, not knowing what a day might bring forth. " The only saving faith," said Luther, " is that which casts itself on God for life or death " ; and Paul, whose faith was of that gallant kind, whose religion was a daily risk, who had no comfortable illusions about the forces antagonistic to Jesus in the great uproarious cities of pagan Asia and Europe where God was sending him to preach, was the least likely of men to be seduced into the intricacies of speculations remote from the urgent realities of life. One name by which Christianity, quite early in its career, came to be known was the simple expression " The Way " ; [2] and whether this description

---

[1] *Grace in the New Testament*, 157.   [2] Acts 9², 19⁹·²³, 22⁴, 24²².

originated with the followers of Jesus themselves, or was coined for them (like the word " Christian ") as a contemptuous nickname by the outside world, the important point is that it referred primarily to a way of living, not a way of thinking. Christianity, on the mission-fields where Paul's work was done, meant first and foremost (as it still means on the Church's mission-fields, and ought indeed to mean everywhere) a new quality of life, a life in Christ, God-given, supernatural, victorious. And when Celsus at a later day parodied the Christian preachers, putting on their lips the parrot-cry " Only believe, only believe," shifting the emphasis from a life to be lived to a system to be credulously submitted to, he knew himself that it was parody, the exact reverse of the truth. The first century mission Churches in Asia and Europe made headway precisely because they confronted the world with a way of life, and not with a speculative system. The situation Paul was addressing demanded a great simplicity. And that is what the apostle offered—the simplicity of Christ, the life in Christ. Deissmann [1] has pictured the consternation, the utter mystification, which would have been produced in any congregation of the Christians of Corinth or Thessalonica or Philippi, if some modern work on Paulinism in a vulgar Greek translation could have been read to them, and concludes that it would have brought them all " into the condition of Eutychus of Troas, the one man who managed to sleep while Paul was speaking."

This leads to the third consideration which ought to warn us against forcing a system upon Paul. We have referred to the subject-matter of his teaching and the situation to which it was addressed. To these we must

[1] *The Religion of Jesus and the Faith of Paul*, 155 f.

add *the man's own view of his vocation*. If it would have
startled the Christians of Corinth and Thessalonica
to be confronted with a dogmatic system, containing
carefully mapped-out sections on Anthropology, Hamar-
tiology, Soteriology, and the rest, the whole being
labelled Paulinism, it would have startled the apostle
himself even more. Paul was not aware when he wrote
that his writings were to become Holy Scripture. He
was not aware that future generations would pore over
these letters and seek to fit together every thought they
contained. Certainly the last thing that he can have
imagined, when he set himself to send a message to one
or other of his Christian communities, was that centuries
later men would be building theologies on words thrown
off to an amanuensis, as many of his words were, in
moments of intense feeling. The fact of the matter is,
Paul had no great love for systems, and very little faith
in the speculations which produce them. The wisdom
of this world [1] was such a poor thing, and mere intellect
so bankrupt, and the best possible formulations of
doctrine so pitifully short of the mark, when they tried
to measure Christ ! Once indeed Paul did conduct the
experiment of philosophizing Jesus ; [2] but his Athenian
experience was the exception which proves the rule, and
the failure of the experiment made him more resolute
than ever not to exchange the herald's calling for the
apologist's. Henceforward he was determined, as he
told the Corinthians, " not to know anything among
you, save Jesus Christ, and Him crucified." [3] It was
faith in Christ, not faith in any creed or articles about
Christ, that was " the master-light of all his seeing."
Men do not gamble with their lives, nor stake their
souls, on abstract truths and systems ; but a great love

[1] I Cor. 1[19-21], 2[13].　　　[2] Acts 17[16-34].　　　[3] I Cor. 2[2].

7

is different. They will do it, Paul did it, for that. " I die daily," he cried—a sudden flash which, to all who have eyes to see, reveals the essential difference between the Christ of Paul's devotion and the Christ of a formal Paulinism.[1] By the use of two Greek words, Deissmann has brought out this contrast most admirably. " Paul is not so much the great *Christologos* as the great *Christophoros*." [2] That goes to the root of the matter. The man knew himself charged to bear Christ, to herald Christ, not to rationalize Christ. Indeed, nothing else was possible, for the fundamental fact about the Christ of Paul's experience was that He was alive. Historical data and reminiscences you can rationalize : a living Lord you can only proclaim. There must, of course, have been considerable difference, both of matter and of manner, between the apostle's preaching and the letters which he wrote ; but let us not forget that he was a preacher first and a writer second. And both spheres—preaching and writing—were ruled by one great fact—the fact of a living, present Lord ; and by one all-decisive experience—the experience of union and communion with Him. This was the apostle's calling. This was his sole vocation and concern. This it was for which he had been born. He came to bring, not a system, but the living Christ.

We cannot, then, help feeling that had these considerations of subject-matter, situation, and vocation been kept in the foreground, the history of Pauline study might have been very different, and intellectualistic theories such as those of Baur and Holsten would never have had such a vogue. It was Holsten's belief that Paul, during his Arabian disappearance,

---

[1] I Cor. 15³¹.
[2] *Op. cit.* 189 : χριστολόγος, χριστοφόρος.

managed by a process of logic and hard thinking to fit
the death of Jesus into the framework of a previously
existing Messianic theology : the resultant was the
Pauline Gospel. That such a Gospel, a clever synthesis
of ideas, a feat of intellectual adaptation, a mere
"*gnosis* of the Messiah's death," as Kaftan in his
criticism describes it,[1] should have made Paul the
passionate herald of Christ which his letters reveal him
to have been, or should through him have come upon
thousands of lives with shattering and transforming and
redeeming power and effect, is frankly incredible. The
theory needs only to be stated to be refuted.

But far more serious than any theories of the kind
has been the tendency, on the part of Roman Catholics
and Protestants alike, to systematize Paul's teaching
into elaborate " plans of salvation," to the details and
order of which the experience of believers has been
required to conform—the tendency, in other words,
to stereotype the grace of God. The Church did not
always realize that the very use of the word " Scheme "
to describe the saving activity of God in Christ was itself
a blunder of the first rank ; and although the Christian
preachers who set God's unfolded scheme before men's
eyes, and begged them to agree to it and accept it and
so be saved, were honestly basing their appeal on Holy
Scripture and on their favourite texts in Paul, their
method was none the less leading them unconsciously
into the very danger on which Paul himself laid a
warning finger when he said " Quench not the Spirit." [2]
The plan, the scheme of salvation, was there, devised
by God, waiting for human acceptance ; the various
elements in it—predestination, repentance, faith, con-

---

[1] *Jesus und Paulus*, 38.   [2] I Thess. 5[19].

version, justification, sanctification, and the like—were set forth, each in its due place ; it was shown that this one must come in time before that other, which in turn would lead on after a due interval to the next. This was the *ordo salutis*, dogmatic Paulinism applied to life, the Church's panacea for the world.

Its strength—and it had a great strength—was not only that generations of passionately devoted men gave themselves to its proclamation, with a fervour born of their own love to Christ and of a sense of the urgent danger threatening all who remained outside of Christ. Its strength was the witness which it unceasingly bore to the solemnity of life's issues, to the glorious achievement of Christ's atoning death, and to the majesty of the will of God. But its weakness was that almost inevitably it gave men the impression that here was a rigid system to be intellectually accepted, a doctrine of salvation whose acceptance was indeed prior to, and the condition of, the experience which it described. Moreover, the logical conclusion of any plan of redemption worked out after this pattern in elaborate successive steps and stages must be the reducing of Christian experience to a drab, colourless uniformity ; and it is hard to believe that the God whose Spirit is like the wind, blowing where it listeth, ever intended anything of the kind. To regularize salvation beyond a certain point is simply to revert from the freedom of the spirit to the bondage of the letter. And Paulinism is always in danger of allowing the evil spirits of legalism which Paul cast out at the door to return by the window.

Nor is it sound to draw a hard-and-fast line, as is often done, between the various elements in the Christian experience, to posit a hiatus, as it were, between repentance and regeneration, or between conversion and forgiveness, or between justification and sanctification. It has been the determination to reduce everything in Paul to a system which has resulted in the dragging apart of justification and sanctification in a way which the apostle himself would simply not have understood. To him, they were but the two sides of a shield. God's justifying act was itself the sanctification of the sinner ; for, as Ritschl, Titius, and others have expressed the matter, it was a " synthetic " judgment, requiring, that is to say, nothing more to be added on to it, but containing in itself the germ of the new life, and creating by its own nature the moral and spiritual character which God wishes to see in men.[1] If less emphasis had been placed on schemes and systems, and more emphasis thrown on the actual realities of life, where forgiveness can in point of fact be seen any day creating goodness in the forgiven, and doing it by its own inherent power and love, many damaging blunders in the interpretation of the Gospel could have been avoided. Who that has ever experienced a great forgiveness does not know that it is the forgiveness itself, and not any subsequent effort of his own, which is the really creative thing, the moral power that secures the future ? But as it is, endless misconceptions have been caused by isolating the various elements in the Christian experience from one another, and assigning each its place on a chronological chart. It would be far truer to say—and this will be brought out at a later point in our study [2]—that in Paul's view everything is gathered up in the one great fact of communion with Christ, and that these other

---

[1] Ritschl, *Justification and Reconciliation*, 80 ; Titius, *Der Paulinismus unter dem Gesichtspunkt der Seligkeit*, 195.

[2] See pp. 147 ff.

elements of the Christian experience are not so much isolated events as aspects of the one reality, not parallel lines with gaps between, but radii of the same circle of which union with Christ is the centre.

We can see, then, that a main cause of the trouble has been the tendency of the constructors of Pauline dogmatic to read themselves back into the apostle, and to ascribe to him the thought-forms of their own age. This process began early. Harnack in a famous saying declared caustically that already in the second century after Christ only one man, Marcion, understood Paul, and that he misunderstood him ; and if that verdict is unduly severe, the element of truth in it is that after the passing of Paul and his contemporaries the work was carried on by a race of *epigonoi* who, brave men and true as they were, could not quite recapture the visionary gleam nor scale the heights of inspiration reached by Christ's greatest apostle. It is open to question whether due recognition has ever been given to the fact that many of the makers of Paulinism have worked with a totally different background from the apostle's own. " The classical theologians of the Christian Church, from Origen onwards, were Greeks, with little inward sense for the Hebrew and biblical ideas which formed the atmosphere of Paul's thinking." [1] So strongly indeed did the thought-forms of the third and fourth centuries colour the interpretation of the Pauline Gospel that our own thinking about Paul bears traces of that colour to the present day. In the same way, an age strong in law stressed beyond all sense of proportion the legal elements in Paul. At another time, the idea of sacrifice was found to be the key to everything. Each age has constructed a Paul in its own likeness. Baur

[1] C. H. Dodd, *Romans*, 60 (*MNTC*).

made Paul a Hegelian, a master of the Hegelian dia-
lectic. Ritschl made him a genuine Ritschlian. " The
heroes of old time," says Von Dobschütz scathingly,
with the apostle and his commentators in mind, " argue
and reason just like the authors of the encyclopaedia." [1]
Paul has been too big for his interpreters; and his
great comprehensive Gospel — " the many - coloured
(πολυποίκιλος) wisdom of God," as he himself called
it [2]—has been lost in a mass of partial and one-sided
reconstructions. Orthodoxy varies from age to age,
and each age has read back its own particular brand
of orthodoxy into the apostle. Often it has been
tragically forgotten that for Paul, and for the Christians
of the early Church who shared with him in the glorious
experience of passing out of bondage and self-consciousness and moral defeat into absolute release and liberty
and victory, into the very life of Christ Himself, many
of the issues which subsequent generations have magni-
fied into essentials of religion and fundamentals of
the faith must have seemed utterly trivial and beside
the point. " For that life," as Raven puts it, " the
minutiae of the theologian were unimportant, indeed
negligible : love, joy, peace, long-suffering were the
marks of orthodoxy." [3] The curious thing is that these
great central realities have scarcely been considered by
Paulinism as part of its data at all. But only when we
begin to give these things the decisive place Paul gave
them shall we be on the way to understand the spirit
of the man and the meaning and permanent validity
of his message.

Two notes of warning must be sounded here. First,

---

[1] *Probleme des apostolischen Zeitalters,* 75.
[2] Eph. 3[10].   [3] *Jesus and the Gospel of Love,* 304.

the danger of too precise definition is always great when
you are dealing with a man who thinks, as Paul so often
thought, in pictures. Thus, for example, it is a mistake
to apply the footrule of an exact theology of the atonement to the great picture in the epistle to the Colossians,
where the apostle describes Jesus coming upon the
scene as the Champion of the condemned, taking the
document that bore the charge against them and nailing
it to His cross (just as His own charge had been nailed
there on the day of Calvary), and finally making the
cross itself His chariot of victory in which He rode in a
triumph greater than any Roman general had ever
known, leading the captive powers of evil behind Him.[1]
That was how Paul, with his intuitive mind, *saw* the
truth of redemption ; and the main idea of the passage
is perfectly clear. It is when we forget that it is a
picture we are dealing with, and begin to measure and
define, that the truth as Paul saw it eludes us, and we
cannot see the wood for the trees. Similarly, it may be
questioned whether the great *kenosis* passage in Philippians [2]—which again is really a picture—can bear the
weight of theory and doctrine loaded upon it. Even the
conception of the Trinity, clothed in such baffling complexities by the analysis of later generations, presented
few intellectual difficulties to an apostle who had arrived
at it, not along the line of speculation, but through the
sheer pressure of experienced fact.[3] Between Paul's
flashing pictures and the definitions forced upon them,
there has often been a difference as wide as that between
Rupert Brooke's magic lines "There are waters blown
by changing winds to laughter " and the mathematical
formula for the action of wind on water which Eddington

[1] Col. 2[14f].   [2] Phil. 2[5ff].
[3] Cf. Gore, *Belief in Christ*, 232.

in his Gifford Lectures so daringly sets alongside them.[1]
Definition was a passion with many of the early Christian
fathers, and no doubt the rise of the great heresies made
it necessary ; but in the days when God let His servant
Paul loose upon the earth, with a heart aflame for Christ,
the forces which carried the new adventure forward on
its amazing career were not precision of doctrine nor
skill of definition, but an open vision, a ringing conviction, and a great love. And often when men have
succeeded in defining Paul's doctrine most closely, they
have lost Paul's Christ most completely.

The other note of warning is this. The practice of
isolating sentences, thoughts, and ideas from their
immediate context is nearly always fatal when applied
to Paul. " Solitary proof-texts," says Professor H. A. A.
Kennedy, " have wrought more havoc in theology than
all the heresies." [2] It is essential to keep our perspective
right. We are not entitled, for example, when we find
Paul using the ransom conception in connection with
the death of Jesus, to press the metaphor, as Augustine
and many others have done, and enquire to whom or to
what the ransom was paid.[3] Again, phrases such as
" having made peace through the blood of His cross " [4]
give no warrant for the elaborate sacrificial theories
which have been deduced from them. More serious still
is the fact that, through a failure to preserve a right
emphasis and accent, the great thought of predestination, which to Paul stood for God's sovereign freedom
and will to save, has come to be entangled with ideas of
reprobation and damnation which can only be described
as repulsive and immoral. If Paulinism has had not a

[1] A. S. Eddington, *The Nature of the Physical World*, 316 f.
[2] *St. Paul's Conceptions of the Last Things*, 310.
[3] Rom. 3[24].   [4] Col. 1[20].

few disquieting results, let us remember that Paul himself was not to blame.

Here it ought to be said quite clearly that a deep spiritual sympathy and kinship with Paul's own inner experience is the first requisite of any generation or Church or individual who would interpret his Gospel rightly. Those in whom that sympathy of experience is lacking, who have never been driven to the point of seeing that their own achievements are nothing, and God's grace everything, and that real religion begins only on the other side of the line where everything human has broken down ; who have not realized the subtle, desperate hold that self lays upon the soul, making its very piety a barrier to Christ, and its morality an offence in God's sight ; who have never stared right into the eyes of moral defeat, nor known the lyrical joy which comes when God floods a life and God's power takes control, nor felt the consuming passion of a Christ-filled man to impart his joyous secret to all the world—they are for ever excluded, they exclude themselves, from the inmost shrine of the apostle's mind and soul. For Paul's life, from the day when he met Christ face to face, was lived in the atmosphere of Christ's Spirit ; and as Weizsäcker does well to remind us, " the man who has this Spirit thinks with the thoughts of God Himself." [1] He is in a new world, a world where the calculus with which other men may be measured ceases to apply. His secret yields itself up, not to any foot-rule of theology nor any logic of Paulinism, but only to those who come to him through the door of spiritual sympathy and through the kinship of a great experience. Hazlitt speaks of some who could translate a word into ten languages, but did not really know what *the thing*

[1] *Das apostolische Zeitalter*, 113.

itself signified in any language ; a statement which the history of Paulinism abundantly corroborates.[1] Something which has been too often forgotten lies in these words which Frederic Myers puts into the apostle's mouth :

" How should I tell or how can ye receive it,
   How, *till He bringeth you where I have been ? "*

The first requisite is that spiritual sympathy of experience. That is why Luther stands out as a supreme interpreter of Paul : the men were blood-brothers in Christ. And that is why, at every point in history where the Church of Christ has been carried on some wave of revival back to reality and self-consecration, thousands of men and women have rediscovered Paul, and have thrilled again to the music of his message.

II

It was only to be expected that the arid scholasticism of traditional Pauline interpretation should lead, sooner or later, to a reaction. In point of fact, two such reactions—both of them of a rather unfortunate kind— have made their appearance.

On the one hand, the suggestion has been put forward that we should cut Christianity free from everything Pauline in it, and revert to the simplicities of Galilee. The original form of Jesus' religion, it is said, has been grossly damaged and obscured by the speculative Christology which Paul substituted for it. Christianity has had two creators, not one : Jesus was no doubt its first begetter, but His simple Gospel of trust

---

[1] Paul's faith, says Dow (*Jesus and the Human Conflict*, 305) " never had the grammarian's, but always the sinner's touch."

in the heavenly Father suffered such a radical transformation, in process of passing through His great suc-
cessor's hands and brain, that what went down to future
generations was virtually a new thing, totally different
from the Master's intention. In short, according to this
view, Paul was the arch-corrupter of the Gospel. God
sent His Son to be a solution : Paul made Him a
problem. Jesus bade men consider the lilies, and trust
like little children : Paul spoke of justifying faith.
Jesus had a cross, Paul a doctrine of atonement. Therefore, it is said, let us away from the Christ of dogma to
the Christ of history. Eliminate the Pauline elements,
and the Gospel in its pristine purity will appear. " Back
to Jesus ! " is the cry.

Now this, of course, raises the whole question of the
relationship between Paul and Jesus, between the
apostle's presentation of the Gospel and that of the
Synoptics—a question which, as Holtzmann declares,
is not only of prime interest for theology, but also of
quite decisive importance for the very fate of Christianity.[1] We shall have occasion to return to this
matter at a later stage.[2] Suffice it here to say that the
alleged twist given by Paul to the Christian Gospel,
turning it out of the channel which Jesus had intended
for it and causing it to flow in a totally different direction, is simply myth and imagination. The truth is that
all the apostle's great central conceptions—the grace
of God, the justifying of the sinner, the adoption of sons,
the death of the Redeemer, and all the rest—came to
him straight out of the bosom of Jesus' Gospel. Jesus
Himself inspired every one of them. It is repeatedly

[1] H. J. Holtzmann, *Neutestamentliche Theologie*, II. 230 n.: " Damit
war der gegenwärtigen Forschung ihre Meisterfrage und dem
Christentum eine Schicksalsfrage gestellt."
[2] See pp. 273 ff.

stated that between Jesus and Paul there was a great
gulf, and that what we call Christianity to-day bears
Paul's signature more clearly than Christ's. A gulf
indeed there was. That ought not to surprise us. How
could there fail to be a gulf, when One was the Redeemer
and the other was the redeemed ? But between the
Gospel which Jesus brought by His life and teaching and
death and resurrection, and the Gospel which Paul in
season and out of season proclaimed, there was no gulf
at all. " Nothing can be more certain than that to
St. Paul himself the question whether he or Jesus was
the originator of the new religion would have appeared
both blasphemous and ludicrous." [1] Even Schmidt's
saying that " the Gospel of Jesus is Theocentric throughout, while Paul's faith is everywhere Christocentric " [2]
is as dangerous and misleading as half-truths always are.
What meets us in the epistles is not a man creating a
new religion, or even giving a new direction to one
already existing : it is simply the Gospel of Jesus in
action, the original, authentic Gospel first changing a
man's life, and thereafter moulding all his thought.
Paul himself, in life and heart and mind, in the totality
of that wonderful experience which breathes through
all he ever wrote, is the most vivid, striking illustration
in history of the very thing which Jesus came into the
world to effect. This " man in Christ," [3] so far from
being a perverter of the simple Gospel, is the mirror
in which the true nature of that Gospel, and the quality
of its influence, have been most accurately revealed.

Accordingly, we gain nothing by seeking to cut
religion free, as some to-day would do, from everything

---

[1] J. Stalker, in *HDAC*, ii. 157.
[2] P. W. Schmidt, *Die Geschichte Jesu*, ii. 74.
[3] II Cor. 12[2].

in it which savours of Paul, and of his presentation of the faith ; on the contrary, we suffer grievous loss. Quite certainly there is no road back to the truth of Christ that way. Between Bethlehem and the Galilean roads and the hill called Calvary on the one hand, and the gates of Damascus and the heights of Galatia and the sea and the Roman prison on the other, there is an indissoluble link ; and we do not know Jesus better by refusing to admit as evidence the most complete and thoroughgoing example of His influence and the most dramatic illustration of His power. That a reaction from the scholasticism fastened upon Paul by successive generations was bound to come is perfectly clear, and we can sympathize with the feelings that produced it ; but that some should react along the line of repudiating Paul's version of Christianity altogether is lamentable. The right antidote to the excesses of Paulinism is to make closer contact with Paul's own Christ-filled spirit. It is certainly not to ignore him.

The other reaction has been of a different kind. It does not make the mistake of ignoring Paul. It accepts him as an evidence, the supreme evidence in the New Testament, of the power of the Gospel. It rightly regards the Christ-experience that lives and throbs all through the epistles as a contribution of quite inestimable value to the religion of the world. But in its zeal to remove from Paul the faintest suspicion of scholasticism, it overreaches itself. *Recoiling violently from the older view which regarded the apostle as a theologian and nothing else, it has gone to the other extreme and concluded that he was not a theologian at all.*

Now this, too, is unfortunate. " Religion without theology " is a familiar modern cry. But it is a foolish cry. Such a religion, supposing it could exist, would at once degenerate into sentimentalism. Spinoza's well-known dictum that faith should "not so much demand that its doctrines should be true, as that they should be pious," [1] will not do. Christian theology became inevitable on the day when the world was faced with the question, " What think y' of Christ? Whose Son is He?" [2] Personal experience is indeed the primary thing, the *sine qua non* of the Christian life ; but experience begets reflection. "Das Denken ist auch Gottesdienst," said Hegel. What does this event in my life imply about the God who sent it? What is the eternal reality to which the specific experience points? These are questions which cannot and ought not to be avoided. In this sense, at any rate, it is true to say that " theology is a necessity of life." [3]

Least of all men did Paul accept experience in an unreflecting way. The tendency to overemphasize the illiterate character of the early Church has obscured the fact that in the membership of that Church there were some of the best brains of the ancient world ; and for sheer mental force, apart altogether from spiritual experience, Paul's place is with Plato and Socrates and the world's giants of thought. We have already referred to his extraordinary powers of intuition : but alongside this we must now set the reflective element of his nature. Life to Paul was a unity. Salvation must also be *truth.*[4] He has to think things out. It is part of his nature. He has to see each event in time *sub specie aeternitatis.* He has to discover the great ruling principles of which the details of experience are illustrations.

---

[1] *Tractatus Theologico-Politicus*, xiv.   [2] Matt. 22⁴².

[3] W. Sanday, art. " Paul," in *HDCG*, ii. 886.

[4] J. Weiss, *Das Urchristentum*, 321 : " Das beseligende Heil muss für ihn zugleich Wahrheit sein, und die Erlösung zugleich Lösung des Welträtsels, wenn sie ihn innerlich befreien soll."

He pushes past the specific situation to the general truth. From the question of meats offered to idols he rises to a meditation on the relationship of freedom and love, from the circumcision controversy to an examination of the nature of faith and true religion. It is probable that this reflective element in Paul owes something to his pre-Christian training in the schools of Rabbinism. The discipline he had undergone as a Jewish theologian could not fail to leave a mark on a mind so keen and forceful. He knows that Christ has saved him, but that is not enough : he craves to understand this salvation in all its implications. He worships Christ, he prays to Christ : but he cannot rest till he has seen how this new worship and the traditional monotheism of his race are to be reconciled. He took time after his conversion to think things out. Before Barnabas fetched him to Antioch and the years of ceaseless strain and travel began, he had ample time to readjust his mind and heart to the revelation which had come upon him with such startling suddenness and bewildering force.[1] Direct experience is everywhere fundamental with Paul, but upon that experience his mind keeps working, working sometimes at white heat ; and to this reflection on experience, which was part of his nature, we owe some of the profoundest and most fruitful ideas about God and Christ and the Spirit which have ever entered the heart of man.

It is clear also that, apart from training and personal disposition, Paul felt himself bound by the exigencies of his pastoral duties to reflect deeply upon the Gospel committed to him. Perversions of his teaching fre-

---

[1] Gore, *Belief in Christ*, 81 : " It is probable that his sojourn both in Arabia and in Tarsus was on the whole a time of retirement and thought."

quently gained currency in his absence, and these had to be countered. Nor were all the heresies which threatened the faith the work of enemies. Some were occasioned by genuine perplexities, and by difficulties which the believing heart in every age has had to meet. These could not be summarily dismissed ; and those who were troubled by them required the most sympathetic consideration and the most careful guidance. It might happen, for example, that some members of a Pauline community, while glorying in the good news of Jesus, were still uncertain about the absolute finality of Jesus, still haunted by the questions, Are there other supernatural forces to be propitiated, other powers and influences to be taken into account ? Christ is the Word of God ; but is He God's last Word, God's final all-sufficient Word ? These were not unreal nor insincere questions. How vital they were may be gauged by the fact that they are living, urgent issues for thousands of hearts to-day. Paul felt the pressure of the problem ; he yearned to lead his converts to a fuller understanding of the faith which they themselves professed ; and his glorious delineations of the cosmic Christ, the ultimate reality of the universe, were the result. " It may be affirmed," says E. F. Scott, " that no Christian thinker since has risen to such heights of speculation as Paul attains to in the first three chapters of Ephesians." [1] This is true, provided we recognize that Paul, differing alike from Greek philosopher and from Gnostic theologian, was interested in speculation, not at all for its own sake, but only for its help in making explicit the meaning of Jesus' Lordship, and so leading to a deeper surrender to Him in faith and hope and love. Such indeed is the grandeur and sublimity

[1] *Colossians and Ephesians*, 129 (*MNTC*).

23

of the apostle's thought when he speaks of Christ's absolute supremacy in the universe, such the heights to which his conceptions soar, that some commentators, holding apparently that Paul had but little of the profound thinker about him, doubt whether such ideas could have originated with him at all, and deny the authenticity of the passages concerned. This, of course, is quite unwarranted. These passages are as characteristic as anything Paul ever wrote. Mind and heart here unite to explore the deepest things in life, " yea, the deep things of God." [1] And for this, all Christendom stands in the apostle's debt.

We have seen reason, then, while agreeing with the reaction from the rigidly scholastic view of Paul, to criticize these two forms which that reaction has assumed. The patronizing way of approving of his religion, while forgiving him for his theology, is as little to be commended as the attempt to ignore him altogether. He was a Christ-apprehended, Christ-filled man, with nothing in his religion that was not rooted and grounded in experience; but the very vividness of that experience, and its daily growth and development, made reflection on it inevitable. Always the experience was primary, the reflection secondary.[2] " He is not a ' theologian ' in the technical or modern sense of the word. . . . Yet neither is he a dreamer, indifferent to history and to reason, satisfied with emotion, sentiment or ecstasy." [3] A systematic theologian he certainly was not. No system in the world could satisfy that untrammelled spirit, that mind of

[1] I Cor. 2[10].

[2] An admirable statement of this whole matter will be found in Kaftan, *Jesus und Paulus*, 39-41.

[3] Anderson Scott, *Christianity according to St. Paul*, 2

surpassing boldness, that heart of flame. This can be seen even in an epistle so elaborate and compendious as that to the Romans. Here Paul, desiring to prepare the way for his visit to a Christian community to which he was still personally unknown, has given a summary of certain main points of his teaching, and it is not without reason that Jülicher calls this letter the apostle's " confession of faith." [1] But beyond that we cannot go : and those who would find here " a compendium of systematic theology," " a manual of Christian doctrine," are certainly mistaken. For Romans, like all Paul's letters, is ultimately not abstract but personal, not metaphysical but experimental. Written on the eve of his last journey to Jerusalem, it looks back on all he had learnt of Christ since he had given Him his heart, and gathers up the ripe fruits of those years of experience and meditation and ever deepened consecration. Passages there are, notably in chapters 3 and 4, where the voice of the theologian trained in the ways of Rabbinism seems to speak almost as loudly as the voice of the herald of Christ (though even there, for those who have ears to hear, the heart is speaking) : but when you turn the page, the trumpet tones ring out again. The section from chapter 9 to chapter 11, to take another instance, has sometimes been regarded as a rather academic discussion of the question of predestination and free-will : in point of fact, right from the impassioned utterance at the beginning, " I could wish that myself were accursed from Christ for my brethren," [2] to the ascription of glory at the end,[3] it

---

[1] Cf. Wendland, *Die hellenistisch-römische Kultur*, 350 : " Er entwickelt erschöpfend Inhalt und Wesen seines Evangeliums. . . Die Gemeinde soll wissen was und wie er predigt. So will er das Vertrauen der fremden Gemeinde gewinnen."

[2] 9^3.   [3] 11^{36}.

is a cry straight from the heart. The man who spoke like that was not interested in abstractions. He cared little, if at all, for logical structure. Romans, the most elaborate of the apostle's letters, the one which, superficially at any rate, shows most resemblance to a treatise in theology, refuses as stubbornly as any of the others to bear the rôle that Bernhard Weiss would assign to it. If it is a " compendium " at all, it is a compendium, not of abstract doctrine, but of vital religion.

Moreover, there is this to be said. You would naturally expect a man who was setting himself to construct a system of thought and doctrine to fix as rigidly as possible the meanings of the terms he employed. You would expect him to aim at precision in the phraseology of his leading ideas. You would demand that a word, once used by your writer in a particular sense, should bear that sense throughout. But to look for this from Paul is to be disappointed. Much of his phraseology is fluid, not rigid. Each of the great terms " faith," " law," " spirit," is found in a variety of meanings. Faith is a conviction of the reality of the unseen,[1] a trust in the promises of God,[2] a surrender to Jesus Christ : [3] the one word does duty for these and other aspects of the religious life, and " he glances from one to another as the hand of a violin-player runs over the strings of his violin." [4] " The law is holy," he writes, " I delight in the law of God after the inward man " ; [5] but it is clearly another aspect of νόμος that makes him say elsewhere, " Christ hath redeemed us from the curse of the law." [6] So too πνεῦμα, spirit, is used by Paul to denote the inner life, that part of human nature which

---

[1] II Cor. 5[7].   [2] Rom. 4[3].   [3] Gal. 2[20].
[4] Sanday and Headlam, *Romans* (*ICC*), 34.
[5] Rom. 7[12.22].   [6] Gal. 3[13].

wars against the flesh, something which exists even in souls that have not reached the full Christian experience ; but far deeper than this are his other usages of the word, for the divine life in men reborn, and for the Spirit of Christ from whom that life proceeds. A scientific precision of phrase is here conspicuous by its absence. Perhaps this may help to account for Holtzmann's declaration that " scarce another writer of antiquity has left his commentators with such puzzles to solve as Paul." [1] It certainly bears out our contention that the construction of a doctrinal system was not the aim of anything the apostle wrote. Greater business was on hand. Mightier, more living, more urgent issues were at stake. One thing, and one thing only mattered—a resolute, ringing witness ; for Christ was marching on.

Exactly the same result meets us when we turn from Paul's use of particular terms to his treatment of many of the great themes that exercise his thought : here too he refuses to be tied down to a rigid, petty consistency. Thus, for example, to the difficult question of the origin of sin among men he gives no fewer than three distinct answers. In one place, all the sins of men are regarded as the direct consequence, the unfolding, of one historic original sin ; [2] in another, sin springs from the " flesh," the constituent part of man's nature which objects to God ; [3] in another, it is the work of certain dark demonic forces which hold the present world in thrall, the " principalities and powers " which beset human life behind and before, against which the man in Christ must wage unceasing warfare.[4] Or take the realm of eschatology. We need only compare and contrast such

---

[1] *Neutestamentliche Theologie*, ii. 236. [2] Rom. 5[12 ff.]
[3] Rom. 7[25], 8[3]. [4] Eph. 2[2], 6[12].

passages as I Cor. 15⁵¹ ᶠᶠ·, II Cor. 5¹ ᶠᶠ·, I Thess. 4¹³ ᶠᶠ·,
Phil. 1²³, to realise the truth of Professor H. A. A.
Kennedy's dictum that, for all Paul's burning interest in
the world beyond death and the coming consummation of
God's kingdom, "he does not even supply the materials
for constructing anything in the nature of a scheme, far
less does he attempt to reach such a construction for
himself." [1] Or, to mention just one other sphere, who
would venture to ascribe to Paul a system of ethics ?
Ethical precepts in abundance his epistles contain ; his
Gospel is ethical to the core ; he will have nothing of a
religion that does not issue in a morally strenuous and
elevated life : yet he makes no scientific classification
of virtues such as the Stoic and pagan moralists of his
day loved, he promulgates no code, he discusses no
" summum bonum." For the spirit is more than the
letter, and life is more than theory ; and Paul's whole
attitude to the deep things of God and of the soul of man
is ruled by the principle which he himself enunciated,
" The letter "—the written code, the system—" killeth :
it is the spirit which giveth life." [2]

It is when we have learnt to cease to look for this
superficial consistency in Paul, this standardized, rigid
system of thought and doctrine, that we begin to discover in him what is far more important—the deep,
inner consistency of the man's religion, and the fundamental unity of all he wrote and taught. " Paul and
Plato," says T. R. Glover, " had this in common :
neither sought to develop a Paulinism or a Platonism ;
they both pursued Truth ; and to keep abreast of Truth
leaves a man little time to be consistent with himself,

[1] *St. Paul's Conceptions of the Last Things*, 21 f.
[2] II Cor. 3⁶.

and little wish for it." [1]   Paul can contradict himself,
can land himself at times in hopeless antinomy, can leap
without warning from one point of view to another
totally different, can say in the same breath " Work out
your own salvation " and " It is God which worketh in
you " ; [2] but through it all and beneath it all there is
a living unity and a supreme consistency—the unity,
not of logic, but of downright spiritual conviction, the
consistency of a life utterly and at every point filled
and flooded with the redeeming love of God.   " Christ
in me "—this overmastering experience which was
" unquestionably the core of his religion," [3] " der eine
Brennpunkt," as Johannes Weiss expresses it,[4] gives to
everything he wrote, even in the midst of his most
startling antitheses and wildest tangents of thought, a
unity far deeper than that of any logical or dogmatic
system.   " By the good faith of God," he declared
emphatically to the Corinthians, " my word to you was
not ' yes and no ' " ; [5] and in an even deeper sense
than the words in their original context held, he had
a right to say it.   In the last resort, his life and work
and preaching and writing and witness were all utterly
consistent, for they were all Christ.   " To me to live
is Christ," [6] he said : " life means Christ to me," as
Dr. Moffatt translates it.   " I determined not to know
anything among you, save Jesus Christ." [7]   It was the
very voice of the apostle that was speaking through
Luther, when he declared " We preach always Him, the
true God and man. . . . This may seem a limited and
monotonous subject, likely to be soon exhausted, but we

---

[1] *Paul of Tarsus*, 3.   [2] Phil. 2[12f].
[3] Inge, *Christian Ethics and Modern Problems*, 73.
[4] *Das Urchristentum*, 341.   [5] II Cor. 1[18] (Moffatt).
[6] Phil. 1[21].   [7] I Cor. 2[2].

are never at the end of it." " He is Alpha and Omega,"
said the early Church ; Christ, as we should say, is simply
everything in life from A to Z : that was literally Paul's
experience. He spoke of " the simplicity that is toward
Christ," [1] meaning that in this difficult, complex, and
often incoherent world the life of a true Christian would
always be conspicuous for a deep, inner coherence and
unity, an integration of experience, a simplicity of
which the secret was a single-hearted devotion and
loyalty to one Master, an undivided heart laid at Jesus'
feet. And if ever a man had a right to speak thus, Paul
had : for that undivided heart was his.

Hence we might take his own confession to the
Philippians and set it as the motto of his life, " This one
thing I do." [2] The quest for a doctrinal system, the
search for a unified Paulinism, ceases when you have
heard that. " If he had been this (a system-maker),"
declares Bishop Gore, " he would have saved the con-
troversial and critical world a great deal of trouble, but
he would not have been St. Paul." [3] No, and he would
not have been the flaming, royal spirit to whom all
generations of Christians look back with gratitude to
God. He would not have been the mighty instrument
he proved himself in God's hand for the converting
of the world. He would not have been the man who
shines as a beacon for ever because he had one master-
passion, Christ. Herein lies the true unity, deeper
than all logical precision, more enduring than all imposing systems. With utter clearness, the great day of
Damascus had revealed to him Christ as the sole meaning
of his own life and of all life, and the very centre of the
universe of God ; and all the days since then had verified
and confirmed the revelation. Possessed, from that

[1] II Cor. 11[8], R.V.   [2] Phil. 3[13].   [3] *Belief in Christ*, 83.

first glorious hour of discovery, with an overmastering gratitude to the Lord to whom he owed it, with an utter conviction that what had then happened to himself could happen to everyone, and with a consuming passion to see it happening all over the earth and to share his Christ with all mankind, he threw everything he had, everything he was, into his response to the Gospel challenge. " This one thing I do "—that is the final, the only real, consistency. Systems, dogmatisms, Paulinisms have no more unity than the shifting sands ; but Paul's Gospel, spoken and written, stands on solid rock. And that Rock is Christ.

CHAPTER II

HERITAGE AND ENVIRONMENT

THE Christian religion was cradled in Judaism. Behind it lay the amazing history of the Hebrew nation. Into the soul of it went all the idealism, the faith, the divine revelation, the providential guidance which had made that history great. Through its veins flowed the blood of generations of Hebrew saints. The Hebrew attitude to life was its inheritance, the Hebrew genius for God its birthright. Jesus came, not to destroy, but to fulfil. Yet Christianity from the first was destined by God for a world-religion. Born and cradled in Judaism, it was to leave its ancestral home and face the desperate need of the whole earth. The seed sown in Palestinian soil was to become a tree whose leaves would be for the healing of the nations. And so when God, seeking a man to herald and proclaim the Gospel of His Son, laid violent hands on Saul of Tarsus, breaking in on his life and claiming him utterly and flooding his whole being with an irresistible passion for Christ, there was a singular appropriateness about the choice. For Paul belonged to both worlds. Before ever he became a Christian, two strains had mingled in him, two influences had been playing upon him. He was at once a Jew, and a citizen of the wider world. Nurtured in the faith and ways of Judaism, he nevertheless had experience of the contact and influence of a Greek environment. Our business in the present study will be to see the man and his religion in relation to this

Jewish and Hellenistic background in which his life was set, and to inquire how far it helped to mould and determine his presentation of the Gospel of Christ.

I

It is clear, to begin with, that all through his life—after his conversion to Christianity, no less than before it—*the fact that he had been born a Jew filled Paul with an intense sense of gratitude to God.* Despised among the nations the Jews might be ; but it never occurred to the apostle, not even when confronting the most cultured and critical Greek audiences, to make any secret of his origin. Jewish lineage, he felt, was not a thing to be apologetic about : on the contrary, it was a unique cause for thanksgiving. He would not indeed boast about it, for when a man has really seen Christ and caught His Spirit (as Paul once said himself) " boasting is excluded," [1] and all that attitude of pride is finished : one thing only is left for him to glory in, the cross by which he has been saved.[2] Still he does tell the Corinthians that if his apostolic authority and his right to speak were questioned, and if it were permissible in answer to forget the Christian spirit just for a moment and " have his little boast as well as others " [3] (so Dr. Moffatt translates it, rightly conserving the playful turn of the apostle's thought), he could soon produce satisfactory credentials. " Are they Hebrews ? so am I. Are they Israelites ? so am I. Are they the seed of Abraham ? so am I." [4] Similarly, he writes to the Philippians that if he chose to rely on outward privilege (meaning, of course, that

---

[1] Rom. 3²⁷.   [2] Gal. 6¹⁴.
[3] II Cor. 11¹⁶.   [4] II Cor. 11²².

he does not so choose—but if he did) he could outvie even the Judaizing teachers themselves: " I was circumcised on the eighth day after birth ; I belonged to the race of Israel, to the tribe of Benjamin ; I was the Hebrew son of Hebrew parents, a Pharisee as regards the Law, in point of ardour a persecutor of the Church, immaculate by the standard of legal righteousness." [1] According to St. Luke's narrative in the Book of Acts, the apostle's defence before Agrippa opened with the plea, " My manner of life from my youth . . . know all the Jews . . . that in the strictest sect of our religion, I lived a Pharisee." [2] The same note is heard again in the letter to the Galatians : " I outstripped many of my own age in my zeal for the traditions of my fathers." [3] Damascus brought many great discoveries in its train, and many new convictions came to Paul as direct corollaries of the revolutionizing experience through which he then passed : one of the greatest was the discovery of a human brotherhood in which the old lines of Jew and Gentile, Greek and barbarian, bond and free, had been obliterated, and the old barriers had for ever vanished. Yet right to the end there remained clearly stamped upon his mind the thought of God's surpassing goodness to the chosen people ; and it baffled and bewildered and hurt him more than he could tell that Israel, " entrusted with the oracles of God," [4] starting with an initial advantage so huge and so decisive, should have stood back watching others, who had no such privilege, pressing forward into a fullness of life and a glory of service that she herself refused to enter. Why should this have happened ? he wonders. Why this startling disloyalty

---

[1] Phil. 3[5f.] (Moffatt).   [2] Acts 26[4f.]
[3] Gal. 1[14].   [4] Rom. 3[2].

to the God whose blessing of Israel had been so un-stinted, so royally extravagant ? Facing the tragic problem, Paul heaps up the splendours his nation had inherited, the unique privileges which ought surely to have made Judaism the first to recognize and hail its Lord : " they are Israelites, theirs is the Sonship, the Glory, the covenants, the Divine legislation, the Wor-ship, and the promises ; the patriarchs are theirs, and theirs too (so far as natural descent goes) is the Christ." [1] All this is the Jew's prerogative, his mandate straight from God, in which Paul claims a share. " I also am an Israelite, of the seed of Abraham." [2] But how much his birth and lineage meant to him may be gathered best of all from the way in which, even in his people's stubbornness and blindness and downright apostasy, he clings to them with the yearning and fervour of his soul, refusing, like God with Ephraim, to let them go. " I could wish that myself were accursed from Christ for my brethren, my kinsmen according to the flesh." [3] Hearing these words, white-hot with love and wild with all regret, words surely as moving as anything in the literature of the world, we seem to watch the centuries falling away, and Paul the born Jew takes his stand with that other great priestly and vicarious soul, the lonely Jew who stood before God on Sinai in the morning of Israel's days, and cried " Yet now, if Thou wilt forgive their sin— ; and if not, blot me, I pray Thee, out of Thy book which Thou hast written." [4] The great, human, god-like cry, wrung from Paul's heart in Romans, is the real index of what his ancestral faith stood for in his experience. To be " a Hebrew of the Hebrews "—that was a priceless and enduring

---

[1] Rom. 9[4f.] (Moffatt).   [2] Rom. 11[1].
[3] Rom. 9[3].   [4] Exod. 32[32].

35

privilege. Even to Paul the Christian, it was a gift of God.

Now the question has sometimes been raised whether that branch of the Jewish faith to which Paul belonged, namely Pharisaism, has been correctly and justly delineated in the pages of the New Testament. The general picture conjured up by the name Pharisee is clear enough. Formalism of worship, pride of goodness and of grace, an orthodoxy almost virulent in its self-righteousness, and that identification of religion with respectability which, in every age down to the present, has been a successful method of eluding the cross— these are the main features of the picture. But is this true to fact ? In its origins, at any rate, the Pharisaic party stood for a perfectly right and healthy reaction against a cosmopolitan drift which was endangering the very foundations of morality. Fired with a passion for religious independence, refusing to be swamped by the denationalizing forces of the time, jealously guarding his historic heritage of faith and morals from the destroying influence of a subtle and pervasive syncretism, the Pharisee rendered a real service, not only to his own land and creed, but to the cause of vital religion everywhere. Righteousness was his keynote, and the honour of the one true God his constant theme. So full of contaminating influences was the age in which he lived, so deadly the pressure of the surrounding paganism, that laxity of any kind could not be tolerated : rigid obedience to law and tradition was the one hope of salvation. These were the circumstances which called Pharisaism into existence, and gave it a name and a place in the world and a work to do for God : nor did it fail, even in New Testament times, to breed men of noble character and genuine spiritual insight.

But the tendency on the whole had been to move away from those first enthusiasms, away from such great centralities as being loyal to heaven and keeping oneself unspotted from the world, towards the unreality and mere pedantry of a dogmatic legalism, and the contemptuous exclusiveness which thinks it has a monopoly of all the virtues and claims vested rights in God. Substantially the familiar picture of Pharisaic religion in the New Testament is true to fact : and it is not only one of the greatest anomalies of history, but also one of the most solemnly significant of facts for every age to ponder, that the men who were, outwardly at least, the most religious people in the land, were ultimately the head and front of the opposition which compassed the death of the Son of God.

To this party, then, Paul belonged. He had indeed the very considerable advantage of studying religion and theology in Jerusalem under Gamaliel,[1] who represented Pharisaism at its best. Gamaliel was a grandson of the great Hillel, and at this time the recognized leader of the school which bore that honoured name. Between the school of Hillel, where a more advanced and liberal Judaism was taught, and the school of Shammai, where the strictest and most unyielding literalism held the field, constant rivalry prevailed : and though Rabbinic conferences were held from time to time in the effort to smooth down the differences and promote unity, the points at issue remained unadjusted. The Talmud records more than three hundred questions of law and observance on which the two schools gave conflicting rulings.[2] Proselytes from other faiths were welcomed by those who shared Hillel's views, but the followers of Shammai barred them altogether. The

[1] Acts 22³.   [2] G. F. Moore, *Judaism*, i. 81.

Mosaic Law was interpreted by the broader school in a more spiritual and more sympathetic way. And the future apostle, sitting at Gamaliel's feet, was undoubtedly in touch with what was best in the religious education of his people. The impression of those student years at Jerusalem would not readily pass away. Yet even Paul, zealous and strong-minded as he was and fearlessly sincere in following the light he had, was necessarily exposed, in his religious life, to the weaknesses and defects that inhered in the very constitution of Pharisaism. We need not imagine for a moment that religion for him ever degenerated into the mixture of self-deception and wilful, rank hypocrisy which thrust itself forward so challengingly into the path of Christ, and brought down upon the very name of Pharisee such crushing words of warning and rebuke and doom. But the essential characteristics of Pharisaism—its dogmatic assurance that the traditions of the fathers contained the whole truth and that therefore no new revelation was to be looked for, its externalizing of a man's duty to God, its glorying in good works, its legal notions of the relation subsisting between the human and the divine, its inner hardness —these things Paul could no more escape than could any other convinced and thoroughgoing Pharisee. Slowly but surely their baleful influence asserted itself, with a grip that began to choke the very life of his soul : and in the end it took the strong hands of the risen Christ to wrench him clear.

But there was one part of Paul's Jewish heritage which, from his youthful student days right on past his conversion to the very end of his life, remained an inexhaustible treasure-store of divine wisdom and blessing for mind and heart. *This was the Old Testament*. All faithful Jews were steeped in the language and thought of the Pentateuch, the Prophets, and the Psalms. The supreme instance of this is, of course, our Lord Himself : no one can read the Gospels without realizing how long and how deeply Jesus, during the silent years in Nazareth, had pored over those sacred writings in which He saw His own mission foreshadowed. Paul was nurtured in the same atmosphere, and drank deep from the same life-giving spring. For him, as for all true Jews, the Old Testament carried an overwhelming authority. Every part of it, every word of it, was the authentic voice of God. Hence any matter under debate could be settled by a quotation from its pages : for obviously when God had given His ruling, when God's own literal words had been heard, nothing more remained to be said. This completely authoritative estimate of the Old Testament was accepted by Paul without question, as can be seen from certain passages in his epistles where a single γέγραπται, " it is written," is deemed sufficient to clinch an argument and foreclose all discussion.

We cannot here attempt to analyse all the religious conceptions which gained firm possession of Paul's mind and heart as he read and studied the great Scriptures of his nation in the Jerusalem school and in his own private devotions. Suffice it to say that the two commanding truths which laid their spell upon him then, and were subsequently carried over by him into his Christian apostolate, were the dogma of monotheism and the concept of righteousness. Long before the young Pharisee sat at Gamaliel's feet, Judaism had given monotheism to the world ; but it was to be Paul's great service to show how this foundation-stone of

Jewish religion could bear the weight of the full assertion of Jesus' Lordship and divinity, and how the most unqualified monotheism and the loftiest Christology could go hand in hand. And the further idea of righteousness had so coloured all Paul's thinking, the age-long question as to how a sinful man could be found righteous before God—or " justified "—had so riveted itself upon his mind, that when in the providence of God the time came for him, a converted man, to interpret and set forth for others the inner meaning of the Gospel by which he had been converted, one at least of the lines which that interpretation was to take was virtually laid down for him in advance. It is a risky business, admittedly, to try to make old categories do duty for a totally new experience, specially when that experience itself directly negates much of the older position ; and it may be questioned whether the concepts of righteousness, justification, and so forth, which Paul inherited from Judaism, were always adequate for the purpose to which he put them. But just as it was the fact of redemption he was dealing with, so the very concepts used have, as it were, been redeemed and born again. The old categories begin to live and breathe with a vitality that Rabbinism had never put into them. Damascus meant a rediscovered Old Testament. Meanings previously unguessed now leapt out at Paul from every page. Hidden truths flashed into view. The student under Gamaliel, the trained Pharisee, the persecutor of all innovators and heretics, had always thought himself learned and adept in the oracles of God ; but Christ laid hold of him, and suddenly what he had pondered and pored over so diligently for years was a new book. Righteousness, justification, all the familiar conceptions, were still there, but shining now with a light how different, how transfiguring, how wonderful! Now at last the man had eyes to see and ears to hear, and on every page was finding living words of God which even noble spirits like Hillel and Gamaliel, master-interpreters of the Scriptures as they were, had somehow utterly missed. The saints of the Old Testament had seen God, and to Paul in his great hour outside Damascus the same vision had now come : hence there sprang up between them a vital kinship. They and he were standing together at the heart of things. Deep answered to deep, insight called to insight; and all the majesty, the spirituality, and the urgency of the Old Testament revelation have passed right over into Paul's proclamation of the good news of Christ.

Something must here be said of the influence upon Paul of the allegorical methods which the Rabbis had by this time developed into a science. Just as Stoic philosophers had learnt to adapt the *Iliad* and the *Odyssey* to their own purposes by the expedient of imposing an ethical or metaphysical interpretation upon the old Homeric myths and legends of the doings of the gods, so the Jewish Rabbis were able, sometimes with a view to edification and sometimes, it must be confessed, with less creditable motives, to make the simplest, most straightforward Old Testament passages yield up many hidden doctrines and unexpected parables. The plain, obvious meaning of the inspired words was rejected, and intricate mystic meanings were superimposed. It was an arbitrary proceeding, but to Jewish minds it was not only legitimate but divinely ordained. God Himself, so ran the argument, had buried those secrets in Holy Scripture, and they were beyond the reach of any but the spiritually enlightened ; but God meant His accredited interpreters, the Rabbis, to dig for them and find them, and share them with the less instructed. Training in this method of allegorical exegesis entered largely into Paul's curriculum, and evidences of it are not wanting in his epistles. The great passage in Galatians where the story of Sarah and Hagar is interpreted in terms of the conflict between legalism and Christian liberty illustrates the method at its best.[1] "Which things are an allegory,"[2] writes Paul after referring to the Genesis narrative, and then proceeds to draw his memorable picture of the Jerusalem above "which is the mother of us all." Another occasion where he uses the Rabbinic method with the sure hand of a master is in his christianizing of the desert wanderings of Israel.[3] "These things were our examples," he declares, using the word τύποι, "types," in the true scholastic way; and again, "These things happened unto them for ensamples"—τυπικῶς—"and are written for our admonition, upon whom the ends of the world are come."[4] Here and there, it is true, the Rabbinic technique betrays Paul into statements and sentiments which are open to serious challenge. The juggling with the singular and plural "seed" and "seeds" in Galatians 3[16] is a case in point. And some may find it hard to forgive Paul for the way in which, having quoted the old law of Deuteronomy, "Thou shalt not muzzle the mouth of the ox that treadeth out the corn," he simply sweeps aside the original intention of the command with a blunt "Doth God care for oxen?" and proceeds to deduce a divine instruction as to the maintenance of the Christian ministry.[5] This is the allegorizing tendency pushed to extremes. One cannot

---

[1] Gal. 4[21-31].   [2] ἀλληγορούμενα, Gal. 4[24].
[3] I Cor. 10[1-11].   [4] I Cor. 10[6, 11].   [5] Deut. 25[4], I Cor. 9[9 f.].

help contrasting Paul and Jesus here. Jesus too spoke about beasts of the field and birds of the air : like Paul, He drew lessons from them about God's care and love for men. But when Jesus raised the question " Doth God care for sparrows ? " it was not, like Paul, to suggest a self-evident negative, but to argue from a clear positive along the line of " how much more "— " How much more must He care for men ! " The Deuteronomy passage itself could have been used in this way by Paul to lead up to the point which he was anxious to make, and the argument *a minori ad maius* was one which elsewhere he has handled with effect : but here the allegorical method prevailed, with a result which we cannot but deplore. It ought, however, to be added that such blunders were due less to the man himself than to the recognized and universally accepted ways of the Rabbinic schools. In any case, he uses allegory sparingly, and generally only in relation to matters of secondary importance : in the central things, he is independent of such aids and speaks out of the fullness of his own heart.

Certain other characteristics of the apostle's handling of the Old Testament may be noted here. He would occasionally pile up quotations, culled almost at random from different parts of Scripture, to reinforce his line of appeal. This was in true Rabbinic style : a striking example of it will be found in the great discussion on Israel's apostasy in chapters 9 to 11 of the epistle to the Romans. In quoting from the Old Testament, Paul did not feel himself rigidly bound by the original context from which the various passages came. Thus in Deuteronomy 30[12 ff.] the great passage beginning " It is not in heaven, that thou shouldest say, Who shall go up for us to heaven, and bring it unto us ? " asserted the claims and the practicability of the law : but when it reappears in Romans 10⁶ ᶠᶠ·, what it asserts is the exact reverse—that faith, not law, is man's salvation.[1] The great bulk of Paul's Old Testament quotations are taken from the Septuagint, and in quoting from it he seems to have relied generally upon memory : inaccuracies of detail are frequent. Occasionally the inaccuracies have the appearance of being deliberately introduced to help the argument.[2] One of the Psalmists had pictured Jehovah " leading captivity captive " and " receiving gifts " among men, accepting the tribute due to a conqueror.[3] Paul, in a well-known passage, seeking to remind his readers of the wonderful spiritual gifts which the exalted Christ had poured out upon His Church, uses the Psalmist's picture and introduces it as a direct quotation with the words " Wherefore He saith " (λέγει, i.e. " it is said in Scripture," or " God says ") : yet the vital word " received " becomes in Paul " gave." [4] It may be that memory here played him false ; or it may be, as E. F. Scott suggests, that it is some old Jewish paraphrase of the Psalm, rather than the Psalm itself, which he is drawing upon.[5] Such paraphrases did sometimes come, through long use and the hallowing associations of the synagogue, to bear

---

[1] Cf. on this point Weiss, *Urchristentum*, 332. Denney, *EGT*, ii. 670: " The Apostle is not thinking in the least what the writer of Deuteronomy meant ; he is putting his own thoughts into a free reproduction of these ancient inspired words."

[2] This is asserted of both Paul and Philo by Kennedy, *Philo's Contribution to Religion*, 44.

[3] Psalm 68⁶. The A.V. " received gifts *for* men " is " an impossible rendering " (Kirkpatrick, *The Psalms*, 388). " Among men " (R.V.) gives the true sense, and Moffatt translates " with tribute taken from men." This is an instance where the A.V. has probably been influenced by a reminiscence of the Pauline quotation.

[4] Eph. 4⁸.

[5] E. F. Scott, *Ephesians*, 207 (*MNTC*).

almost as much authority as Scripture itself. But perhaps the best thing to say about all these inaccuracies, whether deliberate or not, in Paul's use of the Old Testament is that the apostle was conscious, as he himself more than once declares,[1] of sharing in the same Spirit which had inspired the sacred writers, and consequently of being free to apply their message as the needs of his own day demanded. Nothing, at any rate, can obscure the fact that the love of God's Holy Word which possessed Paul from first to last was at once an indispensable *praeparatio evangelica* for the advent of Christ to his soul, and a magnificent equipment for the work which Christ intended him to do.

When we pass from the Old Testament to the other element which entered into the Palestinian Judaism of Paul's day, namely, *apocalyptic literature*, the extent of the apostle's indebtedness is harder to assess. The tendency on the whole has been to exaggerate his debt. Indeed, the influence of apocalyptic in general on the life and thought of Judaism has probably been much overrated—notably by Schweitzer and his school. For the Rabbis themselves this whole body of literature had but little attraction.[2] Its appeal was mainly, not to cultured Jerusalem at all, but to the simpler folk of Galilee and the north.[3] Attempts have been made in recent years to piece together the jumbled, heterogeneous pictures of the apocalyptic writers into something like a coherent theology, but quite without success. At the same time, these pictures do undoubtedly disclose certain deep religious hopes and aspirations which were in the air during the period from a century and a half

---

[1] I Cor. 2[13], 7[40].   [2] G. F. Moore, *Judaism*, ii. 281.

[3] Inge, *Christian Ethics and Modern Problems*, 35 f.   Gore, *Belief in Christ*, 21 ff.

before the birth of Christ to a century after. And as Professor Welch has very cogently pointed out, we dare not ignore a literature which sprang, as apocalyptic did, out of the travail of soul of generations of men to whom life had grown dark and baffling ; a literature moreover which, in days when scribism had largely regularized religion and reduced the world to a closed system, maintained a dogged belief in the direct action of God.[1] When the Maccabaean dynasty, in which such splendid hopes had centred, passed away, and the heel of the oppressor was once more on Israel's throat, the whole nation was in danger of settling down into irremediable despair. It was to counter this growing pessimism that the apocalyptists sought to lift men's eyes to a speedily coming day when God would break in gloriously, not only to subdue the heathen world-powers, but to destroy the old order of things entirely and bring in new heavens and a new earth. Hence the root-conception of all this class of literature is the doctrine of the two ages : everything turns on the contrast between this present evil age (ὁ αἰὼν οὗτος, עוֹלָם הַזֶּה) and the ideal coming age (ὁ αἰὼν ὁ μέλ ων, עוֹלָם הַבָּא).[2] Imaginative pictures, often characterized by crude material features and strong nationalist colours, were given of the blessedness which the transition to the new world-order would bring.[3] On the day of the consummation, God's Messiah, appointed but hidden from the foundation of the world, would be revealed.[4] Not only the heathen, but the whole realm of hostile powers and angels and evil spirits, would be beneath His feet.[5]

[1] A. C. Welch, *Visions of the End*, 18, 23. Cf. Muirhead, in *HDAC*, i. 73 : " the greater the stress the truer the inspiration of the apocalyptist."

[2] IV Ezra 7⁵⁰. [3] Enoch 103 f., Baruch 49 ff.
[4] Enoch 48⁶, 62⁶. [5] Enoch 16³, 65-69.

Such were the ideas which, sometimes dimly and vaguely, sometimes stormily and impetuously, had taken possession of certain Jewish circles. And it was only natural that a man like Paul, whose own life owed everything to a sudden, supernatural intervention, should have had a kindred feeling for a form of faith in which the fact of direct action from the side of God was so steadily and so strongly stressed. But while his eschatological outlook does show clear marks of this influence, it is the general spirit, rather than any of the details, of the apocalyptic picture to which he stands indebted. The basal conception of the two contrasted world-orders meets us in the epistles ; [1] here too we read of the war with the spirits and malignant forces and hostile angels ; [2] here again we encounter the attitude of soul which keeps peering through the dark for the promised dawn of God, and cries out of its tribulation " Marana tha "—" Lord, come ! " [3] But Paul is bound to no apocalyptic scheme, and he treats the materials at his disposal with sovereign freedom. He will have nothing, for example, as Titius has well pointed out, of the nationalist spirit that haunts Jewish apocalyptic like an undertone.[4] Politics are apt to get mixed up even with the day of the Lord : but in Paul, all that is finished, and nothing remains but

---

[1] I Cor. 10[11], Gal. 1[4], Rom. 12[2].   [2] Rom. 8[38], Eph. 6[12].

[3] I Cor. 16[22]. The alternative reading—" Maran atha," " our Lord comes "—is favoured by Weiss, in Meyer's *Kommentar zum NT*, 387. Both readings are given by Milligan, *The Vocabulary of the Greek Testament*, v. 388, and by Lietzmann, I. and II. Korinther, in *HBNT*. The imperative is favoured by Zahn, *Introduction to the New Testament*, I. 304 ; Dodd, *Romans*, 167, etc. It was probably a prayer of the primitive community which became a liturgical formula for the whole Church. Cf. Rev. 22[20], Didache 10[6]. The underlying idea reappears in Phil. 4[5], I Thess. 1[10], Rom. 13[11f.], etc.

[4] *Der Paulinismus unter dem Gesichtspunkt der Seligkeit*, 47-49.

what is spiritual through and through. Moreover, it needs to be said emphatically that Paul's great thought of the eternal Christ owes nothing whatever to the picture of the " Heavenly Man " in the Book of Enoch and elsewhere : it is sheer blindness and banality to suggest, as has not infrequently been done, that a mechanical equating of Jesus with the ready-made concepts of a pre-Christian Messianism was the origin of Paul's glowing and inspired Christology. Not along any such lines was Paul debtor to the apocalyptists. What he did share with them was something different —the rapture of the forward view, the awareness of a life-and-death struggle between supernatural powers in the unseen, and the conviction that the times were moving on to God's great crowning day.

II

Up to this point we have been concerned with Paul's Jewish inheritance. But he was more than a Jew. He belonged to the wider world. Born in a Hellenistic city, and surrounded from his early youth by the varied influences of a Graeco-Roman environment, he brought with him into the Christian Church, as indeed was only natural, a wider horizon than that of the first preachers who had never been outside Palestine ; and it may be that even in his Tarsus days there had begun to stir in his heart some hint of that blunt, decisive question which later he was to fling out so challengingly, " Is He the God of the Jews only? Is He not also of the Gentiles?"[1] It is imperative, therefore, if we are to gain a true understanding of the apostle, to see him as a Jew of the Diaspora, and to watch how he reacted to the

[1] Rom. 3[29]

thought and culture and religion of the world around him.

The dispersion of the Jews among the nations, beginning with the forcible deportations under Tiglath-Pileser and Sargon, Sennacherib and Nebuchadnezzar, had proceeded on more peaceful lines after the Hellenising campaigns of Alexander had unified and opened up the world. The marriage of Europe and Asia—such was Alexander's declared ideal ; and Jewish trade and commerce were not slow to take advantage of the new opportunities thus offered. When it fell to Rome to take up the task that Alexander had laid down, the process of unification was still further developed : frontiers once closed to Judaism now stood invitingly open. The day of separate, self-sufficient, antagonistic nations, gazing suspiciously at one another across bristling defences, was done. All the way from the Atlantic to the Caspian, from Britain to the Nile, from Hadrian's Wall to the Euphrates, the Roman Peace held the world. From end to end of the Empire ran the great highways, triumphs of Roman engineering. Even barriers of language had largely vanished ; for while each province still had its own tongue or dialect, everywhere the people were bilingual and all knew Greek. This was the world into which the Jew penetrated, greatly aided by Roman toleration, which had granted to his worship of Jehovah all the rights and privileges of a *religio licita*. Jewish settlements quickly sprang up everywhere. The New Testament itself bears impressive witness to the fact that in every town of any importance which the Christian preachers visited, alike in Asia and in Europe, they found a Jewish colony : and this gave them a useful point of contact for the initial stages of their mission. According to Philo, there were over a million Jews in Egypt alone : two of the five districts into which Alexandria was divided were predominantly Jewish. Even Rome had its Jewish quarter. In the capital, indeed, their presence was not always welcome, and from time to time attempts were made to evict them : one such edict of expulsion, promulgated by the emperor Claudius, is referred to in the Acts of the Apostles, and corroborated by a famous sentence in Suetonius.[1] But they were too influential to be thus summarily dismissed, and when they began to find friends and adherents within the court itself their position was more or less secure.[2] The distance of these scattered Jewish communities from Jerusalem and the Temple, the headquarters of their ancestral faith, necessitated a change in the centre of gravity of their religion : it shifted from the Temple to the local synagogues. These gradually became the real home of their worship. Indeed, as the Book of Acts makes clear, so vital was the place which these new centres of common devotion and public instruction came to hold in the life of Diaspora Judaism that special synagogues had to be built in Jerusalem itself for the benefit of pilgrims and others temporarily residing in the city.[3] It was in the synagogue of Tarsus that the glory of the one true God and the majesty of the Mosaic Law first laid their spell upon Paul's young mind and heart.

Now when a religion is transplanted from the land of its birth to alien soil, when it is exposed to a totally different mental climate and spiritual temperature,

---

[1] Acts 18[2]. Suetonius, *Claudius*, 25 : " Judaeos impulsore Chresto assidue tumultuantes Roma expulit." The meaning of " impulsore Chresto " is uncertain : see R. J. Knowling, *EGT*, ii. 384.

[2] Poppaea, Nero's wife, befriended the Jews.

[3] Acts 6[9].

there is always the possibility that in the course of a few generations it will change its character. Little by little the new atmosphere begins to tell. Diaspora Judaism seems early to have awakened to this danger, and resolute steps were taken to deal with it. Strict rules were laid down by the Rabbis to regulate the intercourse of Jews abroad with the pagan society around them. No blurring of the lines of difference was to be allowed. With a view to preserving Jewish identity and strengthening the national and religious self-consciousness, careful organization and close communication with the mother Church were enjoined. Temple dues were paid annually, and pilgrimages to Jerusalem were frequent : St. Luke's description of the international character of the crowd present on the day of Pentecost speaks for itself.[1] But what mainly differentiated the Jew in foreign lands from his neighbours, and prevented him from being levelled down to the ways of the Hellenistic world, was his observance of the Law. The keeping of the Sabbath, the distinction between clean and unclean meats, the rite of circumcision, these things marked him off ; and as long as he stressed these with might and main, and remained loyal to them in soul, he could dare the subtle, encroaching influence of his environment to do their worst. Foursquare he stood, dogged in his isolation, and proud of it ; able, like Nehemiah long before him, to say, " I am doing a great work, so that I cannot come down." [2]

That all this stringency of regulation was cordially approved by the young Jew of Tarsus is put beyond doubt by the passages already referred to in Acts and the epistles where he gives reminiscences of his early days.[3] No one could rival him in his determination to

[1] Acts 2[5ff.].   [2] Neh. 6[3].   [3] Acts 26[4f.], Phil. 3[5f.]

remain " unspotted from the world." To use the words of the high-priestly prayer of Jesus, he was *in* the world of Hellenism, without being *of* that world. Its ways he renounced, its wisdom he despised, its literature he largely ignored. Scholars who, on the basis of such fugitive literary allusions and quotations in Paul as " We are also His offspring " [1] or " Evil communications corrupt good manners," [2] immediately declare that he had studied Cleanthes and Menander are committing themselves to a statement which is highly precarious, if not absurd. Tags like these tell nothing : not everyone who says " God tempers the wind to the shorn lamb " has read Laurence Sterne. If ever a Jew of the dispersion strove to be loyal to the land and law of his fathers, that Jew was Paul.

It must, however, be remarked that Diaspora Judaism, for all its aloofness, remained a real missionary force in the world. If it could be said even in Palestine that the scribes and Pharisees would " compass sea and land to make one proselyte," [3] the Jew abroad was certainly no less aggressive. His success as a missionary was due, in the main, to the extraordinary fascination which a lofty monotheism will always exercise upon the better elements in a pagan society which are growing weary of polytheism and its morally degrading accompaniments. It is not in the least surprising that subsequent generations saw an abundant fulfilment of the great, memorable prophecy of Zechariah—" It shall come to pass that ten men, out of all languages of the nations, shall take hold of the skirt of him that is a Jew, saying, We will go with you ; for we have heard that God is with you." [4] Earnest inquirers of this kind were wel-

---

[1] Acts 17[28].   [2] I Cor. 15[33].
[3] Matt. 23[15].   [4] Zech. 8[23].

comed to the synagogue services, and soon every Jewish community throughout the Graeco-Roman world had its own circle of non-Jewish adherents. These were the σεβόμενοι, or φοβούμενοι τὸν Θεόν, so familiar to us from the Book of Acts, including in their number men and women as noble and distinguished as Cornelius and Lydia.[1] Considerable tact and sympathy marked the Jewish attitude to these potential converts. They were not hurried nor driven, but led on little by little ; and as Harnack has shown, their adhesion to Judaism " ranged over the entire gamut of possible degrees, from the superstitious adoption of certain rites up to complete identification." [2] No doubt many of them, like Naaman of old who worshipped Jehovah and yet continued to " bow in the house of Rimmon," were content with a compromise between their old faith and their new.[3] Easy terms of affiliation with the synagogue worship were available : but the ultimate goal to which Judaism sought in every case to bring them was the taking of the decisive step of full surrender to Jewish claims in the threefold ordinance of circumcision, baptism, and sacrifice. One circumstance which greatly stimulated this missionary development was the translation of the Old Testament Scriptures into Greek. It is probable enough that the making of the Septuagint at Alexandria in the time of the Ptolemies had no deliberately propagandist purpose at all, and rose simply out of the needs of a Jewish community which had more or less lost touch with the Semitic original ;[4] but once it was made, its value as propaganda was

---

[1] Acts 10[2.22.35], 13[43], 16[14], 17[4.17], 18[7].
[2] *The Expansion of Christianity*, i. 14.
[3] II Kings 5[18].
[4] Wendland, *Die hellenistisch-römische Kultur*, 196.

immense. It helped, more than anything else, to draw serious-minded pagans within the circle of Jewish influence. And the significance of all this lies in the fact that when the Christian mission to the Gentiles began, it was from these proselytes and " God-fearers " that a great mass of converts came. Paul, the Diaspora Jew, had long been in touch with them ; and now none knew better than he how to win these seeking souls for Christ.

We have seen, then, the vigour and determination with which the Jewish religion maintained its identity against the surrounding paganism. But the best defences, invincible though they may be to direct assault, are not proof against something so subtle and pervasive as an atmosphere ; and if Judaism made a profound and lasting mark on the Hellenistic world, that world did have its reactions on Judaism. That these reactions were largely unconscious ones, so far as Judaism itself was concerned, does not alter the fact that they were real and definite.[1] Continual contact with the outside world along the lines of trade and commerce and thought and social life resulted in the gradual permeating of the Diaspora with a new spirit, whose chief tokens were the passing away of Jewish provincialism and a growing emphasis on the rights and worth of the individual. Paul, like all his co-religionists

---

[1] As specific instances of interaction the following may be mentioned. There were religious communities in Asia Minor where the worship of the Phrygian κύριος Σαβάζιος and that of the Jewish κύριος Σαβαώθ had been harmonized (Cumont, *Les Religions Orientales*, 97 f.). A burial inscription from the Rheneia in Delos invokes τὸν θεὸν τὸν ὕψιστον, τὸν κύριον τῶν πνευμάτων καὶ πάσης σαρκός, which is a blending of Septuagint and Hellenistic usage (Wendland, *op. cit.*, 194). And some strange fusion of Judaism and Hellenism appears to have been partly at least responsible for the Colossian heresy (E. F. Scott, *Colossians*, in *MNTC*, 8 f.).

in Tarsus, breathed a Hellenistic atmosphere. He could not help himself. It was all round about him. His very illustrations and metaphors remind us of that.[1] Judaism might ban Greek amusements and call them of the devil, but there was something in Paul's virile nature that responded to the thrill of the Greek games and the prowess of runners and boxers in the stadium, and he writes of these things as one who had seen them and taken delight in them.[2] Nor can there be any doubt that the proselytes, who in some synagogues were actually in the majority, brought with them new ideas and different ways of looking at life and its problems which passed over into the minds of their Jewish teachers. Moreover, the very use of the Greek tongue involved a certain infusion of the Greek spirit. To some degree this can be seen in the Septuagint itself—as, for example, in the modifying of the earlier Semitic anthropomorphism ; and we have to remember that, though Paul had read the Scriptures in Hebrew, the Septuagint was his Bible. But it is in the branches of Jewish literature represented by the *Wisdom of Solomon* and the work of Philo that Hellenistic influence can be most clearly seen. The former, which Paul almost certainly nad read,[3] is the product of a remarkably keen and able mind almost equally at home in Greek ideas and Jewish religion ; while the latter, coming from one who was an outstanding contemporary of both Jesus and Paul, is a sustained attempt to show that everything best and noblest in‘pagan philosophy can be found within the

[1] Even the Greek theatre may have contributed something : Deissmann refers to an inscription marking the seats assigned to Jews in the theatre at Miletus (*Light from the Ancient East*, 446).

[2] I Cor. 9²⁴ ff.

[3] Cf. Acts 17²⁷ with Wisdom 13⁶ ; Rom. 1²⁵⁻³¹ with Wisd. 14²³⁻²⁸ · Rom. 9²¹ with Wisd. 15⁷ ; I Cor. 15⁴⁵ with Wisd. 15¹¹.

Old Testament. Philo claimed, for instance, to have
discovered the essential harmony between the Mosaic
Law and the Stoic Law of Nature. In any estimate of
Paul's preparation for his Christian apostleship due
allowance must be made for these trends in the Diaspora
Judaism in which he had been reared.[1] On his own
confession, he was " debtor both to the Greeks, and to
the Barbarians." [2] And this raises wider questions still.
For apart from the Hellenistic influences which were
already present in Paul's Jewish environment, there
were others with which his world-wide work as a
Christian missionary must have brought him in contact.
In particular, there were two great contemporary movements, each with a strong popular appeal—Stoicism and
the mystery-religions. To these we must now turn.

III

The Stoic school, founded by Zeno three hundred
years before the Christian era, had gained an enormous
prestige, and by the time of Paul its adherents were to
be found everywhere. It had largely supplanted the
older schools tracing descent back to Plato and Aristotle :
these had now lost the inner vitality of their great days
in the past, and their present leaders were quite incap-
able of rising to any Socratic heights—" mountain-
guides who could not climb," as Gercke has put it.[3]
Stoicism filled the gap, and by its combination of moral
earnestness and humanitarian spirit appealed, not only

[1] H. Bulcock suggests that Alexandrian thought had a new appeal
for Paul after his contact with Apollos (*Religion and its New Testament Expression*, 220).

[2] Rom. 1[14].

[3] Gercke and Norden, *Einleitung in die Altertumswissenschaft*, ii.
323 : " Bergführer, die selbst nicht steigen konnten."

to those trained in philosophy, but also to the popular mind and heart. The common man, no less than Epictetus or Marcus Aurelius, felt its power. Tarsus itself was a prominent centre of Stoic culture, and Strabo mentions by name five distinguished Stoic teachers who resided there. Wandering scholars and orators carried the message far and wide. It was the day of itinerant preachers (the importance of this fact for the work of the Christian apostles has never been adequately stressed), and in the streets and market-places of Asia Minor and Europe the Stoic evangelist was a familiar figure. Wendland compares him to the Salvation Army missioner in the towns and villages of Great Britain to-day.[1] The deep things of the soul, the answer to the universal quest for happiness, the need for moral reformation and spiritual rebirth, the way to victory over life and death—these were the themes on which the Stoic orator discoursed with all the eloquence and appeal at his command. It is no wonder that, in that weary, disillusioned world, men stopped to listen.

Now resemblances in point of style, language, and idea can be found between the Stoics and Paul. Salient features of the style of the Diatribes, as the Stoic discourses were called, were their rhetorical questions, their preference for short disconnected sentences, their use of the device of an imaginary objector, their flinging backwards and forwards of challenge and rejoinder, their concrete illustrations from life.[2] Paul, as we have seen already,[3] was a preacher first and a writer second; and it is in those passages of his epistles where his

---

[1] *Die hellenistisch-römische Kultur*, 85.
[2] A full account will be found in Bultmann, *Der Stil der paulinischen Predigt*, 20-46.   [3] See p. 8.

preaching style breaks through, as for example in Romans 2-3 and 9-11, that the resemblances to the Diatribe are most marked.[1] Here we meet again the dialogue with the imaginary hearer, the swift, lively repartee, the half-ironical apostrophe, the direct personal appeal, and all the other weapons in the Stoic preacher's armoury. The great Pauline sentence " For of Him, and through Him, and to Him, are all things : to whom be glory for ever," [2] has frequent parallels in Stoic literature, and might be called (as Norden has called it) " a Stoic doxology." [3] The word " conscience " ($\sigma\nu\nu\epsilon\iota\delta\eta\sigma\iota\varsigma$) which Paul uses [4] is definitely Stoic in origin, as are also the conceptions of Nature and the law implanted by Nature in Gentile hearts.[5] Here Paul comes very near the Greek preachers of morality. " Live according to Nature," according, that is, to the law of a rational universe which has become immanent in man—this was a recognized Stoic maxim ; and the Christian apostle discovers in this Law of Nature a revelation only less complete and a command only less binding than the Law of Moses itself. The speech on the Areopagus, with its references to the God who " dwelleth not in temples made with hands," who " giveth to all life, and breath, and all things," in whom " we live and move and have our being," who is not " like unto gold or silver or stone, graven by art and man's device," has a definitely Stoic ring about it.[6]

---

[1] C. H. Dodd suggests that Rom. 9-11 is really a sermon on the Rejection of Israel which Paul has incorporated in his epistle (*Romans*, in *MNTC*, 148 ff.).

[2] Rom. 11[36].

[3] *Agnostos Theos*, 240 ff. Norden compares Marcus Aurelius, *Meditations*, iv. 23 : $\dot{\epsilon}\kappa$ $\sigma o\hat{v}$ $\pi\acute{a}\nu\tau a$, $\dot{\epsilon}\nu$ $\sigma o\grave{\iota}$ $\pi\acute{a}\nu\tau a$, $\epsilon\grave{\iota}\varsigma$ $\sigma\grave{\epsilon}$ $\pi\acute{a}\nu\tau a$. (Cf. also I Cor. 8[6], Col. 1[16], Eph. 4[6].)

[4] Rom. 2[15], I Cor. 10[25], II Cor. 1[12], 4[2], 5[11].

[5] Rom. 2[14 f.]. [6] Acts 17[22ff].

Again, when Paul declares to the Colossians that all things " cohere in " Christ,[1] when he depicts Christ as the unifying principle of life, the form of expression at least is reminiscent of Stoic doctrine, and may have been chosen deliberately to bring home Christ's cosmic significance to those whose minds had already been familiarized, by the work of non-Christian preachers, with the thought of a world-soul binding all creation together. It is possible also to trace a connection between the Stoic humanitarianism which was beginning to permeate society with the idea of a brotherhood in which even slaves had rights of equality, and the great, glowing passages in which Paul proclaims the destruction of every barrier of race and class and sex.[2] And when we reflect on the deep moral earnestness by which Stoicism as a whole was characterized, an earnestness which explains Tertullian's remark, " Seneca saepe noster " [3]—Seneca often on our Christian side, one of ourselves—it is surely not surprising that Paul should have acquainted himself with their general outlook and gained a working knowledge of their beliefs : the surprise would have been if he had failed to do so.

That the apostle, then, knew the main Stoic trends of thought, and that here and there he has availed himself of their ideas, seems to the present writer quite certain. The Stoic's " humanitas," his belief in a divine principle or λόγος, his practice of self-examination (σκέψαι τίς εἶ, Epictetus used to say), his call for inward renewal (Seneca speaks of " transfigurari," Marcus Aurelius of ἀναβιῶναι), his stringent criticism of contemporary society, his advice as to the mutual exchange

---

[1] Col. 1¹⁷. συνέστηκεν is a Stoic term.
[2] Gal. 3²⁸, Col. 3¹¹ ; cf. I Cor. 12¹³, Eph. 4⁴.
[3] De Anim. 20.

of spiritual experiences between kindred souls, his habit
of prayer—these and other similar features predisposed
the Christian preacher to see in Stoicism one of the lines
along which paganism was unconsciously being prepared for Christ. At the same time, Paul's debt to Stoic
ideas and terminology must not be overestimated. To
say that his epistles show a knowledge of ideas which
were in the air when he was writing does not at all imply
dependence. It certainly does not imply that Paul had
ever attended lectures in a Stoic school. It simply
implies that the man was intellectually awake. In any
case, theories of dependence must fall to the ground
before the fact that Stoicism itself, for all its nobility
and earnestness, was in certain fundamental and essential
aspects the direct antithesis of the Gospel which Paul
was charged to preach. It is important to notice what
these differences were.

One quite vital difference was this. Paul preached
a historic religion, rooted and grounded in the historic
events of the Incarnation, the Cross, and the Resurrection : the Stoic teachers preached pantheism, a religion
with no roots in history at all. At the centre of Paul's
devotion was a personal God, once for all revealed in
Christ : at the centre of Stoic devotion was a dim, ill-
defined Something, world-spirit, fate, destiny—call it
what you will. Very significant is the well-known
passage in Justin Martyr's *Dialogue with Trypho*, where
he tells how once in his early life, seeking help and
guidance, he had gone to a Stoic philosopher ; but he
turned away in despair when he found that the man
was quite vague about the first article of all religion—
God.[1] Paul speaks of the πνεῦμα ἅγιον, and Seneca
of the " sacer spiritus " ; but the Stoic Holy Spirit, a

---

[1] *Dialogue with Trypho*, 2.

mere principle pervading creation, an almost physical substance extended throughout the universe and having the individual souls of men as its particles, is worlds apart from the Spirit which in Paul cries " Abba, Father." Stoicism suffered from the weakness which has been the doom of all pantheistic systems from the beginning until now : it could speak of a God within, but it could offer no God without. Tὰ ἐπί σοι, " the things in thine own power "—such was Epictetus' watchword. The subjectivism against which in our own generation the prophet voices of Barth and Brunner have been raised was the very hall-mark of Stoic religion. Man was thrust in upon himself for salvation : his, not God's, was the initiative. In short, there was no doctrine of grace. The one thing which to Paul was paramount, the one glorious truth which Christianity existed to proclaim, was nowhere in Stoicism at all. This alone rules out any theory of dependence.

But there are further considerations which should warn us against overestimating Stoic influence on Paul. It is clear, for instance, that the quality of ἀπάθεια, so dear to Stoic hearts (which has given us, significantly enough, our English " apathy "), had but little appeal to a man whose fervent sympathies would sometimes burst out in an impassioned " Who is weak, and I am not weak ? Who is offended, and I burn not ? " [1]—a man who, when speaking of " patience and long-suffering," gallantly added the very un-Stoic expression " with joyfulness." [2] Again, we must not make the mistake of identifying Stoic and Christian humanitarianism. The point of contact here has been referred to above : the difference lay in motive. When the Stoic spoke of brotherhood, he meant that all men had

[1] II Cor. 11²⁹.   [2] Col. 1¹¹.

the capacity of being drawn into one form of culture which would pervade the world ; but when the Christian spoke of brotherhood, he was thinking of something less intellectual, more spiritual, a love binding all together—without any reference to culture—in the great family of the sons of God.[1] It is deeply significant that in apostolic usage the words ἔρως, φιλία, φιλανθρωπία, gave way eventually before the great Christian word ἀγάπη. Once again, the Stoic claim to be αὐτάρκης, self-sufficient, self-controlled, always had something grim and strained about it : Paul uses the word once—but with what a difference ! " I have learned," he says, " to be αὐτάρκης,"—immediately adding, to show where his secret lay, " I can do all things through Christ which strengtheneth me," [2] the αὐτάρκεια, that is, not of self-control, but of Christ-control. " What then ? " asks Epictetus in one place, " is it possible here and now to be faultless ? Impossible ! But this is possible—to have ever been straining every energy towards the avoidance of sin." [3] A fine sentiment, without doubt—the word of a real fighter, thoroughly characteristic of the Stoic outlook at its best. But it is a different world entirely that breaks upon you with the cry " Now thanks be to God who makes my life a constant pageant of triumph in Christ ! " [4] Clearly this second fighter has no need of any weapons borrowed from the first.

The statement is sometimes made that Stoicism bequeathed to Paul a dualistic outlook upon life. In answer to this, two things must be said. On the one hand, a dualism of a metaphysical kind (and it is this

---

[1] For this distinction cf. Wendland, *Die hellenistisch-römische Kultur*, 232.

[2] Phil. 4[11-13].   [3] Epict. iv. 12.   [4] II Cor. 2[14].

that Stoicism represents) is entirely lacking in Paul : it simply does not interest him.[1] On the other hand, the apostle's practical and ethical dualism, appearing in his contrast between the spirit and the flesh, was the outcome, not of theory or study or borrowing, but of his own hard and bitter experience at the hands of life—the experience which we find mirrored so vividly in Romans 7. Of the half contemptuous estimate of the body in which Stoic dualism issued, Paul shows not a trace ; and when the Authorized Version makes him speak of " our vile body," [2] we can only say that it is thoroughly misleading for modern ears. " The body that belongs to our low estate " is what he intended.[3] How far he was from following the Stoics here is made evident by the challenge he flings out to the Corinthians, a challenge which may indeed have been aimed precisely at those who had come too much under Stoic influence, " Know ye not that your body is the temple of the Holy Ghost which is in you ? Glorify God in your body." [4]

Most crucial of all, however, is the fact that Stoicism, worked out to its logical conclusion, is a religion of despair. Now Paul knew this. There were evidences of it all around him. Tens of thousands of souls were seeking release and self-conquest and victory over the world, but Paul could see with piercing clearness that the lines which the Stoic quest for these things was following could never by any possibility lead to the peace and freedom which he himself had actually found in Christ. It was on a wrong track altogether : and was Paul, realizing this, likely to borrow much ?

---

[1] Titius, *Der Paulinismus unter dem Gesichtspunkt der Seligkeit,* 249.
[2] Phil. 3²¹.   [3] So Moffatt.   [4] I Cor. 6¹⁹ ᶠ.

What could the religion of frustration give to the religion of fulfilment ? Across the pages of Seneca, Epictetus, and Marcus Aurelius the shadow lies. Beneath their bravest words the feeling of futility lurks. What is God, after all, but just Fate—εἱμαρμένη ? [1] And what can man do, caught in the toils of a harsh determinism, but bow his head and submit ? Nor can he look forward with any lift of the heart to what may come hereafter, for immortality too has slipped away ; and Epictetus could only bid a father kissing his child remember that it was a mortal thing he loved, and whisper while he kissed " To-morrow thou wilt die." This was the direction in which Stoicism had its face ; and the road led—as Paul saw—straight out towards unyielding despair. We grant that here and there he availed him-self of Stoic terms and ideas. We grant that in these he could find a point of contact with his readers. We grant that he accepted the Stoic message as in some sense a schoolmaster to lead lost souls to Christ. But we shall not be inclined to overestimate the Stoic's contribution to the mind of the apostle when we remember that, whereas the former was living in a twilight deepening into midnight, the latter had already seen the day break and the shadows flee away.

IV

We turn, finally, to Paul's alleged debt to the mysteries. It is here that the " religious-historical " school claims to have produced the most revolutionary results. This school, of which Gunkel's *Schöpfung und*

---

[1] Gercke points out that Vergil, *Aeneid* i. 262, with its reference to " fatorum arcana " is " ganz stoisch " (*Einleitung in die Altertums-wissenschaft*, ii. 345).

Chaos was the protagonist for the Old Testament and Bousset's *Kyrios Christos* for the New, represents undoubtedly one of the most important developments of Biblical study. In particular, it has set the whole question of Christian origins in a new light. Formerly it was taken as axiomatic that early Christianity was an isolated phenomenon, quite without affinities in the world to which it came. But now it has been related to its environment. A multitude of contemporary faiths spoke, like the Gospel, of redemption and salvation. Everywhere hearts were hungry for what Christ could offer. The age was " excessively religious," as Paul told the Athenians.[1] So the Gospel has been set in its historic background. But the process has not been unattended with danger. Certain leaders of the religious-historical school, in the exuberance of the new method, have pushed it much too far. The pendulum has swung right across. Once it was held that everything in Christianity was new : now parallels are found everywhere, and nothing is new. Christianity dissolves into its Hellenistic environment, and all that seemed fresh and original and God-created simply vanishes away. Now it is in relation to Paul and the mystery religions that the most startling results have been obtained. Paul, professedly a " Hebrew of the Hebrews," becomes a " Hellenist of the Hellenists." His chief affinities are found to be with the syncretistic Oriental cults. Jesus, it is said, preached an ethical redemption, but later Christianity, under Paul's Hellenizing influence, preached a metaphysical redemption. Jesus, who came as a prophet and teacher, was raised, again by the same influence, to the rank of divinity. Strange excesses these may seem, but they involve a crucial issue. Did

[1] Acts 17²², δεισιδαιμονεστέρους.

65

Paul come in as an interloper and innovator, and graft
mystery ideas upon the simple Gospel of Jesus and
of primitive Christianity, thus changing the essential
character of the Gospel—or was he loyal to his Master ?
" Is he to be explained," as Wernle demands bluntly,
" from the underworld of ancient magic, or from the
standpoint of spiritual religion ? " [1]

On the general question of the influence of the pagan
cults in the early centuries, there are three facts which
have never been sufficiently stressed. The first is that
*the Church of those centuries consistently refused to
make any terms whatever with the syncretistic religions.*[2]
The great attraction of Isis, Cybele, Mithra and the
rest was their accommodating spirit : they were quite
content to live together and share the honours. But
the young God with the nail-prints in His hands would
not live together or share the honours with any. There
might be, as Paul put it, " gods many and lords many ;
but to us "—note the emphatic challenge of the ἡμῖν
—" to us there is but one God—the Father, and one
Lord—Jesus Christ." [3] In other words, what communion had Christ with Dionysus, or the love of Calvary
with the love of Aphrodite ? " No terms with syncretism " was from the first the Church's spirit.

The second fact is that *it was precisely this refusal
of the Church to syncretize which led to the great
persecutions.*[4] If Loisy and his followers are right, if
Christianity is just another mystery religion, then the
blood of the martyrs is inexplicable. When Isis and
Cybele came to Rome, they were welcomed with open

[1] *Jesus und Paulus*, 67.
[2] Inge, *Outspoken Essays*, ii. 52.
[3] I Cor. 8[5f].
[4] This is admirably brought out by E. F. Scott, *The Gospel and
its Tributaries*, 276.

arms. But when Jesus of Nazareth came, Rome girded herself to fight Him to the death. It was because the Church under no circumstances would play the game of syncretism that the Church, like its Lord, was crucified, dead, and buried. And it was because of the same refusal that the Church—again like its Lord—survived death, and broke from the tomb, and went to work in the world.

> " The men of the East may spell the stars,
>   And times and triumphs mark,
> But the men signed of the Cross of Christ
>   Go gaily in the dark."

The third fact is that *it was the difference, not the familiarity, of the new religion that impressed the pagan world*. A famous passage in Tertullian, in which the autobiographical note is clear, illustrates this : " Every man who sees this great endurance is filled with questioning. He is on fire to look into it, and find its cause ; and when he has found it, immediately he follows it himself." [1] And the unknown author of the Epistle to Diognetus represents the outside world as wondering " what this new society, this new interest, is which has come into human experience, now and not before." [2] It is hard to see why the twentieth century should force upon the first and second centuries parallels which they themselves would not have recognized. Even the syncretizing pagan recognized in Christianity a new thing on the earth.

Turning now to the mysteries themselves, to which Paul is said to have owed so much, we find that definite data about their doctrines and rites are scantier than

---

[1] *ad Scapulam*, 5.   [2] *Ep. ad Diognetum*, 1.

we could have wished. That their influence was widely
diffused is indeed well known : communities for the
worship of Egyptian and Phrygian deities existed all
over the Empire at the beginning of the Christian era.
In all the great centres of population where Paul
founded his Churches, these cult-associations were also
at work. But literary remains are very scarce. This
indeed might have been expected from the fact that the
initiates were bound to secrecy. " I would tell you,"
says Apuleius, " were it lawful for me to tell you ; you
should know it, if it were lawful for you to hear. But
both the ears that heard these things, and the tongue
that told them, would reap the evil results of their
rashness." [1] Chronology, too, is a problem, and in
many cases it is quite impossible to say with any certainty whether a particular mystery rite was contem-
poraneous with Paul or emerged later. The famous
ceremony of the " taurobolium," for example, is sometimes adduced as offering a striking parallel to the
Christian conception of dying to the old life and rising
to life eternal ; but this is quite illegitimate, for though
the ceremony itself may have originated early, it was
at first regarded merely as a sacrifice, and the idea of
the rebirth of the initiate came to be associated with
it only as a comparatively late development. Moffatt
characterizes the efforts of Reitzenstein and Bousset to
read back the main mystery doctrines into the first
century as " more ingenious than convincing." [2] Moreover, the whole matter is further complicated by an
apparent absence of any logical coherence in the ideas
with which these religions worked. Take one illustration
of this—the idea of communion with the deity. Here

[1] *Metamorphosis*, xi. 23.
[2] *Grace in the New Testament*, 52.

a crude, coarse materialism and a spiritual mysticism were inextricably mixed. The methods of attaining communion with the deity ranged from the devouring of the flesh of a bull and from all manner of wild frenzies induced by grossly sensuous means, through the calmer visions of a contemplative ecstasy and the regenerating influence of divinely communicated revelations, up to the blessedness of a mystic trance and incorporation in the life of the eternal spirit : all these strata are present, and it is almost impossible to disentangle them.

Still, the general aim of the mysteries was clear enough.[1] Behind them all lay the age-long yearning for salvation, liberty, rightness with God. Fate, and Fate's worst terror—Death—these were the enemies. Into this situation came the mysteries, offering a regeneration which would draw death's sting and confer immortality. The way to this regeneration was through direct contact with the god, resulting in a change of nature—or deification—partly physical and partly spiritual. Surface resemblances to Christianity are here manifest ; and probably Wendland is right in his opinion that the cults would have welcomed Jesus as a powerful syncretistic ally.[2]

Prominent among the religious influences of the Hellenistic world were the State mysteries of Eleusis, where a passion-play dramatizing the recovery of Persephone from the underworld was used to foster the assurance of immortality.[3] But the cults of Cybele and Isis came to have an appeal and a fascination which the State mysteries lacked. At Eleusis the celebrations,

[1] H. A. A. Kennedy, *St. Paul and the Mystery Religions*, 199 f.
[2] *Die hellenistisch-römische Kultur*, 167.
[3] E. Rohde, *Psyche*, i. 278 ff.

being really of the nature of a national festival, lacked warmth and intimacy; and this the Oriental cults supplied. The centre of the Cybele cult was the myth of the restoration to life of the beloved youth Attis, and the story was enacted in the ritual and carnival of the annual spring-festival. Much of the ritual was flagrantly barbaric; and when we read about the delirious dances, the gashing with knives, the orgies of licence that were tolerated and even encouraged, we begin to realize that the significant thing about the relationship between the Cybele-Attis cult and Hellenistic Christianity was not any superficial resemblance, but their quite startling difference. The Isis-Serapis cult was on a higher plane. Descended directly from the ancient Egyptian worship of Osiris, it had a lofty liturgical tradition behind it, and a moral tone to which the worship of the Phrygian goddess could never lay claim. Thanks to Apuleius and his famous account, in the *Metamorphosis*, of the initiation of Lucius, we can estimate fairly accurately the force and appeal of the Isis Mysteries.[1] Only after long prayer and fasting and ascetic preparations was the candidate for initiation accepted. Careful examination of heart and cleansing of spirit were demanded. Gradually the initiate was led on to the moment of vision (ἐποπτεία), and to the crowning experience of identification with the deity. This spiritualizing of religion, which can be traced in the Isis-cult, was carried a stage further in the Hermetic mystery literature, where we find the conception of regeneration apart from external ritual, and where deification occurs not through outward observance but

---

[1] Kennedy cogently points out that though this account dates from the middle of the second century A.D., it presupposes a long tradition behind it (*St. Paul and the Mystery Religions*, 69).

by attaining to the knowledge (γνῶσις) of God.[1] It is easy for us to understand the powerful influence which the Oriental cults wielded when they emerged into the Graeco-Roman world. They appealed by the very atmosphere of mystery surrounding them, by their exotic flavour, and by the dazzling, spectacular experiences they promised to their initiates. But above all, they appealed by the new hope they kindled in disillusioned hearts, by the gift of immortality they offered, and by their cry to a world sunk in winter and weariness that springtime and the singing of birds had come.

What, then, was Paul's relation to the movement as a whole ? On the positive side, three facts are important. It is clear, first, that the presence, on the fringes of Diaspora Judaism, of those " God-fearers " or proselytes to whom reference has already been made, would bring Paul into direct contact with the main currents of religious thought and practice of the peoples among whom his missions were carried on. Many of the converts were initiates of the local cults. Some of them, as the history of the Colossian heresy would suggest, carried part of the jargon of the cults over into their Christianity.[2] We see here one channel at any rate along which a working knowledge of the mystery religions came to the apostle. Second, due weight must be given to Paul's own words to the Corinthians—" I am made all things to all men, that I might by all means save some."[3] To Paul as a preacher, it was essential to know the background of his hearers' thinking, and to be able to meet them on their own

---

[1] R. Reitzenstein, *Die hellenistischen Mysterienreligionen*, 136 ff.
[2] E. F. Scott, *Colossians*, 8 (in *MNTC*).
[3] I Cor. 9[22].

ground : ideas familiar to an audience born and bred in a Hellenistic atmosphere would be turned to the service of the Gospel. Finally, it must not be forgotten that fundamentally the mysteries at their best and the Christian Gospel were appealing to the same deep human instinct—" My soul thirsteth for God." Philo might call the mysteries " claptrap and buffoonery," [1] but there was more than that in them. " An old, rich world of culture in its death agony, in its yearning for a new creation and a second birth, in its ever restless, ever unsatisfied search for God—this is the picture we have of paganism in its decline." [2] The babel of voices in that dying world and the clamour of its competing religions may have drowned the voice of the Spirit : but Paul with his ear to the ground heard something deeper, something passionate, almost pathetic in its passion, the cry of the souls of men for that very Christ through whom, in the sudden glory of Damascus, his own restlessness had found a perfect rest. And with the Hellenistic religions this was his third and best point of contact.

But granting all this, we should be well advised to go warily in estimating Paul's debt. And that for three reasons. To begin with, *can we say with any certainty that Paul was deeply versed in Hellenistic religious literature ?* Admittedly he was familiar with mystery terms which were current and in the air at the time when he was writing, and occasionally he turned these to his own use ; but to postulate a thoroughgoing acquaintance on his part with mystery literature, or to suggest that his use of current religious terms necessarily implies a borrowing of thought and idea as well

---

[1] *De Specialibus Legibus*, i. 319.
[2] Wendland, *Die hellenistisch-römische Kultur*, 186.

as expression, is a different matter. Here Reitzenstein and his school have all the probabilities against them, and have jumped to conclusions in a perfectly arbitrary way.

More important, however, is a second consideration, namely, that *it is unnecessary and unsound to trace back to the mystery religions Pauline conceptions whose true ancestry might more profitably be looked for in the Old Testament.* Now this is quite crucial. It was in Judaism that Christianity had its roots ; and therefore the exegesis which turns to Hellenistic sources for the genesis of Paul's regulative ideas, without having in the first instance attempted at least to trace the origin of these ideas in the Old Testament, is entirely unscientific. Two illustrations of this may be mentioned. The early Church, as we know, applied to Jesus the title κύριος, Lord. Now Bousset, in his famous book *Kyrios Christos*, laid it down dogmatically that this was derived directly from the usage of the cults, and came into Christianity by parallelism with such phrases as " our Lord Serapis." [1] But why Paul should be indebted to the mysteries for a term with which his own Bible, the Septuagint, was laden, is not explained. What are the facts ? The name Lord was being given to Jesus by the primitive community before Paul had ever appeared on the scene at all.[2] The great Psalm beginning, " The Lord said unto my Lord, Sit thou at my right hand," was already being interpreted in a Messianic and Christian sense.[3] " Jahveh " in the Hebrew Scriptures had become κύριος in the Greek translation : the phrase Χριστὸς κύριος was the Septuagint rendering

---

[1] *Kyrios Christos*, 84 ff. Cf. C. Clemen, *Primitive Christianity and its Non-Jewish Sources*, 337.

[2] Acts 2³⁶.   [3] Ps. 110 ; cf. Acts 2³⁴.

of " the Lord's anointed." [1] This phrase occurs also in
the *Psalms of Solomon*, a Pharisaic work of the first
century B.C. : " They are all holy, and their king is
Χριστὸς κύριος." [2] Very significant, too, is the early
Christian usage of the phrase " the brothers of the
Lord." [3] No doubt the word Lord as constantly applied
to Jesus by Paul and the other apostles must have
carried added weight and force for pagan minds because
of its associations in the realm of the Hellenistic religious
cults with which they were familiar ; but to derive the
Christian usage from the cults, overlooking the Old
Testament altogether, can only be called absurd. The
primitive watchword " Maranatha " would alone be
sufficient to refute Bousset's position. [4] Or take the
word " mystery " itself. If, as is sometimes stated,
Paul took this idea over from the pagan cults, we should
naturally expect its meaning in the epistles to be an
occult rite, or an esoteric doctrine reserved for the
privileged few. In point of fact, the idea in Paul is
entirely different. The Septuagint had used μυστήριον
for the hidden counsel of God, disclosed by revelation ;
and Paul, following this line, makes the word bear the
sense of " open secret." Indeed, the paradox of the
New Testament usage of the word, as Lightfoot has well
pointed out, is that almost invariably it is found in
connection with terms denoting revelation and proclamation. The mystery is " a truth which was once
hidden but now is revealed, a truth which without
special revelation would have been unknown." [5] Thus
Paul uses it of the divine purpose to sum up all things in

[1] Lam. 4[20].   [2] *Psalms of Solomon*, xvii. 36.
[3] Gal. 1[19], I Cor. 9[5]. On this point see Wernle, *Jesus und Paulus*,
20 f.
[4] I Cor. 16[22].   See p. 47.
[5] Lightfoot, *Colossians*, 166 f.

Christ,[1] of the consummation awaiting believers,[2] but
principally of the glorious truth that the saving will of
God includes Gentiles equally with Jews.[3] In all this,
the apostle's independence of the cults is manifest. Nor
should it ever have been forgotten that the whole idea
of an esoteric mystery, an occult doctrine, was foreign
to a religion whose preachers were always and everywhere characterized by their παρρησία, " glad fearlessness of speech," a religion whose invitation from the
Galilean days onwards was " Come and see."

The third consideration which ought to make us
cautious in estimating Paul's debt to the cults is the
most important of all. *This was a man in whose
personality a vital conversion experience had let loose
creative powers.* The Paul whom Bousset and others
would give us is a mere painstaking borrower ; and one
may be pardoned for feeling that much of the haste to
account for Paul by his environment is simply a failure
to give the Holy Spirit, who is always a creative Spirit,
His due. A sentence of Wernle, in the reply he wrote to
Bousset, is worth pondering : " As for religious relationships and experiences such as that known as Christ-
mysticism, one either experiences them, or one does not
experience them ; in no case can they be derived from
the environment."[4] That is the root of the matter ;
and Paul himself expressed it when he said, " There
is a new creation whenever a man comes to be in
Christ."[5] The Churches of Asia and Europe to which

---

[1] Eph. 1[9].   [2] I Cor. 15[51].   [3] Eph. 3[8ff.], Col. 1[26f.]
[4] Wernle, *Jesus und Paulus*, 44. Cf. *ib.* 92 : " ein Mann wie
Paulus nicht von aussen, sondern von innen verstanden werden
muss." T. R. Glover, in an interesting comparison, refutes the idea
that Plato was simply " the product of Periclean democracy and
Orphic religion " (*Paul of Tarsus*, 74).
[5] II Cor. 5[17] (Moffatt).

the apostle wrote had come into existence, not as man-made institutions carefully modelled on the pattern of existing cult-associations, but directly God-made and God-inspired, and on the crest of a divine enthusiasm ; and Paul, with the glory of Christ throbbing in his soul and filling every thought, had no need of second-hand inspiration drawn from Demeter or Serapis or anyone else. The Marcionites raised the question, " What new thing did Jesus bring ? " And the answer of Irenaeus was, " He brought all that was new, in bringing Himself." [1] Clearly the apostle who, writing of that same Lord, could say, " I live ; yet not I, but Christ liveth in me," [2] had within himself the secret of all creative power. And if this fundamental fact had received the prominence it deserved, the exaggerated views of Paul's debt to contemporary religions could never have arisen.

In conclusion, two decisive features of Paul's Gospel, which once for all lift it out of contact with the Hellenistic cults, must be stressed—its ethical insistence, and its emphasis on faith. William James, in a well-known passage,[3] tells of a remark once made by a humble carpenter of his acquaintance : " There is very little difference between one man and another ; but what little there is, *is very important*." So we may say that while here and there, on the surface, there may seem to be little enough difference between the Christian and the Hellenistic use of terms, that little is quite decisively important. Like Paul, the mysteries spoke of salvation ; but what a new Christ-given energy, what a moral

---

[1] " Omnem novitatem attulit semet ipsum afferens."
[2] Gal. 2[20].
[3] *The Will to Believe, etc.* 256.

dynamic, marked Paul's use of the word ! In the cults, σωτηρία was redemption from ignorance and from fate : hence its method was purely ritual, its nature non-ethical. " Neither Demeter nor Isis was very squeamish," says Glover pointedly.[1] Sometimes indeed it is suggested that when Christianity faced the Gentile world it accommodated itself by subordinating the ethical aspects of redemption to the metaphysical : Jesus aimed simply at changing men's wills, whereas Paul thought in terms of a change of essence. But this is extremely precarious. For on the one hand, both things, the renewal of the will and the change of essence, were already present in the teaching of Jesus, and not only present but inextricably bound up together ; and on the other hand, Paul's Gospel remained moral to the core. Indeed, the ultimate difference between the Hellenistic and Pauline views of salvation lies just here, that in the former the ethical implications were continually being lost sight of, while in the latter they were deliberately set in the foreground and kept there. No priest of Cybele ever bound an initiate with such a terrific moral obligation as this—" The love of Christ constraineth us . . . that they which live should not henceforth live unto themselves, but unto Him which died for them." [2] Wrought out under the shadow of the Cross, the apostolic doctrine of salvation stands on a different moral plane from Hellenism, and indeed from all other creeds for ever.

The other feature which, along with this ethical insistence, sets Paul's Gospel apart is its emphasis on faith. Here we touch on the comparisons which are often drawn between the facts of the death and resur-

---

[1] *Paul of Tarsus*, 133.
[2] II Cor. 5¹⁵ f.

rection of Jesus in the Christian preaching and the myth of the dying and rising god familiar in mystery lore. All these efforts to assert parallelism, it must be stated explicitly, are built on a radical fallacy—the fallacy on which G. K. Chesterton, referring to this very matter, put his finger when he declared, " There can be no parallel between what was admittedly a myth or mystery and what was admittedly a man." [1] The Jesus of Paul was a historic Being who had died on a historic Cross : the Osiris and Attis of the mysteries were " mythological personifications of the processes of vegetation." [2] But besides this, there is another consideration which is frequently overlooked altogether, but which seems to the present writer decisive. Paul himself states that the preaching of the death of Jesus was " unto the Greeks foolishness." [3] *Why* should it have been foolishness if, as we are confidently told, that Greek world would recognise the story at once and have half a dozen parallels ready ? The plain fact is that there was no such recognition. It was precisely because no parallels could be found, because the Hellenistic world had nothing to compare it with and therefore could not place it or grasp it, that the death of Jesus seemed " foolishness." And it follows from all this that the cognate conception of dying and rising with the Saviour-god, which finds a place in the mysteries, has nothing to do with Paul's doctrine of the believer's death and resurrection with Christ. In the cults, this conception is sensuous and external and ritualistic : in Paul, the heart and soul of it is faith. So, too, we come to see that between pagan and Christian Sacraments there is a great gulf fixed—

[1] G. K. Chesterton, *The Thing*, 215.
[2] Kennedy, *St. Paul and the Mystery-Religions*, 213.
[3] I Cor. 1[23].

the former crass and gross and materialistic, the latter spiritual through and through ; the former appealing *ex opere operato*, the latter founded on faith alone. This is the final, irreconcilable divergence. The Hellenistic religious world had nothing to say about faith, and Reitzenstein's effort to show that πίστις had a place in the mysteries fails completely : [1] Christianity had everything to say about it. Osiris and Cybele never thought of including faith in their vocabulary : Jesus of Nazareth made it the alpha and the omega of His, and His followers saw in Him its author and perfecter.[2] Initiation into the mysteries left faith out of sight, but baptism into Christ enthroned it. With the one, faith was nowhere ; with the other, it was everywhere. That is the last, decisive difference between the mystery religions and the apostle Paul, the final, fathomless gulf ; and across it no bridge can be thrown.

Within recent years an effort was made, in connection with a great international missionary advance, to assess the main non-Christian religions of to-day and to compare them with the faith of the New Testament. The striking words in which Dr. John R. Mott [3] summed up the results of that investigation may well do duty to close our present study and stand as a verdict on the relationship between the religions of the Hellenistic world nineteen hundred years ago and the message which Paul came preaching. " It proved that the more open-minded, thorough, and honest we were in dealing with these non-Christian faiths, and the more just and generous we were, the higher Christ loomed in His absolute uniqueness, sufficiency, and supremacy—as

[1] *Die hellenistischen Mysterienreligionen*, 94 ff.
[2] Heb. 12[2].
[3] *International Review of Missions*, Jan. 1931, 105.

One other than all the rest, strong among the weak, erect among the fallen, believing among the faithless, clean among the defiled, living among the dead—the Fountain-head of vitality, the world's Redeemer and Lord of all."

CHAPTER III

DISILLUSIONMENT AND DISCOVERY

"WE cannot really speak of God," says Eckhardt; "when we would speak of Him we do but stammer." "We are like young children learning to speak," exclaims Luther, "and can use only half words and quarter words." So Paul felt, whenever he tried to set down in words the great decisive experience of his life. All the resources of language could not communicate it. Strive as he might to express it, the inmost secret remained inexpressible. Once he falls back on the word "unspeakable," "God's unspeakable gift," [1] and the adjective there was no mere vague hyperbole, as often in our modern usage: it was the literal conclusion to which the failure of all attempts to capture in words the glory of the fact had driven him. The thing could not be spoken; and the apostle, like the poet, was always conscious of

> "Thoughts hardly to be pack'd
> Into a narrow act,
> Fancies that broke through language and escaped."

Secretum meum mihi, as the mystics love to say.

But Paul has one description of his conversion which does suggest something of the splendour of the new life into which that experience ushered him. Writing to the Corinthians, he declares: "God who said, ' Light shall shine out of darkness,' has shone within my heart." [2]

[1] II Cor. 9[15]. [2] II Cor. 4[6] (Moffatt).

81

In other words, something had happened comparable only to the great *Fiat Lux* of creation's dawn. That the sublime passage in the Genesis prologue was actually in the apostle's mind seems beyond doubt.[1] "The earth was without form and void"—had not his own soul known that chaos? "And darkness was upon the face of the deep"—was not that a very picture of his experience before Christ came? "But the Spirit of God was hovering over the waters"—and looking back, Paul could see how true it was that from his very birth Providence had set him apart, and that, through all his blindness and rebellion, the Spirit of God had been brooding over him and guiding his destiny.[2] "And God said, ' Let there be light ' : and there was light." To me, says Paul in effect, it was just like that—sheer miracle, a word proceeding out of the mouth of God, a creative act of omnipotence. To me, it was the birth of light and order and purpose and beauty, the ending of chaos and ancient night. And to me, as at that first creation, the morning stars sang together, and all the sons of God shouted for joy. God who said, " Let there be light," has shone within my heart ; He has scorched me with His splendour, and remade me by His strength ; and I now walk for ever in a marvellous light—the light of the knowledge of the glory of God in the face of Jesus Christ.

This conversion experience was far and away the most vital and formative influence of Paul's life. Compared with this, everything else—his Jewish ancestry, his Rabbinic training, his Hellenistic contacts, every factor of heredity and environment—was completely secondary. To see the decisive event aright, however, and to understand the consequences that flowed from

[1] Gen. I$^{2.3}$.　　　[2] So *e.g.* Gal. I^{15}.

it, we must approach it along the line of the religious experience of his pre-Christian days. And here at once we meet the striking fact that for years before the call came the dominating note of Paul's inner life had been one of utter failure and frustration and defeat.

I

We have seen above[1] how zealously and whole-heartedly Paul had embraced the religion of his fathers. Judaism never had a better champion. No one could rival him in enthusiasm for the spiritual heritage of his people.[2] He plunged eagerly into the life to which law and tradition seemed beckoning him. He flung himself into the observance of their commands with unmatched ardour. But that boundless enthusiasm of the young devotee was doomed to receive a check. He found that the more keenly he pursued his ideal, the further it receded. The righteousness on which his heart was set stood afar off, mocking his endeavour. Feelings of doubt and disillusionment began to creep in. Was he perhaps on the wrong track after all ? Had he accepted a challenge that was beyond his strength ? He was missing the mark, and he knew it, and he was unhappy. But it was an unhappiness of the kind which, as Carlyle knew and proclaimed, springs from a man's greatness. It was the disillusionment which is one of the surest proofs that the human clay has the divine fire mingled with it. Already into the secret mind of the Pharisee the thought was stealing, which later the Christian apostle was to shout from the housetops, that the religion of Mount Sinai, " Jerusalem which now is," was a yoke of bitter bondage : already the first faint yearn-

[1] See pp. 33 ff.   [2] Gal. 1[14].

ings for release had entered the man's soul, the first dim far-off vision of the " Jerusalem which is above," which " is free, the mother of us all." [1]

Before proceeding further, then, we must try to arrive at a clear understanding of Paul's reactions to the religion of the law. There is a widespread idea that this whole side of his experience and thought is nowadays irrelevant, and that the numerous passages in his epistles where these reactions are mirrored may more or less be ignored as being the product of controversies which have long been dead. No mistake could be greater. True, the intricacies of the Jewish Law have but little appeal for twentieth-century minds, and any interest that we have in them is mainly historical : religion has more pressing business on hand than raking among the cold ashes of extinguished fires. But the spirit of legalism—which was really the thing Paul was concerned about—is by no means extinct. The idea underlying the words " righteousness by the law " still commands the tacit assent of multitudes, even within Christendom. Still the old error takes, in every generation, a new lease of life. Still the very elect are deceived. Confronted with Paul's strenuous and repeated grapplings with this subject, his constant wrestlings with it in thought and in experience, we cannot afford to set all this part of his message aside with an airy gesture as though it were obsolete now. It carries permanent validity. It goes right to the roots of our modern problem, lays its finger on the Church's deepest need, and concerns the spiritual experience of every soul. For what does " legalism " mean ? What are the main marks of this form of religion ?

In the first place, it is a religion of *redemption by*

[1] Gal. 4[25 f.]

human effort. Man is thrown back on his own resources.
In front of him stands the law, challenging him to work
out his own salvation. He is summoned to toil un-
remittingly at the moral life in the hope of winning
acceptance with God at last. He has to fight down the
world, the flesh, and the devil in his own strength. He
has to build his own highway to the heavens. And
what happens ? He starts building, but it is a tower of
Babel that results. It reaches nowhere near to God ;
and it ends in shame and confusion of soul. Thus the
shadow of Pelagianism—which is really just Jewish
legalism in another form—has fallen across the Christian
centuries ; and wherever it has come, it has blighted
hope and peace. The soul of man, setting out gallantly
enough on the crusade to conquer besetting sin and
weakness and to establish personal righteousness, has
found the road too hard and the foes too stubborn ;
and gallantry has given way to disillusionment, and
aspiration to a sense of downright futility. No man can
save himself : this was Paul's great discovery. A
drowning man does not want a lecture on the art of
swimming : he wants a rope to cling to. Nor does a
lame man ask for a guide-post to point him out the
way : he asks for an arm to lean upon. But the very
weariness of those unavailing efforts to achieve its own
salvation may prepare the soul of man to hear the cry,
" Stand still, and see the salvation of God." And if it
was Paul's first great discovery that no man can save
himself, it was his second that salvation is of the Lord.
In Horatius Bonar's words—

> " Thy love to me, O God,
>   Not mine, O Lord, to Thee,
> Can rid me of this dark unrest,
>   And set my spirit free."

This is Grace appearing on the battlefield of human defeat. A better way than that of legalism has been opened up. A greater than Moses is here.

A second mark of the legalist spirit is *its tendency to import a mercenary spirit into religion*. This is almost inevitable, as righteousness on this view is something which may be earned. A man, seeking salvation, is to stand before God and point to his own piled-up moral achievements and say—" There is what I have done : now give me my reward ! " Having earned it, he can claim it as of right. The soul which keeps the law of God will be able, to quote Browning's words in *Johannes Agricola*, to—

> " Make out, and reckon on, His ways,
> And bargain for His love, and stand,
> Paying a price, at His right hand."

Legalism always tends to develop this mercenary attitude. It is ever seeking to increase its claim upon God by multiplying the regulations and ordinances which it proposes to obey. The great central requirements of doing justly and loving mercy and walking humbly with God are not always easy of fulfilment : but what matter a few failures there, if you can point to a whole host of meritorious actions—prayers, fastings, tithes, and the like—faithfully and rigorously performed ? Thus arises the strange and rather terrible spectacle of a man bargaining with his Creator. What this spirit has forgotten is, that if God should mark iniquity, there is not a soul anywhere which could stand before Him for one moment ; while as for the idea that a man may put God in his debt by his obedience, the fact is that even if he were to wear his fingers to the bone in God's service, even if he were to burn out his brain and beggar his soul in utter devotion, he still would not so much as have begun to establish a claim upon God. No man can ever have God in his debt : God has every man immeasurably in His.

A third mark of legal religion, alike in the twentieth century and in the first, is *its fondness for negatives.* " Thou shalt not " is the foundation on which it is built. It bids men preserve the house of life swept and garnished and free from the desecrating intrusion of marauding spirits by keeping the doors permanently bolted and the windows tightly shuttered. It fails to realize that that method of keeping the evil things out is defective in two directions. On the one hand, a negative religion is always apt to defeat itself : the evil spirits which are repressed and refused entrance at the front may quite possibly, as every psychologist knows, burrow underground and come up from the basement. So long as the place is untenanted, that danger will remain. On the other hand, even if the soul were to succeed in shutting these things out, it shuts out something else as well—God's good light and air and sunshine : legalism can never hope for the width and freedom and gladness and release which have been Christ's great gifts to men. It is a burdensome creed, and never sings nor exults. It is a dead-weight the soul has to carry, not (as a true religion ought surely to be) wings to carry the soul. The secret of all power and gladness, as Paul was later to discover, lies in three words, " Christ in me." For while legal religion is a burden bearing a man down from above, Christ is a living power bearing him along from within. To be in union with Christ means the joy of possessing interior sources of a super-natural order, and of feeling within you the power of an endless life. But legalism knows, and can know, nothing of that.

This brief analysis will serve to show that the problems confronting Paul as he lived out his life under the religion of the law can by no means be regarded as of merely historical or antiquarian interest, nor can we dismiss the passages in his epistles where these matters hold the field as being irrelevant to our own generation's most urgent needs. The words with which Barth first launched his now famous commentary on Romans are worth repeating : " Paul, as a child of his age, addressed his contemporaries. It is, however, far more important that, as Prophet and Apostle of the Kingdom of God, he veritably speaks to all men of every age." [1] In his attack on the legalist spirit, and in his heralding of a better way, the way of surrender to the Spirit of Christ—this is pre-eminently true. To say that Paul is simply *ein antik denkender Mensch* is to miss the truth completely. His problem is our problem. And the hope of our generation is to make his answer ours.

But here the question inevitably rises—*Is Paul's picture of Jewish legalism historically correct?* How far are we justified in taking his experience of the law as typical ? Is it not possible that the dark side— the element of bondage—has been overstressed ? Certain Jewish scholars and others have argued strongly that Paul, consciously or unconsciously, has given a misleading version of the facts, that his evidence on the whole matter is hopelessly biased, and that alike by temperament and by experience he was totally unfitted to construct a fair picture of what Judaism meant

[1] *The Epistle to the Romans* (Eng. tr.), 1.

to the average orthodox Jew of the time. Thus Kohler declares bluntly that " those who define Judaism as a religion of law completely misunderstand its nature and its historic forces." [1] Montefiore accuses Paul of a pessimism quite uncharacteristic of Judaism at its best.[2] And Schechter, with more than a touch of asperity, complains that " with a few exceptions our theologians still enlarge upon the ' Night of Legalism,' from the darkness of which religion only emerges by a miracle supposed to have taken place about the year 30 of our era." [3]

But those who challenge Paul on this matter, alleging his representation of Judaism to be historically unsound, are hard put to it to substantiate their claim. After all, it proves little to adduce from Jewish literature, as Schechter does,[4] Rabbinic expressions of thankfulness for the law and of joy in its service : it is the deep undertone of a religion that matters, and the undertone of Judaism is not joy. Nor does Kohler's attempt to rebut the charge of legalism succeed. It is simply not possible to evade the plain meaning of statements such as that of Rabbi Benaiah, " The world and everything in it was created solely for the sake of the law " ; [5] the veneration of the law did not stop short of a doctrine of pre-existence. Other elements Judaism certainly contained, but the fact remains that fundamentally it was in terms of law that man's relation to God was conceived. And the shadow which has always been, and always must be, inherent in and inseparable from that conception was lying

---

[1] *Jewish Theology*, 355.
[2] *The Old Testament and After*, 275, 575.
[3] *Some Aspects of Rabbinic Theology*, 117.
[4] *Op. cit.* 148 ff.
[5] Quoted by G. F. Moore, *Judaism*, i. 268.

heavy upon the soul of Judaism, like a great dark cloud across the sun. Paul's picture cannot be set aside. It is no distortion, but a true presentation of the facts.

It is necessary to remember that the " Torah," or Law, included more than the Mosaic prescriptions. Sometimes the use of the term was extended to cover the entire Old Testament, or even the whole sum of divine revelation.[1] But as a rule it denoted the law of the Pentateuch *plus* the great mass of interpretations and rulings and traditions which centuries of later scribes had built upon that foundation. It is this last addition which is crucial. Alongside the original law there had grown up a new body of legislation, far more extensive and far more detailed, possessing in Jewish eyes an authority as binding as that of Moses himself. What the developing experience of later generations had felt to be lacking in the guidance offered by Leviticus and Deuteronomy on points of civil and ceremonial law was now supplied. Prohibitions which had been left vague and general were now worked out with extraordinary care and minuteness in their application to every conceivable situation of life. As new situations arose, juristic exegesis working on the revealed law of God in Scripture produced new rulings ; and these rulings in turn had come to be regarded as part of the content of revelation, bearing an equal sanctity.

No doubt the aim of all this was excellent. So severe were the penalties of disobedience which the law of Moses had enunciated that nothing, it was thought, should be left to chance : it was not safe, it was not right, to ask the common man to make his own particular

[1] Examples of this usage in Paul will be found in Rom. 3[19], I Cor. 14[21].

applications of the general law. Left to himself, he might easily blunder as to what was permissible and what was prohibited ; and where the penalties to be visited on a false move were so grave, the man, for his own sake, must be protected. He must have everything worked out for him to the smallest detail. And doubtless, in that age as in this, there were minds of a certain type which found the way of unquestioning submission to detailed mechanical guidance a positive relief : doubts and dilemmas were automatically excluded, and the whole duty of man mapped out and regulated from the cradle to the grave. Why should any man be left to go through clouds and darkness and travail of soul to find out God's will for him at some specific point of his life ? Here it was set down in detail—given, authoritative, infallible. The motive, no doubt, was excellent.

What was not so clearly realized was the soul-destroying burden that this meticulousness was laying up for future generations. Heavy as the burden would have been even if the Halachah—the applied rules— had concerned the realm of moral character alone, it became quite intolerable when every ridiculous triviality of ceremonial observance was exalted to a place of importance and dignity alongside the weightiest matters of the law. "The Jewish teachers," as G. F. Moore in his great work on *Judaism* has well expressed it, "recognized the distinction between acts which the common conscience of mankind condemns as morally wrong and such as are wrong only because they are made so by statute ; but the former are not the more properly sin because of their moral quality nor the latter less so because in themselves they are morally indifferent. The sin is in either case the same, violation of the revealed will of God." [1] Rabbi Johanan and Rabbi Simeon ben Lakish worked out the number of regulations imposed by the law of Sabbath observance, and arrived at a grand total of 1521.[2] And when it is remembered that to each of these was assigned an authority and sanctity no less binding than that of such great primary requirements as the duties of honouring parents and of refraining from idolatry, it will begin to be evident why Paul, bred to worship the law and to regard the slightest criticism of it as dangerous blasphemy, broke out against it at last as slavery and bondage and a curse.

Within Judaism itself, at the time when the soul of Paul was entering on its struggle, four attitudes towards the law can be distinguished.

There were, first, *the people who were frankly irreligious.* They had neither the time nor the inclination for the study of the law. Not for them the scruples of a pious and sensitive conscience, not theirs to vex themselves with things too high for them. Willingly they abandoned all that to others, and took their own careless, unashamed way. Towards this lawless rabble many of the Pharisees had nothing but the most undisguised contempt. " This people which knoweth not the law is accursed," they said, and passed by on the other side. Some there were, however (and Paul, in his Pharisaic days, was one), who could not dismiss the problem so lightly. Was it not the plain teaching of Deuteronomy that the favour of God to His people was dependent on national obedience ? [3] And, therefore, might not this multitude which ignored the law or openly flouted its demands be a menace to the highest

---

[1] *Judaism*, i. 462.   [2] *Ib.* ii. 28.
[3] Deut. 27. Paul quotes Deut. 27²⁶ in Gal. 3¹⁰.

hopes of Israel, or even a threat to her very existence ?
It was a haunting problem, with which the mind and
heart of the future apostle must have wrestled long.

At the opposite extreme from those to whom the
law meant little or nothing were *the saints, to whom it
meant everything*. " Under the shadow of the law,"
says Ottley, " there grew up a rich and deeply-rooted
life of personal religion, the character and tone of
which are best illustrated by the Psalter." [1] Some of
the choicest souls in Israel, looking to the spirit rather
than the letter of the law, saw in it a symbol of a divine
inflexible faithfulness. As they meditated on it, and
studied it, and prayed over it, they found that it gave
them the assurance of a dependable God and the com-
fort of a rational universe.

" Thou dost preserve the Stars from wrong ;
    And the most ancient Heavens, through thee, are fresh
        and strong."

Nor did such elect souls experience any insuperable
difficulty in holding the two ideas of law and grace
together in their minds. What was the gift of the law
itself if not just the most signal token of God's gracious
kindness to His people ? In point of time, indeed, as they
saw and acknowledged, grace held the priority—a fact
on which Paul was later to base a famous argument :
such outstanding historic events as the call of Abraham
and the Exodus made it clear that grace had been in the
field before law appeared. But law, when it came, was
grace reaching its climax. A cleft between God's mercy
and God's justice there could not be. He was " a just
God and a Saviour." [2] There is an interesting Midrash
on Gen. 2[4] which represents God deliberating as follows :

---

[1] *Religion of Israel*, 166.   [2] Is. 45[21].

" If I create the world in my merciful character (alone),
sins will abound ; if in my just character (alone), how
can the world endure ? I will create it in both the just
and the merciful character, and may it endure ! " [1]
Hence there were devout hearts in Israel who thanked
God day and night for His law, and could say with
perfect truth, in the words of the writer of the 119th
Psalm, " Thy statutes have been my songs in the house
of my pilgrimage." [2] It must, however, be clearly
understood that this attitude of quiet assurance was not
typical of Judaism as a whole. Such childlike souls,
standing untroubled and grateful in the shadow of the
law, were not the rule in Israel, certainly not in Paul's
day, but the exception. And even of them it would be
true to say that it was the spirit, not the letter, of the
law that had won their gratitude. It was the inward
spirit . . . on which their soul's anchor was cast.

Midway between these two classes in Judaism, the
saints and the sinners, there was a third class, whose
attitude to the law was *compromise*. When Paul, looking back on his own younger days, declares " I outstripped many of my own age and race in my special
ardour for the ancestral traditions of my house," [3] he
is obviously implying that many a worthy Jew, despair-
ing of the impossible perfection which the law demanded,
had patched up some sort of working arrangement by
which a less strenuous line of conduct could be accepted
without offending conscience unduly. The law itself
seemed to offer certain loopholes in this direction. Thus,
for example, occasionally it happened, as we have already

---

[1] Quoted in Moore, *Judaism*, i. 389. Jewish exegesis interprets
" Jahveh " as God in His merciful character, " Elohim " as God in
His character of judge : Gen. 2⁴ contains them both.
[2] Ps. 119⁵⁴.   [3] Gal. 1¹⁴ (Moffatt).

noted,[1] that different schools of Rabbis, such as those of Hillel and Shammai, interpreted one and the same command in quite different ways ; and where doctors disagreed the common man might well feel that implicit obedience was not to be looked for. Another loophole offered itself in the distinction which was drawn between unwitting transgression of the law and wilful, defiant sin ; and still another was provided by the practice of certain Rabbis who, holding that the division of mankind into two categories—the righteous and the wicked—was too simple to fit the facts, recognized a third category, the " middling " people, who inclined now to the one side and now to the other, and in whom the workings both of " the good impulse " and of " the evil impulse " were apparent. In addition to all this, any Jew who wanted to compromise and to accept a second-best could easily enough settle the qualms of conscience by bringing in the Rabbinic doctrine of repentance ; for however lofty and noble this doctrine was as originally conceived, its all too frequent practical effect was to minister to a superficial view of sin. The snare of compromise has always been religion's most serious enemy, and the higher the religion the greater the danger. Men will always find ways and means of eluding a religion's stern demands while still calling themselves its followers and signing its creeds and continuing to bear its name ; they will always be able to convince themselves that, even on that basis of compromise, they have a right to bear its name, and will grow indignant with anyone who challenges that right ; they will always regard the half-allegiance they are prepared to give with a wonderful complacency and satisfaction, feeling that anyone—even God Himself—might

[1] See p. 37.

be gratified with the interest they show and the patron-
age they offer ; not realising that that attitude, which
seems so reasonable and respectable, is dealing religion
a blow and doing it a damage compared with which
all the direct, frontal attacks of its open enemies are
a mere nothing. So it was in Judaism. Compromise
and religious unreality were rife. Endless discussion
of the minutiae of the law was a screen behind which
men hid from the inexorable claims of conscience.
It was as much easier then as it is now to spend a
dozen hours discussing religion than one half-hour obeying God.

Over and above these three classes of people whose
attitude to the Jewish law differed so widely—the
sinners who ignored it, the saints who gloried in it, and
the half-hearted who compromised with it—there
existed a fourth class, whose main feeling was one of
profound disappointment and dissatisfaction ; and to
this class Paul belonged. He had inherited far too
deep a respect and love for the law ever to dream of
ignoring it. But to glory and rejoice in it, as did
some free, childlike souls, to declare with the Psalmist
that God's hardest marching-orders were the music of
his life, was not in his power : it would not have been
true to his experience. And the middle way, the way
of compromise, was impossible. Others might find
relief and a solution there ; but for a man of Paul's
vehement, downright temperament, that road was
barred. Indeed, it is one of the marks of Paul's
inherent bigness of spirit, even in his pre-Christian
days, that nothing less than the best would satisfy him.
A temporizing, middle course he could not tolerate.
The very idea of neutrality was repugnant. To be
content with an indifferent morality and a second-rate

religion seemed to him thoroughly immoral and irreligious. And if the easy plan of compromise was thus ruled out from the start, and if his most heroic efforts to drive himself by sheer relentless force of will along the road of perfect conformity to the mind and command of God were unavailing, where in the whole world was peace to be found ? He seemed doomed to live out his days in unrelieved disappointment and frustration, and to die defeated at the last.

In one place, it is true, Paul claims that as a Pharisee he had been "immaculate by the standard of legal righteousness." [1] This suggests (and we may well believe it) that in observance of the ritual demands of the law Paul had reached an extraordinarily high standard. None could accuse him of the least degree of carelessness or neglect. His zeal was unparalleled and unique. But behind the multifarious requirements of the Rabbinic law stood the moral challenge of God Himself ; and no amount of ritual observance was ever going to bring peace if that inward, ultimate claim was not being met.

It was a hopeless situation. Nor was it in any way improved or lightened by the conviction, deeply rooted in the Jewish mind, that failure at one point meant failure everywhere : " whosoever shall keep the whole law and yet offend in one point, he is guilty of all." [2] With everything that was best in him, Paul yearned to fulfil the demand of God ; he felt that it was to satisfy that holy will that he had been born ; and yet something was beginning to tell him that, along the road which he had been trained to travel, he would never satisfy it—not in a thousand years. The law, so an inward voice kept telling him,

[1] Phil. 3⁶ (Moffatt).   [2] James 2¹⁰.

" Will bind thee by such vows, as is a shame
   A man should not be bound by, yet the which
   No man can keep."

What then was he to do ?   Reject the law altogether ?
But that would mean signing his birthright away.
For the inward voice went on—

   " but, so thou dread to swear,
Pass not beneath this gateway, but abide
Without, among the cattle of the field."

Was that to be the end of it ?   It was a bitter problem.
   And yet Paul could not bring himself to believe that
the law itself was in any way to blame for this hopeless
situation.   If that thought crossed his mind, resolutely
he put it away.   " What shall we say then ?   Is the
law sin ?   God forbid." [1]   But what did grow clear to
his mind, as he struggled with the problem, was this—
that the blame lay in human nature.   " We know that
the law is spiritual : but I am carnal, sold under sin." [2]
That was the root of the trouble, that radical weakness
in the very constitution of humanity.   " I delight in
the law of God after the inward man : but I see another
law in my members, warring against the law of my
mind, and bringing me into captivity to the law of sin
which is in my members." [3]   One phrase sums it all
up : " what the law could not do, *in that it was weak
through the flesh.*" [4]   Here we have come upon one of
the apostle's great regulative ideas.   His teaching on
the law is at every point conditioned by his experience of what he calls " the flesh."   This we must now
examine.

[1] Rom. 7⁷.   [2] Rom. 7¹⁴.
[3] Rom. 7²² f.   [4] Rom. 8³.

II

The *locus classicus* for this whole side of Paul's thought is, of course, Romans 7. This famous passage, so crucial for an understanding of the apostle's life and religion, has raised two questions. Is the struggle here described that of an unconverted soul, or does it enter also into the experience of the redeemed ? And is this a general statement, or is it autobiography ?

On the former of these questions we need not linger long. The very fact that the name of Christ is not heard until the closing verse, that Jesus is nowhere in all this chapter until He comes in suddenly in the doxology which proclaims the conflict ended and the victory won, is a clear indication that it is *the experience of a life still requiring to be born again* which is here being described.[1] Anyone who reads the two chapters 7 and 8 consecutively will assuredly feel that in passing from the one to the other he has entered a totally different atmosphere. If it is one soul's experience which is being described in both, then we can only say that between them something decisive has happened. There has been a clean break of some kind. There has been rebirth, conversion. Phrases such as " sold under sin " (verse 14), " O wretched man that I am " (verse 24), are not the normal notes of a life that Christ has changed. " What would be the use of the new birth or redemption at all," asks Johannes Weiss hotly, " if it could not end that miserable stress and slavery ? "[2]

[1] There is much to be said for Moffatt's arrangement : he puts the second part of verse 25, which certainly seems out of place in our A.V., immediately after verse 23 ; and the chapter then ends with the climax of verse 24 and the first part of verse 25. Reasons for the displacement of the text are suggested by Dodd, *Romans*, 115.

[2] *Das Urchristentum*, 399 n.1.

Deissmann indeed inclines to another view. " It is bad psychology," he declares, " to refer the words significant of depression exclusively to Paul's pre-Christian period, and to make only Paul the Christian speak the words from on high. Even as a Christian Paul was swallowed up by the deep." " Even in his Christian period St. Paul is capable of such cries for help when the old distress wakes in him again." " Side by side with all his moral exhortations to Christians to battle against sin there are confessions of Paul the Christian himself, witnessing that even the new-created feels at times the old deep sense of sin." [1] That there is truth in this need not be denied. The Christian who has made his peace with God is not exempt from struggle and conflict, and history can testify that it is often the noblest saints who feel their unworthiness most. But the point to be noticed is that the struggle and conflict are now faced in a spirit utterly different from anything that went before ; the whole tone of the life is altered ; and from the man who is " in Christ " the feelings of sadness and disillusionment and futility which cry aloud in Romans 7 are fled and vanished. Were he to fall from grace or even for a moment to have his connection with Jesus severed, then indeed the misery there described would come rushing back upon him ; and it may be that in writing the chapter Paul was saying, " There is what my life is, and yours, and the life of all the world—apart from Christ. This is what happens when a man lets Jesus go." Denney certainly has right on his side when he maintains that " no one could have written the passage but a Christian," and that the experience to which it refers is being " seen through regenerate eyes " ; [2] but

[1] *St Paul*, 68, 95, 156.   [2] *EGT*, ii. 639.

fundamentally it is the pre-Christian life which is here delineated, a life which passes away when Christ makes all things new.

There remains the other question raised by this chapter in Romans—*Is it autobiographical, or purely general?* Weiss inclines to the latter view, and holds that the absence of specifically Jewish colouring and the use of the present rather than the past tense make it impossible to regard it as a transcript of Paul's own experience : the first personal pronoun is no more than a literary convention. " So ist das ' Ich ' ein allge-meines." [1] To the present writer this seems entirely unconvincing. " It will in fact be found on examina-tion," says C. H. Dodd, " that Paul rarely, if ever, says ' I ' unless he is speaking of himself personally, even if he means to generalize from the particular instance." [2] But quite apart from that, there are certain canons which enable one to decide with a high degree of ac-curacy whether a man is giving a personal confession or whether he is simply speaking at large : and if ever words bore all the evidences of having been wrung from the agony of a man's own soul, these poignant sentences most surely do. No literary convention makes a man speak as Paul has spoken here. In his very heart's blood this page was written.

This, of course, is not to say that a wider reference is excluded, for in his own bitter conflict Paul sees the struggle of unredeemed humanity mirrored. But all the way and in every word, as Holtzmann has well remarked, one hears a *crede experto* that cannot be denied.[3] This was *my* struggle, says Paul, this *my* defeat ; and this, thank God, *my* victory !

---

[1] *Das Urchristentum*, 399 n.1.   [2] *Romans*, 107 (*MNTC*).
[3] *Neutestamentliche Theologie*, ii. 32 n.2.

Let it be said in passing that we cannot be too grateful to Paul for thus admitting us to the inner sanctuary of his life and sharing with us the deepest secrets of his soul. The contrast between a message of this kind and one which is general and impersonal is well illustrated, as Denney has pointed out, by a comparison of the *Confessions* of Augustine with the writings of Athanasius.[1] Certainly what has given Paul's Gospel its force and grip and appeal for every age is the fact that it is experimental through and through. Just as Paul's Master once drew back with His own hands the curtain that hid the secrets of His desert conflict with the tempter, just as Jesus with His own lips told His friends the story of that lonely titanic struggle in order to help and strengthen them when their dark days should come, so Paul here, realizing that the man who is to lead others to God must " walk in the light " [2] and make no secret of the redeeming experience that has delivered him from sin and shame and death, has opened his whole life to us without reserve. " No man," says Raven, " has ever given himself away more generously or to better purpose. Such self-giving is the finest and the hardest task of discipleship." [3] Of Romans 7 and 8 it is surely true to say that nowhere in the literature of personal confession could a nobler fulfilment be found of the Psalmist's injunction, " Let the redeemed of the Lord say so, whom He hath redeemed from the hand of the enemy." [4] *Let the redeemed say so*—and Paul, by disclosing the wretchedness and misery in which Christ had found him, and the glory and romance into which Christ

---

[1] *The Christian Doctrine of Reconciliation*, 44.
[2] I John 1[7].
[3] *Jesus and the Gospel of Love*, 293.
[4] Psalm 107[2].

had ushered him, is bearing his witness to bowed and burdened spirits everywhere : " This, by God's grace, happened to me, and this, under God, can happen to you." In the service of Christ and of humanity, the man has opened his very heart, and written in his very blood, and taken us into the shame and glory of his secret soul ; and for this the world stands for ever in his debt.

We can now turn to the conception to which this page from the apostle's life introduces us, the conception of " *sin in the flesh.*" The prominence of this idea here and elsewhere has occasionally led readers of his writings to conclude that his life must have been harassed by some special sensual sin, and that Paul more than others had an evil bias in the moral sphere to contend with. But that is to misunderstand the terms he is using. " There is no reason whatever to suppose, with Lagarde and others, that he had ever been a careless or loose liver." [1] Everything points in the opposite direction. Nor is it necessary to find in the chapter we are discussing a reference to some definite sin committed in youth ; and when Deissmann states that " even in his old age there stood out clearly to his soul one experience of his childhood, concerning which he gives pathetic hints in his letter to the Romans. We might speak of it as his fall " [2]—he is going beyond what is warranted by the evidence. The point at issue is this : what does Paul mean when he speaks of " the flesh " ?

The word σάρξ in Paul's epistles has various shades of

[1] Inge, *Christian Ethics and Modern Problems*, 72. Cf. Garvie, in *Expository Times*, March 1925, 250.
[2] *St. Paul*, 93.

meaning, ranging from the strictly literal usage in such
a phrase as " flesh and bones " [1] to the idea of carnal
sin. [2] But in the great majority of passages it stands for
human nature on its material side. It includes " all that
is peculiar to human nature in its corporeal embodiment." [3] Elsewhere Paul has used the contrast of ὁ
ἔσω and ὁ ἔξω ἄνθρωπος—the inward and the outward
man [4]—and the flesh comprises everything (impulses,
thoughts, desires, and the like) belonging to the latter.
" Carnem appellat quidquid est extra Christum," says
Calvin. [5] It is human nature in its frailty and weakness
and need of help. It is man apart from God. " What,
indeed, does *flesh* mean," exclaims Barth, " but the
complete inadequacy of the creature when he stands
before the Creator ? " [6] It is not in itself base ; and it
is well to remind ourselves that of the notion of the
inherent evil of matter, which was a characteristic
Gnostic doctrine, there is not a trace in Paul. His
dualism is not cosmic nor metaphysical, but practical
and moral. But though not evil in itself, the flesh is that
part of man's nature which gives evil its opportunity.
It is the thing on which sin impinges and to which it
attaches itself. It becomes sin's " willing and obedient
organ and instrument." [7] " With the flesh," says Paul,
" I serve the law of sin." [8]

Here we come in sight of another important element
in the apostle's thinking—*his view of sin as personal.*
" The flesh is a substance, but sin is a force." [9] It is

---

[1] Eph. 5[30].   [2] Rom. 13[14].
[3] Cremer, *Biblico-Theological Lexicon of NT Greek*, 519.
[4] II Cor. 4[16].
[5] Quoted by Michael, *Epistle to the Philippians*, 139 (*MNTC*).
[6] *The Epistle to the Romans* (Eng. tr.), 89.
[7] H. J. Holtzmann, *Neutestamentliche Theologie*, ii. 43.
[8] Rom. 7[25].   [9] Holtzmann, ii. 44.

a living power, the subtle adversary of man's soul. " Sin," he says, " sprang to life." [1] " Sin deceived me, and slew me." [2] " It is no more I that do it, but sin that dwelleth in me." [3] All this, it should be noticed, is in direct line with the teaching of Jesus. There also we find sin regarded personally. It is the " strong man " who has to be bound.[4] It is the Satan who falls as lightning from heaven.[5]

It is but another aspect of the same idea which Paul is using when he speaks of " principalities and powers." [5] The world, as he conceived it, was full of spirit-forces hostile to God. When he speaks of the στοιχεῖα, or " elements," it is most probably such supernatural beings, or elemental spirits, which he has in mind.[6] This, too, runs back to Jesus' teaching. Round about the lives of men was an unseen realm full of malign influences, emissaries of the Evil One ; and suffering, sickness, and sin were regularly attributed to demonic agency. Hence Jesus could say that when, through His own and His followers' mission, the work of saving and healing suddenly began to go forward on a gigantic scale, it was a token that the whole kingdom of Satan was being shaken to its foundations, was indeed breaking up, and that the kingdom of goodness and light and God was at last coming into its own. " If I with the finger of God cast out devils, no doubt the kingdom of God is come upon you." [7] Here, then, we have one of Paul's working hypotheses : sin is a personal force, which first exists outside of a man altogether, and then comes and launches its attack upon him. And the point of attack is the flesh.

---

[1] Rom. 7[9] (Moffatt).   [2] Rom. 7[11].
[3] Rom. 7[17-20].   [4] Matt. 12[29].   [5] Luke 10[18].
[6] Gal. 4[3.9], Col. 2[8.20].   [7] Luke 11[20].

It lies outside the scope of our present inquiry to examine in any detail Paul's view of *the origin of sin*. We have already had occasion to remark that the apostle did not feel it necessary to unify his own thinking on this matter.[1] Side by side with his belief in the existence of a world of hostile spirits deceiving man into sin stands the thought of Adam's transgression as something in which all future ills were implicit : " sin came into the world by one man." [2] Traces of the Jewish conception of " the two impulses " can also be found. According to this doctrine, sin, viewed on its subjective side, originates with the *yeser ha-ra'*, the evil impulse, the tempter within.[3] But in truth Paul was little anxious to discuss how sin had been born and whence it had come : the one thing that filled his mind was the fact that sin was there, doing the devil's work, and that only the power of God could destroy it.

He went far beyond the Rabbis in his view of *sin's seriousness*. Moore has pointed out that the definition of sin in the Westminster *Shorter Catechism*—" any want of conformity unto, or transgression of, the law of God "—might have come from the Jewish doctors of the law themselves.[4] That is perfectly true : the definition is identical with the Rabbinic position, and could have been arrived at even if Christ had never died and Paul had never preached. But it is also true that the very point where the Rabbis and the Catechism are at one is the point where the latter most conspicuously fails. Certainly Paul's view went far beyond any such definition. Sin was not something a man *did* : it was something that took possession of him, something the man *was*, something that turned

---

[1] See p. 27.   [2] Rom. 5[12] (Moffatt).
[3] G. F. Moore, *Judaism*, i. 479 ff.   [4] *Ib.* i. 460.

him into an open enemy of the God who loved him. It brought outward penalties : " whatsoever a man soweth, that shall he also reap." [1] But far more appalling than these were its inward results. It tormented the conscience : " O wretched man that I am ! " [2] It brought the will into abject slavery : " the good that I would, I do not, but the evil which I would not, that I do." [3] It destroyed fellowship with God : men were " alienated," [4] "without God in the world." [5] It hardened the heart, and blinded the judgment, and warped the moral sense : " God gave them over to a reprobate mind." [6] It destroyed life itself : " the wages of sin is death." [7]

Such is the apostle's estimate of sin's overwhelming gravity. And through it all, even where sin is regarded as an external force waiting to take advantage of human nature in its frailty, he will allow no blurring of the fact of personal accountability. Principalities and powers may lie in wait, but in the last resort man's is the choice, man's the responsibility, and man's the doom.

No one has ever described more strikingly than Paul the torment of the divided self. Many writers have dwelt on this state of inward civil war—Epictetus, with his ὃ θέλει οὐ ποιεῖ καὶ ὃ μὴ θέλει ποιεῖ ; Ovid, with his " video meliora proboque, deteriora sequor " ; Plato, in his picture of the horses and the charioteer ; Shakespeare, in his delineation of the conflict in the soul of Hamlet, a conflict which, as Bradley has told us,[8] is the very essence of all tragedy ; but for vividness and simple poignancy none has surpassed Paul in the passage which

---

[1] Gal. 6[7]. [2] Rom. 7[24]. [3] Rom. 7[19]. [4] Col. 1[21].
[5] Eph. 2[12]. [6] Rom. 1[28]. [7] Rom. 6[23].
[8] A. C. Bradley, *Shakespearean Tragedy*, 18.

is the *De Profundis Clamavi* of the New Testament.
Into this picture, memories of years of struggle and
impotence and unhappiness deepening into desperation
have entered. Romans 7 is Paul as he was right up to
the eve of the Damascus journey—torn in spirit, disintegrated in personality, sunk into an abyss of self-
loathing and despair. " Out of the depths have I cried
unto Thee, O Lord."

III

This, then, was the situation in the midst of which
Paul saw one fact standing, stern and challenging—the
law. What we have now to do is to observe how his own
experience of defeat at the hands of sin (in which, let
it be emphasized again, he saw humanity's problem
mirrored) reacted on his view of the law itself. It is
practically certain that, for a considerable time before
the great crisis of Damascus came, there were taking
shape in his mind and heart some at least of the
criticisms of the law and of legal religion in general
which later, in the light of Christ, he was to proclaim
with all the strength and energy of his being. Here let
us try to assess his position as a whole, and for the sake
of clearness let us notice the following points.

First, Paul never to his life's end lost the sense that
the law, in spite of all its defects and dangers, *had something noble in it*. This is an aspect of the matter which
has not received the emphasis it deserves. His attitude
to the Scriptures, of which mention has been made
above,[1] rendered it certain that the law of Moses at
least would always claim his regard and honour. The
Old Testament was divinely inspired, and therefore
completely authoritative ; and in so far as " law " in

[1] See pp. 39 ff.

the apostle's mind was associated with this total historic revelation of God, there could be no question of its cancellation. Even Jesus, he realised, came " not to destroy, but to fulfil." [1] " Do we make void the law through faith ? God forbid ; yea, we establish the law." [2] Hence Paul found himself perfectly able, even where attacking legalist religion, to reinforce his arguments by quotations drawn from the books of the law : notable instances of this will be found in Romans 9-11. If this proceeding is considered arbitrary and inconsistent, it should be remembered that not only in psalms and prophets but even in the Pentateuch itself the prophetic note can be heard ; and it is to this strain of his ancestral religion, as distinct from the legal strain which had latterly taken precedence, that Paul makes his appeal. [3]

In this sense, then, his estimation of the law never wavered. To his own question " What advantage hath the Jew ? " he gives the answer " Much every way : chiefly, because that unto them were committed the oracles of God." [4] And even in the passage over which the shadows of frustration and futility lie most deeply, he can declare " The law is holy, and the commandment holy, and just, and good." [5] All the moral commands God had ever promulgated remained valid. " The Law is given," says Augustine, " that Grace may be sought ; Grace is given that the Law may be fulfilled." [6] As Anderson Scott has aptly put it, " Paul, as a Jew, had thought that men should keep the Law in order that they might be saved. As a Christian he saw that men

---

[1] Matt. 5[17].   [2] Rom. 3[21].
[3] On this point, see Dodd, *Romans*, 50 (*MNTC*).
[4] Rom. 3[1, 2].
[5] Rom. 7[12].
[6] Quoted art. *Law*, in *HDAC*, i. 691.

must be saved in order that they might keep the Law." [1]
The idea of a religion where the demand for absolute
obedience to God was abrogated never entered his
horizon. The type of attitude, familiar to us to-day,
which rebels at discipline, and resents the thought of
obligation, and grows irritated at the apostolic injunction to " humble itself under the mighty hand of God," [2]
Paul would not have countenanced for a moment.
Against any such attitude, his Gospel stands like a
bulwark. Against it he declares uncompromising downright defiance ; announcing that God was from the
beginning, is now, and ever shall be, absolute monarch
in His own world, and that the discipline of God, the
moral demand of God, is the very keystone of the arch
of life : remove it, and collapse and chaos must result.
Noble the law of God had always been, and noble in the
Christian dispensation it remained ; and the time would
never come when the demand on human nature would
be anything less than the full, direct, and absolute surrender of itself to the high God of its salvation.

Second, we have to remark on Paul's growing conviction of *the law's powerlessness to save*. It was his great
Christian discovery that what God had achieved by
sending Christ into the world was something which
the law, " weak through the flesh " as it was, could
never have done. [3] The law itself was " spiritual,"
πνευματικός ; [4] and, granted an ideal situation where all
men were spiritual too, it might have carried through
what it had set itself to achieve. Paul himself says as

---

[1] *Christianity according to St. Paul*, 45.

[2] I Peter 5⁶.

[3] Rom. 8³.

[4] Rom. 7¹⁴. The law is spiritual, says Holtzmann, as being
" Inbegriff dessen, was von Gott, dem Inhaber des Geistes, gewollt
und gefordert wird " (*Neutest. Theol.* ii. 29).

much when he writes to the Galatians, " If there had been a law given which could have given life, verily righteousness should have been by the law." [1]   The trouble was that the human nature, over against which the law stood, was not πνευματικός but σάρκινος, a creature of the flesh : and therefore true kinship and co-operation there could not be.   Jewish legalism might point man the road to travel, but actually to set him upon that road and give him strength for the journey was more than it could do.   The law might be noble ; but for dealing with the practical situation of a humanity labouring under the thraldom and the inevitable limitations which sin imposes, it was pitifully weak.

It cannot be concealed that a good deal of modern religion, even when bearing the Christian name, is in a like case, and suggests nothing so much as the picture of a man endeavouring to lift himself up into mid-air by the hair of his own head, or going through gymnastic exercises to increase his own muscles.   The most vital question for religion now, as in Paul's day, is the question of power ;   and much of what passes as Christianity is still on the far side, the Jewish side, of the line that runs through Damascus and the vision of Christ.   To this question, and to the answer which the Gospel gives, we shall have to return later.   Suffice it here to say that once it was the very crux of Paul's own most haunting problem ;   and what made the Christian revelation, when at last it came to him, a discovery so surpassingly wonderful and joyous was this, that at the flaming heart and centre of the new religion lay precisely the thing he needed most, the one thing for lack of which humanity was perishing—power, supernatural and divine.   " I am not ashamed of the gospel : for it

[1] Gal. 3[21].

is the power of God."[1] " Now unto Him that is able to do exceeding abundantly above all that we ask or think, according to the power that worketh in us, unto Him be glory."[2]

Third, let us observe that one function of the law, as Paul came to see it, was *to reveal sin.* " Had it not been for the law," he writes, " I would never have known what sin meant."[3] Here was an absolute standard of morality by which each man had to measure his life ; and those who might have been content to turn a blind eye to certain ways and habits of their own, or to use the argument (which indeed is the stock-in-trade of complacent souls in every age) that while they might not be saints they were at least as good as most of their neighbours and that nothing more was necessary, were likely to be rudely shaken out of their contentment and to have that complacent argument silenced when the searchlight of the law fell across their path. A day was coming when Paul was to find another and more searching test of life, another standard by which his own sins and the sins of men would be revealed for what they were and shown up in their true colours—namely, the cross of Jesus Christ. But in the meantime this was the function which legal religion in its own degree fulfilled. " What the law imparts," he declared bluntly, " is the consciousness of sin."[4]

Fourth, not only did the law reveal sin : *it actually promoted sin.* It instigated human nature to evil. As an illustration of this, Paul takes the tenth commandment of the Decalogue, and shows that the very prohibition stirred a desire for the forbidden thing within

---

[1] Rom. 1[16].   [2] Eph. 3[20].
[3] Rom. 7[7] (Moffatt)·   [4] Rom. 3[20] (Moffatt).

his soul.[1] Here, of course, the apostle has simply hit upon a truth with which everyone who knows anything of modern psychology is perfectly familiar. But the amazed horror with which the average orthodox Jew would greet his statement may well be imagined. " That the law ceremonially given to the nation by Moses, the privilege and pride of the chosen people, should not only be powerless to promote righteousness, but actually serve to let sin loose, bearing the brand of terrible guilt ; and that the whole history of the chosen people from the time of Moses should be simply an illustration of the truth of this dictum—nothing more than this was needed to stamp the name of Paul with utter infamy for every Jewish circle. . . . This alone amply explains the opposition which came to him from the Judaizers." [2] But Paul is quite clear about it. " The commandment, which was ordained to life, I found to be unto death." [3]

Fifth, Paul came to see that law, as a system of religion, was no more than *a temporary expedient*. It was not God's last word to man, any more than it had been His first. Four hundred and thirty years before the legal dispensation began, free grace had prevailed, in the covenant which God had made with Abraham ; [4] and in the case of Abraham himself, the promise was prior to the circumcision which ratified it.[5] Hence it could not be said that legalism was of the essence of religion. Appearing on the earth at a particular point of time, and for a special set of circumstances, it was no doubt destined, when it had served its purpose, to

---

[1] Rom. 7[7 f.]

[2] H. J. Holtzmann, *Neutestamentliche Theologie*, ii. 31 f.

[3] Rom. 7[10].   [4] Gal. 3[17].

[5] This is the point of Rom. 4[9-12], which looks back to Gen. 15[6], 17[10].

pass away. "The law *entered*," [1] says Paul, it came upon the scene : but something else had been there before. Law was an intermediate stage, [2] an intermezzo. [3] By way of strengthening this argument, Paul further points out that the law, according to Jewish doctrine, had been transmitted to man by a roundabout road, first through the mediation of angels, and then through the great lawgiver Moses [4]—a circumstance which must obviously place it in a lower rank than a revelation which came direct from God.

All this side of the apostle's thought may seem to us remote enough from the religious outlook of our own day. But in truth, what he is insisting upon is the entirely relevant and extremely important principle that God is not a prisoner in His own laws : God is alive, and therefore at any moment new truth may come breaking in. Blindness to this cardinal fact of religion was largely responsible for the fanatic outburst that nailed Jesus to the cross ; and if there is one lesson which, after Calvary, ought to be written upon the world's conscience as with a pen of iron on the rock, it is this, that the obscurantist attitude, the closed mind in every form, is a thing fundamentally irreligious and heathen. "Quench not the Spirit," wrote Paul. [5] It was really this great thought of a living, acting, working God, a God of endless resource, that was filling the apostle's mind when he inveighed against the overestimation of the law current among his contemporaries. Let them not regard as final and absolute what could, in the nature of things, be no more than temporary and provisional. Let them not think that they had

---

[1] Rom. 5[20].
[2] "Mittelstation." Holtzmann, *op. cit.* ii. 35.
[3] Wrede, *Paulus*, 75.   [4] Gal. 3[19].   [5] I Thess. 5[19].

exhausted the divine revelation, or that heaven's last word had come through. Let them open their closed minds and hearts to God's unsearchable riches. Such was Paul's appeal and challenge ; and beneath it there lay the thought which Whittier's familiar words have expressed so nobly—

> " Immortal Love, for ever full,
>   For ever flowing free,
> For ever shared, for ever whole,
>   A never-ebbing sea ! "

Sixth, Paul's reflection on the course of history and Providence convinced him that the main positive function of the law was *to prepare the way for the coming of the Christian revelation.* It was an integral part of the *praeparatio evangelica.* " The law was our school-master to bring us unto Christ."[1] Lightfoot has pointed out that the παιδαγωγός was the tutor, " frequently a superior slave," who " was entrusted with the moral supervision of the child," and remained in charge of him until such time as he came of age.[2] It was an apt illustration for Paul's purpose, for not only did it bring out clearly the positive service which the law had been put into the world to fulfil ; it also emphasized legalism's temporary character and inferior rank. That the discipline of life and morals to which the law subjected the Jewish nation was in a real sense preparing the way of the Lord, and making straight in the desert a highway for God, is abundantly clear ; and still to-day there are souls in whom the experience of the shackles of a code and the bondage of the letter creates a yearning and a hunger and a restlessness which, under Providence, lead on and out

---

[1] Gal. 3[24].   [2] *Galatians,* 147 f.

at last to the freedom of the Spirit of Christ and the liberty of the children of God.

Seventh, the conviction in which Paul's mind, as it explored the whole matter, finally came to rest was this, that the law, having fulfilled its purpose, *was destined to pass away*. To cling to it when its work was done would be to do irreparable damage to the cause of vital religion. " Christ is the end of the law for righteousness to every one that believeth."[1] This truth is expressed with vivid pictorial effect in the letter to the Colossians. There Paul depicts Christ, the champion of defeated souls, coming suddenly upon the scene when the verdict of condemnation had been pronounced, taking the document on which the sentence of death stood written, blotting out the fatal decree and nailing it to His cross.[2] We know that in those days it was the common custom, when a criminal was executed, publicly to placard his crime : a brief description of the charge on which the man had been condemned was written out and nailed to the cross itself. And it is possible that Paul, in the famous picture in Colossians, is referring to this practice. With a stroke of imaginative genius, he sees above Jesus' head, not the historic superscription " The King of the Jews," but the condemnation pronounced on mankind by the law ; and the truth which he wishes to drive home is that Christ, by dying, had ended the law's claim on man, and satisfied its ultimate demands, and thus finished its tyranny for ever.

Another way of expressing the same truth occurs in the letter to the Galatians. " Christ hath redeemed us from the curse of the law, being made a curse for us : for it is written, Cursed is every one that hangeth

[1] Rom. 10⁴.   [2] Col. 2¹⁴.

on a tree." [1]   Here the line which the apostle's thought follows seems to be this : Jesus, by His birth as a Jew, was "made under the law." [2]   He took His stand by His brethren's side. He involved Himself in their distress. He subjected Himself to the tyranny under which they laboured. By His death on the cross, He took upon Himself the full weight of the curse under which the law had brought them ; and by His resurrection, which was death's defeat, He declared that the curse was finished. In other words, Jesus had allowed the tyrant law to have all its way with Him ; in the dread deed of Calvary it had spent itself, and had exhausted all the curse ; and when He came out victorious on the other side, it meant that the evil bondage was lifted off humanity's heart once for all. The curse was dead. The law was ended.

A position so radical and revolutionary was bound to bring upon Paul the charge of antinomianism. How he met this charge, and how his central doctrine of union with Christ safeguarded the Gospel which he preached from any danger of an antinomian taint, we shall have occasion to see in a later study.[3] Suffice it here to record the apostle's intense conviction that to hark back to the law, after what Christ had done, could only defeat God's purpose in sending Christ, which was to help men to righteousness along a new and better way. Jews and Judaizing Christians might denounce Paul for an attitude to the law which, they declared, was bound to reduce morality to chaos : but they were wrong. As Moffatt well expresses it, " They had made the Law their Christ, and God intended Christ to be the Law." [4]

One circumstance which no doubt strengthened Paul

---

[1] Gal. 3[13], Deut. 21[23].   [2] Gal. 4[4].
[3] See pp. 194 ff.   [4] *Grace in the New Testament*, 266.

in this radical attitude to legalism was the discovery that, as long as the law was tolerated, the feud between Jew and Gentile would continue. Between them, the law was nothing more nor less than " a wall of partition " ;[1] and it would be foolish, to say the least of it, to do anything to reconstruct the barrier which Christ had swept away. " In His own flesh," writes Paul, " He put an end to the feud of the law with its code of commands, so as to make peace " between the two parties.[2] Hence Paul's working policy " was not *first* a course of the Law and *then* a course of Christianity— but Christianity straight away for every man."[3] Nothing could be more explicit than the clear-cut alternatives presented to the Galatians : *either* the law, *or* Christ— you cannot have both. A Christianity cramped in its action by the accoutrements of legalism was as little fit to face the world as David in Saul's hampering armour was fit to face Goliath. And any Christianity which hankered after the law was virtually denying the finality of Jesus. Were men slow to realize this ? Bluntly Paul would force on them the question, Has Christ done all, or has He left something undone ? You say, He has done all : then go on and draw the obvious conclusion—the law can add nothing. You cannot say "All is of grace," and yet assert (for instance) the religious importance of circumcision. " If righteousness comes by way of the law, then indeed Christ's death was useless."[4] " You are for justification by the law ? Then you are done with Christ."[5]

---

[1] Eph. 2[14]. There may be a reference here to the dividing wall in the Temple at Jerusalem. So E. F. Scott, *Ephesians*, 171 (*MNTC*).

[2] Eph. 2[15] (Moffatt).

[3] L. P. Jacks, *The Alchemy of Thought*, 268.

[4] Gal. 2[21] (Moffatt).   [5] Gal. 5[4] (Moffatt).

That is Paul's final word, and a drastic word it is.
But our study of the law, of its aims and limitations and
dangers, has now shown that, for Paul, no other final
word was possible. " Of all the stars," says Holtzmann,
" which fell to earth in the mighty firmament-shaking
experience of Paul's conversion, the law was the
greatest." [1] What need was there of stars, when the
full noonday glory had come ?

IV

In two of the three accounts of Paul's conversion,
given in the Book of Acts, there occurs the sentence " It
is hard for thee to kick against the pricks " ; [2] and the
vivid little picture of the recalcitrant animal which, as
it is being yoked to the plough, kicks out at the man
behind it and only hurts itself by doing so, suggests
very forcibly the condition of Paul's mind and heart
immediately prior to his apprehension by Christ.

One of the sharpest and most stinging goads was *his
own growing sense of the failure of Judaism*. Whatever
else his religion had done for him, it had certainly not
yet brought him peace with God, and he was beginning
to feel that it never would. Against that feeling he
fought with might and main. To toy with it would be
treachery. To countenance it would be to blow out the
light of faith and piety. Hence the fury of his attack
on the new sect. Action might relieve his brooding.
The wild whirlwind campaign might dissipate the uneasy shadows and questionings which were hanging
about his mind. But stubbornly the shadows refused to
lift. The questions persisted. Kick as he might, the
goad still stung.

---

[1] *Neutestamentliche Theologie*, ii. 37.   [2] Acts 9⁵, 26¹⁴.

Again, there was *the fact of the historic Jesus*. That, too, was strangely haunting. We shall not here discuss the question whether Paul as a young Pharisee in Jerusalem had actually seen Jesus. Certainly he had spoken to men who had seen Him. The leaders of the Pharisees had kept a watchful eye on Jesus all through His ministry ; they had sent their agents hither and thither to spy on Him ; they had followed Him north to Galilee ; they had cross-examined men and women who claimed that Jesus had healed them ; they had been the prime movers in His trial, condemnation, and death. Hence there can be little doubt that a certain knowledge of Jesus came to Paul through his Pharisaic associates ; and even if their version of the facts was hopelessly prejudiced and one-sided, that could not altogether prevent something of the nobility and majesty of the real Jesus from shining through. Nor is it at all credible that a man like the young Pharisee from Tarsus, with a mind so keen and alert and wideawake, and a soul so passionately religious, would allow any contemporary movement of thought or any new trend of religion to escape his scrutiny. He knew of Jesus' Messianic claim. He had conducted a considerable personal research into the blasphemous heresy, as he regarded it, with which the new faith was seeking to poison the very life of Judaism. Contact with the victims of his persecution added to his knowledge of their fundamental beliefs and stimulated his curiosity about a Man who, even when He was dead (as this Man assuredly was), could rouse such devotion in His followers. Bitterly as the Pharisee reviled Jesus and His memory, vehemently as he swore eternal enmity, destruction, and death to all that Jesus stood for, he could not quite cast off an impression of another kind which his own inquiries into Jesus' teaching and character had produced, nor silence a still small voice that bore a different witness. It was hard to kick against the goads.

A third fact Paul had to reckon with was *the lives of the Christians*. Their bravery under persecution, their absolute conviction that they had found the truth, their calm confidence and peace of heart that stood every imaginable test, their unconquerable happiness, their glad fearlessness (to quote the favourite New Testament expression [1])—all this could not but make a deep mark on Paul's mind. Paul certainly had no intention of being infected with the new heresy; but that, in Tertullian's words,[2] he was " struck with an inward misgiving," unconfessed probably even to himself, in witnessing the lives which its protagonists led, seems beyond doubt. Had they found something— some power, some peace, some joy—to which he himself, for all his seeking and striving, was a stranger? " Then said they among the heathen, The Lord hath done great things for them " [3]—so a Psalmist had envisaged the outside world's impression of God's elect people; and on Paul as a non-Christian, the lives of the Christians whom in his rôle of persecutor he encountered were beginning to produce an impression strangely similar, which refused to be thrust quite away, and against which his angry spirit kicked in vain. The Lord had done great things for them.

Finally, there was *the death of Stephen*. Remorse for his share in the work of that wild day may well have troubled him, though the records say nothing on this point. But if there were one circumstance of the martyrdom to which Paul's mind would frequently return, it must have been the strange way in which

---

[1] παρρησία.　　　　[2] See p. 67.　　　　[3] Ps. 126[2].

the martyr's last words appeared to tally with and verify the central Christian belief, that Jesus who had died was alive and exalted in glory. To Paul as he was then, this was the most pestilent and impossible of creeds ; yet had not Stephen with his dying breath declared, " I see the heavens opened, and the Son of man standing on the right hand of God " ? [1] Had he not spoken to One unseen, and cried, " Lord Jesus, receive my spirit ? " [2] Vigorously Paul repelled the deduction to which such questions pointed ; scathingly and contemptuously he reaffirmed his own dogmatic assurance that the Christian resurrection theory was a lie. Yet the memory of Stephen's eyes as he gazed heavenward in death, and of Stephen's colloquy with some living Spirit whom he called by Jesus' name, troubled the Pharisee's soul.[3] It was hard to kick against the goads.

We have seen, then, something of the inward conflict which was agitating Paul's mind when he set his face towards Damascus. It must not, however, be imagined that when you have traced the conflict you have explained the conversion. Too often the line has been taken of interpreting the event which revolutionized the man's life as the product of natural causes or the climax of ascertainable psychological processes. Against such a view, it is necessary to record a very definite protest. This is not to say that God does not work upon men along the lines which psychology indicates. Quite obviously He does ; and the idea that the discovery of the laws of nature and of

[1] Acts 7[56].   [2] Acts 7[59].
[3] For a vivid reconstruction of the influence of this event in Paul's life, see J. A. Hutton, *Finally : With Paul to the End*, chs. vii. and x.

thought which regulate human life means the progressive elimination of God and of God's action is manifestly unsound and absurd. It is still *God* who acts, though the mode of His action may now be traced. But what we are here concerned to maintain is that naturalistic explanations, even the best and fullest, are a hopelessly inadequate measuring-line for an event like Paul's conversion. No doubt his experience under the law, and the secret " goads " that we have mentioned, prepared the way ; but it was no mere projection of an inward state that suddenly changed his life and redeemed his soul. No doubt it was " in the fulness of the time " that the heavenly glory broke upon his vision, just as (in his own words) it was " in the fulness of the time," when the waiting world was ready, that God sent forth His Son ; [1] and yet the one event can as little be accounted for from below, from the purely human side, as the other. The Barthian school of theology has vulnerable points ; but its supreme service to our generation is the deliverance it heralds from the morass of subjectivism in which much recent religious thinking has wallowed. Christ's words to Simon Peter, in response to the great confession at Caesarea Philippi, might have pealed out again like a trumpet to Paul lying prostrate on the Damascus road : " Flesh and blood hath not revealed it unto thee, but My Father which is in heaven." [2] " In the end," as Dr. W. R. Matthews does well to remind us, " the problem of the supernatural resolves itself into the question of the existence of the living God." [3] Had anyone suggested to the apostle that the truth which enveloped him in a blaze of light was something to which, by the experience of the years

[1] Gal. 4⁴.   [2] Matt. 16¹⁷.   [3] *Essays in Construction*, 40.

behind him and by his own reactions to life, he had won his way, he would most certainly have considered such a suggestion as dangerously akin to blasphemy. His own account of it was very different. " It pleased God," he declares, " to reveal His Son in me." [1] No horizontal line of cause and effect could explain it : it had come vertically from above. The living God, unsearchable in His sovereign freedom, inscrutable in His absolute wisdom, had there and then interposed. And if the thought of a divine initiative runs like a red thread through all Paul's subsequent religion, if he is never tired of reiterating the great evangelical truth that nothing man may do or endure can bring peace and victory and that salvation is of the Lord, if his whole life is given to proclamation of the glorious paradox of a God who justifies the ungodly, it is because his own soul owed everything to an experience of which he could say with utter certainty that it was no mere resultant of human and natural forces, but a direct, original act of supernatural grace.

In that high moment of revelation, two things came to Paul, even as they had come to Jesus Himself at the baptism in Jordan—a Vision and a Voice. The efforts which have been made to empty this part of the conversion experience of all reality need not detain us here. Some have seen in it a product of an overheated and unbalanced imagination. Kohler calls it bluntly " a strange hallucination." [2] Others connect it with a particular theory of the " thorn in the flesh "—the theory of epilepsy. Others speak of the perils of a neurotic temperament. Others hint at sunstroke. A deeper knowledge of spiritual experience on its mystical side would have made such vagaries of interpretation

[1] Gal. 1[15 f.]   [2] *Jewish Theology*, 437.

unlikely ; and a more believing grasp of what is surely one of the main consequences of the Resurrection—namely, that in a world where Christ is alive and present, men may sometimes come upon Him face to face—would have made them impossible.[1] Why a living Jesus should *not* be able to reveal Himself to Paul is a question which many critics have not even troubled to consider ; but it is the crucial question. And when we find the three Lucan narratives reinforced by the apostle's own explicit statements, it is superfluous to continue searching for explanations, pathological or other. The man means precisely what he says. Jesus revealed Himself to him. Writing to the Corinthians, Paul enumerates the various appearances of the risen Lord to His disciples, and adds " Last of all He was seen of me also, as of one born out of due time." [2] The verb ὤφθη which Paul uses throughout this famous passage is the regular Septuagint expression for the revelation of the Deity to man ; [3] and here it denotes, as Weiss rightly remarks, " no subjective ' vision ' in the modern psychological sense, but a real beholding of the glorified Christ." [4] When Paul thus sets his own encounter with Jesus in direct line with the Resurrection experiences of the first disciples, he is deliberately stressing the fact that the revelation which

---

[1] Prof. C. E. Raven, in his noble book, *A Wanderer's Way*, ch. iii., has told how at one stage he accepted the Resurrection on intellectual grounds and was convinced of the evidence, without realizing the full consequences of the belief ; and how he was enabled, through a personal vision of Christ which came to him, to draw the practical deductions implicit in the Resurrection faith.

[2] I Cor. 15⁸.   [3] Deissmann, *St. Paul*, 120.

[4] J. Weiss, *Erster Korintherbrief*, 349 (in Meyer's *Kommentar*) : " Dass ὤφθη bei ihm nicht eine subjektive ' Vision ' im modern-psychologischen Sinne bedeutet, sondern ein wirkliches Sehen des Verklärten, ist selbstverständlich."

he received was in every way as real and as objective as theirs. It is significant, moreover, to find that on occasions when his apostolic authority was called in question and attacked, he reminded his critics that in the Damascus experience there lay a full vindication of his claim. No one could bear apostolic rank—so the mind of the Church decreed—who had not personally seen the risen Jesus. "An apostle must necessarily have been an eye-witness of the resurrection. He must be able to testify from direct knowledge to this fundamental fact of the faith." [1] And Paul always insisted that he possessed this essential qualification. "Am I not an apostle? Am I not free? Have I not seen Jesus Christ our Lord?" [2] In the face of all this, to speak of Paul's vision as "illusion," "projection," "hallucination," and so on, simply betrays a lack of spiritual perception and a defective understanding of the ways of God. What shattered the flaming career of persecution, wrenched the stubborn Pharisee right round in his track, killed the blasphemer, and gave birth to the saint was nothing illusory: it was the most real thing in life, as real as the fact of God, as real as the risen life of Christ. It was, in the apostle's own words, an "arrest." [3] It was a "revelation." [4] It was a new divine "Let there be light!" [5] And the glorious words in which Paul's great disciple of a later day, St. Augustine, described his own redeeming experience of God in Christ might have come straight from the apostle himself: "With Thy calling and shouting Thou didst break my deafness; with Thy flashing and shining Thou didst scatter my blindness. At the scent of Thee I drew in breath, and I pant for Thee. I have

---

[1] Lightfoot, *Galatians*, 98. [2] I Cor. 9[1].
[3] Phil. 3[12]. [4] Eph. 3[3]. [5] II Cor. 4[6].

tasted, and I hunger and thirst. Thou hast touched me, and I am on fire for Thy peace." [1]

Johannes Weiss, in his book *Das Urchristentum*, has raised the question whether Paul's religion, based upon this tremendous event and determined by it at every point, can be taken as normative for other Christians. The point at issue here is a vital one, and demands careful thought. That Paul's personal experience is the foundation of his Gospel goes without saying. Damascus coloured all his theology. It is " conversion-theology," to use the familiar phrase.[2] Through all his religious thinking, there can be traced his own sudden apprehension by Christ. Now some have felt that this raises a serious difficulty. Can a man whose experience was of this cataclysmic sort be the best guide in religion for those who have come into the Kingdom of God by another way ? Must not the very individuality of his message prove a hindrance rather than a help ? Is it not inevitable that much of his teaching should sound alien and remote ? Is it not natural that many Christians to-day should feel no real kinship for some of the distinctive elements in his Gospel ? Weiss considers that it is. The matter is so important that his words deserve to be quoted.

" Just as it was by a complete break in his life that Paul himself reached his convictions, so it is to people who have passed from one religion to another that all the fundamental ideas of his theology are directed. For later ages this constitutes a serious difficulty in Paul's

---

[1] *Confessions*, x. 38.

[2] H. J. Holtzmann, *Neutestamentliche Theologie*, ii. 238 : " Die Explikation des Inhalts der Bekehrung, die Systematisierung der Christophanie."

theology, and it has given rise to endless debate and confusion. In view of the authoritative place held by that theology in the Church, his road and that of his converts came to be regarded as the normal way for every Christian to travel, and Paul himself as the type of the converted sinner, whose experiences all who wanted to rank as ' believing ' and ' converted ' in the true sense must needs recapitulate. But in point of fact, the necessary conditions for this were lacking in the case of the overwhelming majority of Christians. The most of us have not moved over to Christianity from Judaism or heathenism ; we did not first come to know the Gospel in our middle years, after living in outer darkness. We have grown up in the Christian community, have been reared by Christian parents, have received from childhood the message of the heavenly Father and of the Lord Jesus, and have in perfectly normal fashion been so trained in the basal laws of Christianity that we have no personal knowledge of the thick darkness of a sin-sunk paganism. Hence in many a life the question arises, How can I manage to experience ' justification ' and ' redemption ' ? When will the great moment come when I shall be a converted believer ? It has often been the most earnest spirits who have felt it a sacred obligation to have their ' day of Damascus,' and have sought with this end in view to bring about a crisis that would not come of its own accord. . . . But without a doubt there are many whose whole nature rebels against going through such a conversion process—not at all because they are impenitent or self-willed, but precisely because they are deeply sincere and honest. They realize themselves to be God's children, just as Jesus taught His disciples ; and do not feel called on to travel the long difficult road of conversion through the valley of despair, in order ' to receive the adoption of sons,' as Paul puts it, as though that were something new and fresh. That is why they find such difficulties with all those expressions, ' justification,' ' redemption,' and the rest, which denote a single occurrence ; they are not conscious of having ever experienced justification or the forgiveness of sins as a special act, seeing that from the earliest days they have lived in the atmosphere of God's grace ; and to be reborn as a ' new creature ' seems to them organically impossible, because they are well aware that the question for them can only be one of slow and gradual progress, not without moments of stumbling and retreat. Such is the position of the normal Church member, reared in the discipline of a Christian family, towards Paul's doctrine of redemption. There are, of course, other Christians, those, for example, who through a serious fall and long-continued carelessness have lost all Christian character and fellowship with God. Moreover, there are millions to-day who, in spite of Church and school, have never really been in inward sympathy with the spirit of the Gospel : there is a modern paganism springing up within the Church itself. And it may be that, both for those fallen Christians and for this great indifferent multitude, the ' conversion-theology,' the ' mission-theology,' is the true way of salvation : that we cannot exclude. But it is quite certain that there are countless men to-day for whom Paul's Gospel with its intense and dramatic form is simply incomprehensible, and out of harmony with their own life's experience." [1]

I have quoted this passage at length because it involves a practical issue of first-class importance. We can agree with Weiss at once when he emphasizes the

[1] J. Weiss, *Das Urchristentum*, 337-339.

intensely individual character of Paul's Gospel. No one was more conscious of that than the apostle himself. " My Gospel," he called it ; [1] and frankly declared his inability to preach anything except what had been given him, and what had passed through the flames of his own soul. And, indeed, no Gospel that lacks an intensely individual touch can be worth very much. Again, it is perfectly true to say, as Weiss does, that Christian truth and training and lifelong fellowship in the beloved community are factors of incalculable value. A cataclysmic change from Christ-hatred to Christ-devotion (as in Paul's case), or from arrant, God-denying paganism to spiritual religion (as in the case of many of his converts), is obviously not the only gateway into the Kingdom ; nor is it necessary for a soul to have gone wildly and dramatically astray in order to appreciate the peace of reconciliation. But where Weiss surely is seriously mistaken is in assuming a radical antithesis between the two types of experience. There is no such antithesis. It is one of the most certain facts in the world that no man—whatever his faith or folly may have been—can save himself : and this fact alone would make Paul's Gospel universally cogent, for it is the burden of everything he has to say. All alike, those nurtured in a Christian atmosphere no less than those arrested in sin's mid-career, are dependent utterly upon God : here at least there is neither Jew nor Greek, bond nor free. Hence it is simply not true to say that, for those whose road has been different, Paul's message is " unintelligible." It is not true to history : it is refuted by the fact that that message has been, as Denney has pointed out, " incomparably the greatest source of spiritual revivals

[1] Rom. 2[16].

in the Christian Church for nearly two thousand years." [1] And it is not true to individual experience : vast multitudes of men and women, who have had no such violent revolution as Paul lived through, have yet heard in his words the very voice of God to their souls. Indeed, it is precisely the intense individuality of Paul's experience that makes his Gospel universal. That is the great paradox which we have to grasp if we are to understand him at all. Had the experience been something less than the individual, singular, distinctive thing it was, the resultant Gospel would have been something less than the universal, catholic thing it is.

The fact is that the real antithesis is not, as Weiss supposes, between those who have entered the Kingdom by the one way and those who have entered it by the other : it is between those who, whatever their way may have been, have personally committed their lives to God, and those who have not. And if a man cannot read Paul's " conversion-theology " without a sense of unreality ; if he is " not conscious of having ever experienced the forgiveness of sins as a special act " ; if when he hears the words, " Jesus Christ came into the world to save sinners," there is no inward urge to go on and add " of whom I am chief " ; if the apostolic ardours and appeals seem somehow strangely irrelevant ; if all he can say about the transition from darkness to light and from death to life is that " it is out of harmony with his own experience "— then such an one would be well advised to ask, not whether Paul was limited and made one-sided and largely unintelligible by the particular mode in which Christianity gripped him, but whether he himself has ever really committed his soul to God, and allowed

[1] *The Christian Doctrine of Reconciliation*, 179.

Christ and His religion to get possession of his life. The ordinary Christian to-day, working out his salvation with fear and trembling, knowing that it is God who worketh in him, has far fewer difficulties with Paul than Weiss's words would lead us to suppose. He does not feel that the apostle is talking in an unknown tongue. He does not complain that between this man's life and his own there is a great gulf fixed. If he is sensitive at all, he feels that there is a kinship. He finds himself at home, eminently so, with this great ardent soul who knew life's heights and depths so well. He believes that he can understand him. And he is right. For Damascus, so far from setting Paul apart from us and keeping him away, has made him brother of us all.

V

We have now to examine the immediate consequences for thought and life and religion which the revelation at Damascus brought with it. It would, of course, be a mistake to suppose that the full implications of his amazing experience were evident to the apostle from the first, or that everything which subsequently found a place in the Gospel he preached took shape at once within his mind. The first disciples, to whom the original resurrection appearances of Jesus Christ were granted, required time in order to grasp all that their Master's return involved for themselves and for the world ; and most of life's great spiritual experiences are of necessity followed by a period of rethinking and readjustment. In Paul's case, the withdrawal into Arabia, which St. Chrysostom and many of the fathers interpreted, with rather curious exegesis, as a mission for the conversion of the Arabs, suggests rather a deliberate seeking of seclusion for the purpose of deep reflection and communion with God : the context of the passage—particularly the declaration " I conferred not with flesh and blood "—makes this almost certain.[1] The converted man realized that time was needed for the consolidation of his position. But while that is true, the fact remains that some of the results of Damascus— and these precisely the most crucial, life-changing results —came *with the conversion itself*. No interval elapsed. They were *given*. They were immediate and direct. They were flashes of discovery. They were glories of certainty. They were sudden facts that gripped the man's mind and soul. Our question now is, What were these results, these facts which stood thus immediately revealed ?

First and foremost, *Jesus was alive*. Here it is of the utmost importance to realize that what Paul saw was no vague " Heavenly Being," no impersonal Messiah : it was Jesus Himself, the Person of whom he had heard so much, whose life and character and lineaments had become well known to him through his persecuting con- tacts with the new sect. The vision of a heavenly Messiah would never by itself have made Paul a Christian : indeed, it might only have served to strengthen his Jewish pride and to confirm him in his antagonism to those who dared to claim divine rights

[1] Gal. 1[16f.]. See Lightfoot, *Galatians*, 90. It is very doubtful' however, if Lightfoot is right in saying that " Arabia " here means the Sinaitic peninsula. The name might quite well refer to the desert hinterland east of Damascus. It is " a singularly elusive term. Originally it meant simply ' desert ' or ' desolation,' and when it became an ethnographic proper name it was long in acquiring a fixed and generally understood meaning. ' Arabia ' shifted like the nomads, drifted like the desert sand " (J. Strahan, in *HDAC*, i. 88).

for a crucified Nazarene. We cannot therefore too strongly underline the fact that it was Jesus, and none other, the Jesus who had been crucified, who appeared to Paul in the way. So came the great discovery that Jesus was alive. Then His followers had been right after all ! .Then the faith on which they had staked their lives was really true ! Then Stephen's dying declaration that he saw Jesus on the right hand of God had been, not blasphemy, but sober, literal fact ! Then all that those persecuted men and women had said about having their Leader with them still, about holding daily intimate communion with Him, had been no fabricated, preposterous story, as it had seemed, but strictly accurate and genuine ! It was a staggering discovery.

It meant, moreover, that everything that Jesus had been and had done, every title that He had claimed or that His followers had claimed for Him, was now attested by God Himself. For Jesus' conquest of death and defeat could be nothing less than God in action, God's right arm made bare, God's seal set convincingly to the Messianic claim, God's final vindication of His Son. In this connection it ought to be remarked how frequently, in describing the resurrection, Paul uses the passive in preference to the active voice : occasionally he says " Jesus rose," but much more often " He was raised " or " God raised Him." [1] This is deeply significant. The resurrection was *God's* act. It was God's authentication of Jesus as Messiah and Son. The following passages may be taken as typical. " Christ was raised up from the dead by the glory of the Father." [2] " If the

---

[1] That Paul was here in line with the practice of the primitive Church is evidenced by such passages as Acts $2^{24. 32. 36}$, $3^{15. 26}$, 4^{10}, 5^{30}, 10^{40}.   [2] Rom. 6^4.

Spirit of Him that raised up Jesus from the dead dwell in you, He that raised up Christ from the dead shall also quicken your mortal bodies." [1] " We have testified of God that He raised up Christ." [2] " Ye are risen with Him through the faith of the operation of God, who hath raised Him from the dead." [3] " To wait for His Son from heaven, whom He raised from the dead." [4] Most striking of all are the great statement to the Philippians, " He became obedient unto death, even the death of the cross ; wherefore God also hath highly exalted Him," [5] and the famous words in the prologue to the Romans, " declared to be the Son of God with power, according to the spirit of holiness, by the resurrection from the dead." [6] All this points back to the startling truth which broke upon Paul in the hour of his conversion, that the new religion stood, not on any human credulity or invention, but on the very word and guarantee of God. As the apostle himself once put it, in Jesus risen and alive there had sounded forth the great divine " Yes," affirming all the most glorious promises that God had ever given. [7]

This, then, was the first immediate consequence of Paul's conversion experience. Jesus, he now knew, was alive, by the power of God. From this point right on to the end of his life, the resurrection was central in the apostle's thinking. It could not be otherwise. Protestant theology, concentrating on the atoning sacrifice of the cross, has not always done justice to this apostolic emphasis on the risen life. We can certainly agree with Denney when he says that " nothing could be more curiously unlike the New

---

[1] Rom. 8[11].   [2] I Cor. 15[15].   [3] Col. 2[12].
[4] I Thess. 1[10].   [5] Phil. 2[8f].   [6] Rom. 1[4].
[7] II Cor. 1[20].

Testament than to use the resurrection to belittle or disparage the death." [1]   But it is not a case of belittling or disparaging the death.   It is a case of recognizing with Paul that without the resurrection the death would have been powerless to save ; and that without a risen, living, present Christ, with whom through faith the believer can come into union, all the benefits of the death would have had to stand unappropriated for ever.   It was on the resurrection fact that the Church was built.   It was the resurrection Gospel that the apostles preached.   It was the experience of union with the risen Christ that made them the mighty men of God they were.   The fact of the matter is that, so far from belittling the death by laying all the emphasis we can upon the resurrection, we are doing what is most likely to interpret that death in its full redeeming value ; and we are in far graver danger of belittling it when the resurrection emphasis is lacking.   In short, no good service can be done to religion or to Pauline study by separating the two events and setting one over against the other.   The single verse, " who was delivered for our offences, and was raised again for our justification," [2] should warn us that any such isolation is unwarranted and quite unreal.   The point which we are here concerned to make is that Protestant theology, in some of its phases, has unconsciously altered the apostolic accent by almost isolating the cross, and failing to see Calvary with the resurrection light breaking behind it.

About Paul's own position there can be no doubt. No one who reads the epistles will ever be likely to minimize the power and glory of the cross : it con-

---

[1] *The Christian Doctrine of Reconciliation*, 287.
[2] Rom. 4[25].

strained the man's love, and subdued his stubborn will. But sentences like " We preach Christ crucified,"[1] and " I determined not to know anything among you, save Jesus Christ, and Him crucified,"[2] do not alter the fact that all through Paul's religion there runs the overwhelming experience of a Christ at his right hand, a living Presence with whom he can commune, in whom he can confide, from whom he can draw all the daily guidance that he needs ; and that all through his Gospel there sounds the trumpet note, " Christ, being raised from the dead, dieth no more."[3]

To Paul, the resurrection was a historic event of the past, but it was also much more : it was a present reality. Dr. R. H. Strachan has drawn attention to the significant fact that, in the summary of the apostle's teaching set down in the opening verses of I Corinthians 15, while the verbs " died," " was buried," " appeared " are all aorists, the word " rose " is given in the perfect tense. " The perfect $\dot{\epsilon}\gamma\dot{\eta}\gamma\epsilon\rho\tau\alpha\iota$ reverberates like the stroke of a bell right through the chapter."[4] Not only has Jesus risen, Paul meant to say : He is alive— now ! For I have seen Him, and I know. Chesterton in one place, speaking of Plato and Shakespeare, begs us to " imagine what it would be to live with such men still living, to know that Plato might break out with an original lecture to-morrow, or that at any moment Shakespeare might shatter everything with a single song."[5] Paul needed no such imagination where Jesus was concerned. At any moment Jesus might break out with a new self-revelation, or shatter Judaism and heathenism alike with the new song of salvation.

[1] I Cor. 1[23].   [2] I Cor. 2[2].   [3] Rom. 6[9].
[4] *The Historic Jesus in the New Testament*, 46.
[5] G. K. Chesterton, *Orthodoxy*, 285.

Such was the first direct message of Damascus—Jesus was alive.

The second immediate result of the conversion experience was *the revolutionizing of Paul's whole attitude to the cross*. As a Pharisee, he had always held that the death of Jesus put the Messianic claim out of court. Who of Israel's prophets or Rabbis had ever dared to envisage a Messiah suffering death ? The idea was monstrous, unthinkable. It played havoc with Jesus' pretensions. It finished His foolish followers' creed. It reduced their cause to mockery. But even stranger than the delusion that One who had died could be Messiah was the arrant madness which could go on maintaining that belief in the face of such a death as Jesus had endured. Crucifixion was the very abyss of ignominy. Had not the law declared, " He that is hanged is accursed of God " ? Had it not warned the people that one dead body, if allowed to hang a few hours too long upon the tree, would defile their whole land ?[1] Jew and Gentile were at one in regarding the cross as the symbol of final condemnation and uttermost shame. " Servile supplicium " was the Roman designation ; and in Cicero's words something almost like a shudder can be felt—" crudelissimum taeterrimumque supplicium."[2] Hence we may be sure that when Paul, writing to the Corinthians, admits that " Christ crucified " is " unto the Jews a stumbling-block, and unto the Greeks foolishness,"[3] he is doing something more than reporting what he saw

[1] Deut. 21[23].
[2] Cicero, *In Verrem*, v. 66. Cf. *Pro Rabirio*, v. 10 : " Far be the very name of a cross, not only from the body, but even from the thoughts, eyes, and ears of Roman citizens."
[3] I Cor. 1[23].

around him. He is drawing upon first-hand experience. He is remembering his own pre-Christian reactions to the story of the cross. No one had cried out more loudly against the σκάνδαλον of it than Paul the Jew ; and no one had more scathingly denounced its μωρία than Paul the Roman citizen. Again, when we hear him declaring that " no man speaking by the Spirit of God calleth Jesus accursed (ἀνάθεμα)," [1] it is another autobiographical echo of the same kind that we are listening to. As a Christian, Paul could cry " If any man love not the Lord Jesus Christ, let him be anathema ! " [2] But once it had been Christ Himself on whom his anathemas had been showered. How could a would-be Messiah whose career had ended in the appalling disgrace of crucifixion be anything but a pretender and a charlatan ? What else was there to say than that God's curse was upon Him ?

All this the flash of light at Damascus changed. Jesus had conquered death. He had passed through it and beyond it to eternal glory. There can, of course, be no question that it was only after long, deep, prayerful meditation that Paul came to see the full and many-sided significance of the cross, as we have it set forth in his epistles. But from the very moment when the exalted Jesus was revealed to him, he knew that the curse was gone. To regard as a victim of the divine denunciation One whom God had so triumphantly vindicated was henceforth impossible. The σκάνδαλον was removed. The death of the cross was the wisdom and glory of God. Jesus had not been driven to it helplessly, broken and defeated : He had accepted it in the freedom of His own unconquered soul. Along the line of the cross lay the world's redemption. Cal-

---

[1] I Cor. 12³.   [2] I Cor. 16²².

vary was in the divine plan for mending a broken earth. All this Paul began to see. It was the hour of Damascus that taught him the first notes of what was one day to become a great, jubilant battle-song of faith—" God forbid that I should glory, save in the cross." [1]

This leads to a third direct consequence of the encounter with Jesus on the road—*the man's surrender to the divine love which now stood revealed*. That Jesus Christ, whose name he had maligned, whose followers he had harried, whose cause he had striven to bring down to destruction, should nevertheless have come to meet him, and to lay His hands upon him, was a thought at once gloriously uplifting and terribly subduing. For him, then, blasphemer and persecutor as he was, Jesus had been seeking! For him, grace and mercy had entered the field. For him, the Lord had climbed Calvary. In that hour of revelation Paul realized that right on to the end of his days he would be immeasurably Christ's debtor. With endless wonder he now could speak of " the Son of God who loved me, and gave Himself for me." [2] And never for a moment did he doubt that the love which had come seeking him was the love of God Himself. The order of the clauses in the great Trinitarian benediction, where " the grace of the Lord Jesus Christ " stands first, followed by " the love of God," may be taken as a transcript of Paul's own experience : [3] it was through his meeting with Christ, a Christ who was all grace, that he entered on the knowledge of love divine. All his feverish quest for peace and righteousness and certainty was now over, for God in Christ had taken the initiative.

[1] Gal. 6[14].　　[2] Gal. 2[20].　　[3] II Cor. 13[14].

The poor, smoking lamp of legalism had flickered out in the glory of the dawn. God had reconciled him. While he was yet a " sinner," an " enemy "—how deep dyed in Paul's own heart's-blood the great words in Romans are !—Christ had died for him.[1] Gone was the stern, inexorable God of Judaism, watching His creatures toiling for a justification He knew they could never win. Now there stood revealed a Father yearning for His child. Face to face with that seeking grace, that reconciling love, Paul's whole being went down in uttermost surrender. With all the passion of his soul he responded. He gave himself to God. He worshipped Christ. Grace on the side of God had met faith on the side of man : and from the white-hot crucible of that experience there emerged a new life. The cataclysm of that hour ushered Paul into a totally different sphere of being. He was now as unlike the man who had set out from Jerusalem as noonday is unlike midnight, as life is unlike death. His outlook, his world, his nature, his moral sense, his life-purpose— all were changed. He was a man " in Christ."

Out of this there arose the last direct consequence of the conversion which we shall notice here—*the vision of a waiting world*. Paul suddenly knew that he had found the truth for which all men everywhere were seeking, the truth for lack of which Jew and Gentile alike were perishing ; and there rang through his being the imperious command that to the proclamation of this truth his whole life must henceforward be devoted. This was Paul's prophetic call, the source of his apostolic consciousness, the origin of his doctrine of election, and the mainspring and motive of the evangelizing passion which

[1] Rom. 5[8, 10].

was to carry him tirelessly over land and sea as a herald of the risen Lord.

It is interesting to compare his call with that of his great predecessor Isaiah.[1] In the one case as in the other, the decisive experience came with startling suddenness : a day in the temple, an hour on the road, and two lives were changed for ever. For both men, moreover, it was a personal vision of God which proved the turning-point. " I saw the Lord sitting upon a throne," declared Isaiah. " Who art Thou, Lord ? " said Paul. Again, in the heart of both, the first reaction to the vision was an overwhelming sense of personal unworthiness and sin : " I am a man of unclean lips," cried Isaiah ; " Jesus, whom thou persecutest," were the words that revealed to Paul his shame. Once again, there came to both, lying prostrate in self-loathing and despair, the wonderful sense of a cleansing, pardoning, divine love which was taking the initiative. " This hath touched thy lips, and thine iniquity is taken away." And finally, to these visions of God, of self, and of redeeming grace, there was added, for both prophet and apostle, the further vision of a lost world waiting for their evangel. " Here am I ; send me," cried the one. " Necessity is laid upon me," declared the other, " yea, woe is unto me, if I preach not the gospel ! "[2] Paul knew, and Isaiah knew, what in some degree all who have ever truly come face to face with the eternal know, that the vision of God is never an end in itself, that indeed it is the very death of religion when it hugs its glories to itself instead of scattering them abroad, and that every disciple who has seen the light must be more than a disciple, must be a herald—or else fail miserably the God of his salvation.

[1] Is. 6[1 ff.]   [2] I Cor. 9[16].

" I knew that Christ had given me birth,
To brother all the souls on earth."

" They who have the torch," says the old Greek
proverb, " must pass on the light."

Hence Paul would never tolerate any minimizing of
his apostolic office. It was expressly to claim him for
God's work that Christ had appeared outside the
Damascus gates. " I am an envoy for Christ," he tells
the Corinthians.[1] " Paul, a servant of Jesus Christ,
called to be an apostle, set apart for the gospel of God,"
is his introduction to the Romans.[2] " The man who is
now speaking," comments Karl Barth, " is an emissary,
bound to perform his duty ; the minister of his King ; a
servant, not a master." [3] Elsewhere he rebuts the
insinuations of those who charged him with grasping at
an office to which he had no claim, by declaring that he
had actually been predestined to it by God. " The God
who had set me apart from my very birth called me by
His grace. . . . He chose to reveal His Son to me, that
I might preach Him to the Gentiles." [4]

Here we are at the very nerve-centre of Paul's great
thought of election. We shall never understand this
doctrine as it appears in the epistles until we realize that
it runs back to the personal experience of a man who,
by the fact of his conversion, discovered himself to be
elected by God, marked out by divine decree for service
and ambassadorship. " He hath chosen us in Him (in
Christ) before the foundation of the world." [5]   Predestination, in this aspect, is just another name for
grace. It is safe to say that if Paul's interpreters had
always kept this personal background adequately in

[1] II Cor. 5[20] (Moffatt).   [2] Rom. 1[1] (Moffatt).
[3] *The Epistle to the Romans* (Eng. tr.), 27.
[4] Gal. 1[15 f.] (Moffatt).   [5] Eph. 1[4].

view, many of the enormities of interpretation which
have overshadowed the whole idea of election, making
it productive of misgiving and even of misery for
thousands of pious souls, could never have been per-
petrated. What Paul is really trying to do is not to
suggest misgivings but to remove them. He is bidding
anxious souls reflect that their religion stands in the last
resort, not upon their choice of Christ, but upon Christ's
choice of them. What a note of ringing confidence, he
seems to say, that fact ought to impart to your personal
religion !

The Pauline doctrine of election, in short, resolves
itself into the words of Jesus in the fourth Gospel : " Ye
have not chosen Me, but I have chosen you." [1] And if
the apostle kept stressing this thought with might and
main, it was because he had found it such a mighty help
and strength and support in the vicissitudes of his own
life and religion. " The gifts and calling of God are
without repentance," he declares ; or as Dr. Moffatt
strikingly translates it, " God never goes back upon His
call," [2] a statement which every doubting soul, in the
twentieth century as in the first, would do well to ponder.
You are " called to be saints," [3] he tells his converts ; as
though to say, " Let no doubt from within, no criticism
from without, destroy your quiet assurance or make you
question the reality of the experience that has come to
you. It is the eternal will and decree of God, nothing
less, on which your new life rests." It is the same
magnificent confidence, generated by a personal experience of Christ, which breathes through his words to the
Corinthians, " As I hold this ministry by God's mercy to
me, I never lose heart in it." [4] His own moods might

---

[1] John 15[16].   [2] Rom. 11[29].   [3] Rom. 1[7], I Cor. 1[2].
[4] II Cor. 4[1] (Moffatt).

change, feelings might come and go, difficulties that he had never bargained for might suddenly crowd in upon his path : but behind all that stood God, and God's word was rock ; and he could no more question the validity of his apostleship than he could doubt the truth of God Himself.

And yet, sure as he was of this, Paul never took it for granted, nor lost the sense of overwhelming amazement that he, of all people in the world, should have been called to proclaim God's Christ. Why should the choice have fallen on the chief of sinners ? That was the thought which, right to the end of his life, filled his soul with breathless wonder. " Unto me, who am less than the least of all saints "—ἐλαχιστοτέρῳ, a reinforced superlative—" is this grace given, that I should preach among the Gentiles the unsearchable riches of Christ." [1] Isaiah, in his day, may have experienced that same feeling ; for had not his vision shown him all the shining seraphs round the throne, ready at any moment to go forth at the King's command and do His bidding, and why, then, should God look to him—a being not only mortal, but actually sunk in sin, who just a moment before had been crying " Unclean, unclean "—to be the messenger of redemption ? Perhaps to Isaiah, meditating on these things with deepest wonder, there came the thought that the very depths in which he had wandered and in which God had found him explained his commission ; that he knew something about divine forgiving grace which the seraphs in the untroubled bliss of heaven could never know ; and that therefore there would be a passion and an urgency in his proclamation of the message that would drive it deep into the heart and conscience of the world. Such, at any rate, was Paul's

[1] Eph. 3⁸.

feeling. That God in grace should have looked upon the sons of men at all was a thing to bring any man to his feet with shouts of joy : but that God should have looked upon *him*, the persecutor of God's cause, the man who more than any other had crucified God's Christ afresh, was a thing to bow him to the ground in amazed, adoring gratitude. It was this that took Paul and grappled him to Christ with fetters of deathless gratitude. Henceforth he was literally a bondslave of the evangel. For one thought now possessed him like a passion : to lead men everywhere to the source of all salvation and the fountain of living waters, to that stream in the Damascus desert of which his own soul had drunk, whose name was the grace of God and the everlasting mercy of Christ.

CHAPTER IV

MYSTICISM AND MORALITY

THE heart of Paul's religion is union with Christ. This, more than any other conception—more than justification, more than sanctification, more even than reconciliation—is the key which unlocks the secrets of his soul. Within the Holy of Holies which stood revealed when the veil was rent in twain from the top to the bottom on the day of Damascus, Paul beheld Christ summoning and welcoming him in infinite love into vital unity with Himself. If one seeks for the most characteristic sentences the apostle ever wrote, they will be found, not where he is refuting the legalists, or vindicating his apostleship, or meditating on eschatological hopes, or giving practical ethical guidance to the Church, but where his intense intimacy with Christ comes to expression. Everything that religion meant for Paul is focused for us in such great words as these : " I live, yet not I, but Christ liveth in me." [1] " There is, therefore, now no condemnation to them which are in Christ Jesus." [2] " He that is joined unto the Lord is one spirit." [3]

I

The growing recognition of the fact that union with Christ is the centre of Paul's personal religion and of the Gospel he proclaims marks a definite and important advance in New Testament interpretation. There are

[1] Gal. 2[20].　　[2] Rom. 8[1].　　[3] I Cor. 6[17].

indeed those who, partly through the influence of a traditional Paulinism, and partly from a rooted dislike and distrust of anything to which the word " mystical " may be applied, still fail to give this cardinal reality the place that is its due. Protestant theology, throughout a great part of its history, has concentrated on the thought of justification. This it has regarded as more typically Pauline than anything else. To elucidate the circle of ideas associated with justification was all that was necessary, it held, to understand Paul. This was the first axiom with which generations of investigators went to work. Now no one who realizes the deep religious principles that are at stake in all the apostle's references to this matter will wish for a moment to set justification aside, or indeed to regard it as anything less than crucial for a true evangelicalism. All that we are here concerned to insist is that it was a one-sided development which made this idea central and saw in it the final clue to Paul's religion. Ritschl, taking a wider view, spoke of Christianity as " an ellipse with two foci " : these were justification and the kingdom of God.[1] But the great Pauline phrase " in Christ " received too scant attention from the Ritschlian school ; and perhaps J. K. Mozley was not going too far when he declared that " Ritschl is an entirely unreliable guide in any interpretation of a New Testament passage, which points in the direction of mystical union."[2] In Denney's view, " reconciliation " was the solving word. " Just because the experience of reconciliation," he wrote, " is the central and fundamental experience of the Christian religion, the doctrine of reconciliation is not so much one doctrine as the inspiration and focus

---

[1] *Justification and Reconciliation*, 11.
[2] *Ritschlianism*, 139.

of all. . . . In the experience of reconciliation to God through Christ is to be found the principle and the touchstone of all genuine Christian doctrine." [1] Denney's work has put all students of Paul deeply in his debt ; but here again the criticism may legitimately be urged that the conception of union with Christ occupies something less than the quite decisive place in which Paul sets it. It is at this point, too, that the Barthian theology has left itself most open to attack. Sentimental mysticism Barth cannot endure : it is the apotheosis of all that is most misguided in religion. But there is a mysticism that is not sentimental, and this school is in real danger of rejecting the true with the false. In his treatment of Paul's great doctrines of the indwelling Spirit and the fellowship of believers with Christ, Barth has nothing at all comparable to his own noble discussion of such themes as the righteousness of God. If the awe of a human soul lying prostrate at the feet of God, " the wholly Other," is essential to religion, the joy of the soul which is taken into fullest and most intimate communion with God in Christ is no less religious ; and the Barthians, who have served their generation so well in the emphasis they have laid on the former, will not be able to escape the charge of onesidedness until they make room for the latter. Without a doubt, the great words of Faber's familiar hymn will always awaken a responsive echo in the truly religious soul :

> " O how I fear Thee, living God,
> With deepest, tenderest fears,
> And worship Thee with trembling hope
> And penitential tears ! "

But that, as Faber saw and as some of the present-day

---

[1] *The Christian Doctrine of Reconciliation*, 6 f.

interpreters of Christianity have failed to see, is not the whole of religion. What Paul once described as " the fulness of the blessing of the Gospel of Christ "[1] is known only to the soul which has made the further discovery :

> " Yet I may love Thee too, O Lord,
>   Almighty as Thou art,
>   For Thou hast stooped to ask of me
>   The love of my poor heart."

That is what union with Jesus Christ means ; and until we realize the central place which this always held in Paul's thought and experience, many of the richest treasures of his Gospel must remain sealed from our sight.

On the whole, however, the tendency of Pauline study in recent years has been to give increased attention to this most vital element of the apostle's religion. As illustrating the growing consensus of opinion, the following verdicts may be cited. " Just as the thought of life," declares Titius, " is the decisive one for religion, as over against that of righteousness ; and as the resurrection thought, in consequence, takes precedence of that of judgment in delineating the way of salvation ; so the idea of the spiritual life in Christ takes precedence of the thought of justification."[2] " This personal union with Christ," says Garvie, " is the constant dominating factor in the religious experience and moral character of Paul."[3] Deissmann, who has always been a protagonist of this point of view, holds that " the various Pauline testimonies about salvation are refractions of

---

[1] Rom. 15[29].

[2] *Der Paulinismus unter dem Gesichtspunkt der Seligkeit*, 270.

[3] Art. *Paul's Personal Religion*, in *Expository Times*, March 1925, 252.

the one single ray, the faith of Christ. . . . As a matter of fact, the religion of Paul is something quite simple. It is communion with Christ." [1] Dean Inge is equally emphatic. " This intimate relationship with the Spirit-Christ is unquestionably the core of his religion. . . . The critic of St. Paul must give full weight to the constantly repeated words ' *in* Christ.' The mystical Christ could do what the idea of a Messiah could never have done. This conception, developed in the Fourth Gospel, has been the life-blood of Christianity ever since." [2] " Christ-faith," says J. Weiss, " Christ-piety, Christ-worship, Christ-mysticism—this is the one focus of Paul's religion ; this is the special form in which he experienced Christianity." [3] Professor H. A. A. Kennedy's verdict is a notable one. " This supremely intimate relation of union with Christ constitutes for Paul the pre-supposition of everything that counts in salvation." [4] " Union with Christ," according to Professor H. R. Mackintosh, " is a brief name for all that the apostles mean by salvation. For St. Paul and St. John oneness with Christ is to be redeemed, and to be redeemed is oneness with Christ . . . the classical Christian experience, not a peripheral eccentricity." [5] Schweitzer's recent book *The Mysticism of Paul the Apostle*, while marked by the same rather exaggerated eschatological bias which characterized his earlier work, has this great merit, that it fixes on the experience of union with Christ as the very core of Christianity. And Professor C. E. Raven's conclusion about Paul is that " his whole many-sided philosophy is based upon the

[1] *The Religion of Jesus and the Faith of Paul*, 207, 223.
[2] *Christian Ethics and Modern Problems*, 73.
[3] *Das Urchristentum*, 341.
[4] *The Theology of the Epistles*, 124.
[5] *The Person of Jesus Christ*, 334.

belief that such personal union achieved by faith and consummated in love is the essence of religion. . . . Life ' in Christ ' is not peculiar to St. Paul and is indeed the essential and creative element in Christianity." [1]

Further evidence of the same kind could be quoted ; but these passages will serve to illustrate what has been one of the most important and hopeful trends in Pauline study in recent years.[2] If it be now asked, *Why* is it so vital to keep the conception of union with Christ in the centre ? the answer is clear. For one thing, to assign to this fact any place other than the centre is to endanger the whole doctrine of atonement. The redemption achieved by Christ becomes something that operates mechanically or almost magically : it is altogether outside of us, independent of our attitude. Gore was not speaking too strongly when he declared that the tendency to isolate the thought " Christ for us " from the other thought " Christ in us " has been historically " an abundant source of scandal." [3] It is certain that such an idea as justification, for instance, can only be gravely misleading, when it is not seen in the light of a union with Christ in which the sinner identifies himself with Christ in His attitude to sin. Similarly, the thought of sanctification, dissociated from union, loses all reality. It is left, as it were, hanging in the air. It becomes an " extra." It is not organically related to the rest of redemption. Only when union with Christ is

---

[1] *Jesus and the Gospel of Love*, 296, 301.

[2] A Roman Catholic testimony may be added here : " the fundamental idea of the Church " is " the idea of the incorporation of the faithful in Christ " (Karl Adam, *The Spirit of Catholicism*, 22).

[3] *Belief in Christ*, 299. Cf. E. Brunner, *The Mediator*, 528 : " That which is expressed outwardly and that which is spoken within the heart, the Christ for us and the Christ in us, are one and the same God."

kept central is sanctification seen in its true nature, as the unfolding of Christ's own character within the believer's life ; and only then can the essential relationship between religion and ethics be understood. In short, the whole meaning of the atonement is here at stake.

Of all this Paul was well aware. There is one very important passage which summarizes his general thought about it, and also shows in particular how definitely union with Christ held precedence over all the other conceptions with which his mind worked. The passage is this : " But God commendeth His love toward us, in that, while we were yet sinners, Christ died for us. Much more then, being now justified by His blood, we shall be saved from wrath through Him. For if, when we were enemies, we were reconciled to God by the death of His Son, much more, being reconciled, we shall be saved by His life." [1] Here by the use twice over of the *a fortiori* argument, Paul declares his conviction that in Christianity the final stress must ever fall on one thing, and on one thing only, union with Christ, life in fellowship with Christ. It should be noted, moreover, that in many of the passages where justification is the theme (though not indeed in all) there can be felt the influence of the Judaistic controversy—another fact which would warrant us in regarding such passages as being at least one degree further from the centre of things than those in which, with all thoughts of controversy stilled, his own most intimate Christ-experience speaks.[2] It is perhaps also a point worthy of remark that, while justification and reconciliation un-

[1] Rom. 5[8-10].
[2] The influence of controversy must not, however, be exaggerated. See p. 244.

doubtedly look forward and contain in germ all the harvest of the Spirit that is to come, yet—by the very nature of the terms themselves—they carry with them, and can never quite shake off, a memory of the old life left behind ; their positive implies a negative ; they speak of a transition, a break, an end and a beginning ; and their brightness has a dark background to set it off. Union with Christ, on the other hand, means the steady, unbroken glory of a quality of life which shines by its own light, because it is essentially supernatural ; allows no hint of any negative, because " the fullness of God " is in it ; and knows no before and after, because it is already eternal.

We turn now to the brief but most important phrase in which Paul's intimacy with the risen Lord finds expression, the phrase " *in Christ*." So frequent and even commonplace has this phrase become in latter-day Christian usage that it is quite possible to miss its significance and fail to realize just how striking it is. It is worth reminding ourselves that no such words have ever been used, or indeed could ever be used, of any of the sons of men : we do not speak of being *in* St. Francis, or *in* John Wesley. The fact is that when we speak of being " in Christ " we are consciously or unconsciously making a confession of faith ; we are framing a Christology ; if we are saying something about ourselves, we are saying something far more tremendous about Jesus. We are declaring that Jesus is no mere fact in history, no towering personality of the past, but a living, present Spirit, whose nature is the very nature of God. So far-reaching is this favourite apostolic phrase.

It was a dictum of Luther's that all religion lies in

the pronouns ; and that there is a real truth in this, everyone who can speak with Paul of " the Son of God, who loved *me*, and gave Himself for *me*," [1] must realize. But Deissmann, going a step further than Luther, has virtually declared that religion resides in the prepositions, and in one of them in particular. The publication in 1892 of *Die neutestamentliche Formel " in Christo Jesu "* heralded the dawn of a new era in Pauline study. Starting from the fact that " in Christ " (or some cognate expression, such as " in the Lord," " in Him," etc.) occurs 164 times in Paul, but never in the Synoptics, Deissmann carried out a thorough examination of the use of ἐν with a personal dative in Greek literature in general and in the Septuagint in particular, and came to the conclusion that Paul " was the originator of the formula, not indeed as being the first to employ ἐν with a personal singular, but in the sense that he used an already existing idiom to create a new technical term " [2] of religion. It is an instance of the way in which the creative power of the Christian experience makes itself felt even in the domain of language. New wine requires new bottles ; and traditional thought-forms are often poor vehicles of expression for a man who has had his Damascus day. Where the Synoptics speak of the disciples' fellowship with Jesus, the preposition they use is μετά, never ἐν. Paul, on the other hand, uses ἐν constantly, μετά never. Take the long, typically Pauline sentence at the opening of the epistle to the Ephesians : within that single sentence " in Christ " (or some derivative) occurs a dozen times. It is indeed the most characteristic phrase in the apostle's terminology.

Is Deissmann correct in regarding Paul as its originator ? It is a point on which it would be unwise to be

---

[1] Gal. 2[20].   [2] *Die neutestamentliche Formel*, 70.

dogmatic. The phrase is certainly absent from the Synoptics, but it is at least possible that the idea comes from Jesus Himself. Is there not a hint of it, for example, in the great promise, " Where two or three are gathered together in My name, there am I in the midst of them " ? [1] And while we cannot enter here into a discussion of the historic basis of the Johannine discourses, it seems probable that the parable of the vine and the branches, with its reiterated emphasis " Abide in Me, and I in you," [2] represents a definite element in our Lord's teaching. But there can be little doubt that it was Paul who made the phrase regulative for Christian thought and experience : thus far at least, Deissmann's position commands our assent.

Now the obvious clue to an understanding of this whole circle of ideas lies in the cognate phrase " *in the Spirit.*" Paul's thought of the living Christ is so closely bound up with his thought of the Holy Spirit that he seems on occasion to use the two names almost interchangeably. To say this is not to agree with Weiss when he declares that Christ and the Spirit are simply identified. [3] The New Testament doctrine is that it is the Spirit who makes Christ real to us and mediates Christ's gifts to us : and this is not " identity." Still, so close are the ideas of Christ and the Spirit in Paul's mind that he can pass almost without any sense of distinction from the one to the other. It is, therefore, natural and legitimate to use the phrase " in the Spirit " to elucidate the harder phrase " in Christ." Let us take, for example, the statement : " Ye are not in the flesh, but in the Spirit, if so be that the Spirit of God dwell in you." [4] There the idea " in the Spirit " and its

---

[1] Matt. 18[20].　　　　　　　　　　[2] John 15[4].
[3] *Das Urchristentum*, 356.　　　　[4] Rom. 8[9].

reverse " the Spirit in you " are brought together in a most illuminating way. Plainly, Paul thinks of the Christian as living and moving and having his being in a πνεῦμα element which is the very breath of life. Just as it might be said that the human body is in the atmosphere which surrounds it on every side, and yet that atmosphere is also within it, filling it and vitalizing it, so it may be said of the Christian soul that it both exists in the Spirit and has the Spirit within it. Here, then, is the key to the phrase " in Christ." Christ is the redeemed man's new environment. He has been lifted out of the cramping restrictions of his earthly lot into a totally different sphere, the sphere of Christ. He has been transplanted into a new soil and a new climate, and both soil and climate are Christ. His spirit is breathing a nobler element. He is moving on a loftier plane. As Principal W. M. Macgregor has well expressed it, " Just as a bird lives in the air and needs the air to live in, just as a fish lives in the water and can live nowhere else, so, in Paul's view, a Christian man requires the presence of his Master ; and if that is withdrawn, he must speedily die." [1] He lives, as Deissmann puts it vividly, " *innerhalb* des Christus." [2] Or, in Paul's own succinct confession, " Life means Christ to me." [3]

The question may, however, be raised—Is the full mystical meaning present in *every* occurrence of the phrase in Paul's epistles ? Probably not. This is Deissmann's mistake. Having made his discovery, he is inclined to apply it everywhere without exception. He forces his key into every lock. He gives to certain passages a weight more than the words can really

---

[1] *Repentance unto Life*, 231.
[2] *Die neutestamentliche Formel*, 84.
[3] Phil. 1[21] (Moffatt).

bear.[1] It is possible, for instance, that sometimes *ἐν* has
the sense of *διά*, and the translation " through Christ "
would best convey the meaning. It is more than likely,
too, that occasionally " in Christ " is simply synonymous with " Christian." At the time when Paul was
writing, " Christian " was still a term of reproach, and
was therefore not in the vocabulary of the Church ; and
the apostle may well have fallen back on his favourite
phrase where we to-day should use the single word.[2]

But if it is a mistake to read the full mystical
significance into all the passages where " in Christ "
occurs, it is a far greater mistake to whittle down the
phrase until it carries no such significance at all. In
his main contention, Deissmann is perfectly right. The
words have what may almost be called a local meaning.
With wonderful vividness they convey something akin
to, but even deeper and more intimate than, the truth
contained in the Psalmist's cry, " Lord, Thou hast been
our dwelling place in all generations," [3] or in Words-
worth's great expression " God who is our home." [4] And
unless we realize this fact, and give it its due, we are sure
to miss Paul's meaning again and again. Take a case
in point. The Authorized Version, in a famous passage,
reads " Let this mind be in you, which was also in Christ
Jesus." [5] The Revised Version is practically the same.
On the face of it, that means simply, " Let Jesus'
attitude be yours " ; and this is how the words have
frequently been understood. " Reflect in your own

[1] See Titius, *Der Paulinismus*, 260 ; Weiss, *Das Urchristentum*,
360 ; Morgan, *The Religion and Theology of Paul*, 118 ; Wernle,
Jesus und Paulus, 69 f. But Wernle's criticism goes much too far.

[2] Philemon [16], " both in the flesh and in the Lord," is translated
by Moffatt " as a man and as a Christian."

[3] Psalm 90[1].

[4] *Intimations of Immortality.*   [5] Phil. 2[5].

minds the mind of Christ Jesus," is Lightfoot's rendering.[1] To obtain this meaning, however, involves straining the Greek, and supplying a most unlikely verb in the relative clause. But now, all that is needed, not only to overcome the linguistic difficulty, but also to discover a far richer and more pointed challenge in the words, is to interpret the phrase " in Christ Jesus " in its strict Pauline sense. The meaning which then emerges is this: " See that you apply among yourselves, in your community life, the spirit which has been born within you by union with Christ." [2] Clearly, what Paul is hinting at is the danger—as common to-day as it was then—of a hiatus between personal religion and public relationships. He reminds the Philippians that their own experience " in Christ " must be the controlling and directing factor in all their treatment of one another. Very similar is the passage, later in the same epistle, where he begs Euodia and Syntyche to " be of the same mind in the Lord." [3] Here again, " in the Lord " must be given full weight. It is as though he said to those two Christians who had unhappily become estranged, " Remember your common union with Christ. Remember that it is not in two different spheres that your spirits are living ; the two spheres coincide, there is but one, and it is Christ. Realize this and act on it, and your present differences will vanish. *In the Lord* you will agree." These passages illustrate the important

---

[1] *Philippians*, 1 10.

[2] The verse reads—τοῦτο γὰρ φρονείσθω ἐν ὑμῖν ὃ καὶ ἐν Χριστῷ Ἰησοῦ. In supplying a verb for the relative clause, some form of the verb in the principal clause is more natural than A.V. " was," and φρονεῖτε is more natural than ἐφρονεῖτο. In this case, the natural reading is the correct one. The point to notice is that it has been the failure to give the words " in Christ " their strict meaning and full value which has been responsible for the confusion.

[3] Phil. 4 2.

fact that very often Paul's real meaning will yield itself up only when we refuse in any way to thin down or reduce his great watchword " in Christ." For always, to Paul, it was this conception that struck the keynote of religion, and echoed the deepest experience of his soul.

II

In the foregoing discussion, we have had occasion more than once to use the word " mysticism " ; and it is necessary to grasp quite clearly what this term means, as applied to Paul's religious experience. Efforts are periodically made to banish this conception altogether. But it is hard to destroy ; it has a way of reasserting itself, and coming back into its own. Indeed, the stubborn survival-power of this term, in face of trenchant criticism and attack, suggests that it stands for something quite indispensable and essential in religion. A hundred years ago, Schleiermacher declared that an idea so vague was better avoided ; [1] and with this many to-day are disposed to agree. They imagine that mysticism represents something so shadowy and ill-defined and non-intellectual that to use the term is simply to " darken counsel by words without knowledge." Others go further, and proclaim a personal aversion to the mystic and all his works. He is accused of a selfish absorption in his own individual experience. He is regarded as culpably negligent of religion's roots in history. He is criticized for an alleged indifference to moral judgments. It is even suggested that he has not escaped the deadly sin of the superior person.

Behind all this there lies a serious confusion of thought. The type of character which seeks religious

[1] *The Christian Faith,* 429.

emotions and ecstasies for their own sake, which dissolves history in speculation and is defective in respect of moral duty, is unfortunately not unknown : the pity is that to religion of this kind the noble name of mysticism should ever have been applied. Linguistically, we are not so well equipped here as are the Germans : for where they have two words, *Mystik* and *Mysticismus* (the former standing for the true religious attitude, the latter for its debased and spurious imitation), we have to make the one do duty.[1] But the confusion goes deeper than that. It is not only a case of distinguishing between what is genuine and what is forged. We have to realize that there are important differences even within the range of what may properly be called mystical experience. A very striking illustration of this lies to our hand in one of Paul's epistles.[2] Writing to the Corinthians, he relates an extraordinary event which had happened in his own spiritual life. He was caught up to the third heaven. He was given the beatific vision. He had a direct experience of the presence of God. He heard divine secrets which no man was at liberty to repeat. Now the precision with which he dates this event is highly significant. It happened fourteen years before this particular letter was written. That is to say, even in the apostle's own career, it was quite exceptional. This was not the level on which he habitually lived. The rapture and ecstasy came—and passed. The trance marked an epoch in his life. That glorious experience of the open heavens, of

> " God's presence, and His very self
> And essence all-divine,"

[1] Deissmann, *The Religion of Jesus and the Faith of Paul*, 194.
[2] II Cor. 12[1 ff.]

meant to Paul something akin to what Bethel meant to Jacob. Undoubtedly this was one aspect of the apostle's mysticism. *But only one.* And Paul himself —this is the point to be emphasized—would have been the first to recognize and to insist that such experiences form only a comparatively small part of the soul's deep communion with God in Christ. His whole teaching about special gifts of the Spirit, their value and their limitations, makes it perfectly clear that, while attaching great importance to these unique " visions and revelations " and glorifying God for them, he would never dream of using them to disparage the more normal experiences of souls " hid with Christ in God." [1] On the contrary, it was in the daily, ever-renewed communion, rather than in the transient rapture, that the inmost nature of Christianity lay. This was the true mysticism. This was essential religion. This was eternal life.

In some degree, then, *every real Christian is a mystic in the Pauline sense.*[2] It is here that Paul differs very notably from his great contemporary Philo. For Philo as for Paul, a direct apprehension of the eternal was the goal of religion. But this union with God was the reward only of a privileged minority. Outside the comparatively small circle of elect, initiated souls, the crowning experience remained unknown. And even the few who were taken into inmost fellowship with God had but broken glimpses of the glory : God was an intermittent, not an abiding, presence. This was the Philonic mysticism—noble so far as it

[1] Col. 3³.

[2] W. R. Inge, *Vale*, 38 : " In truth the typical mystical experience is just prayer. Anyone who has really prayed, and felt that his prayers are heard, knows what mysticism means."

went, but too esoteric to be a Gospel, far too restricted and aloof to be good news for a perishing world. What Paul by the grace of God discovered was that the glorious experience was waiting for any soul which gave itself in faith to Christ. Not only so : such union with the divine, he knew, need be no transient splendour, flashing for a moment across life's greyness and then gone ; it could be the steady radiance of a light unsetting, filling the commonest ways of earth with a gladness that was new every morning. Unhealthy reactions such union never could engender. The crushing sense of world-weariness which has marked too many types of mysticism, the contempt of life, the absorption in unproductive emotion, were foreign to it altogether. Its effect, as the apostle saw and as his own career in Christ convincingly proved, would be the very opposite. It would make men not less efficient for life, but more so. It would vitalize them, not only morally and spiritually, but even physically and mentally. It would give them a verve, a creativeness, an exhilaration, which no other experience in the world could impart. It would key life up to a new pitch of zest and gladness and power. This is Pauline mysticism ; and great multitudes who have never used the name have known the experience, and have found it life indeed.

Mention should here be made of a fruitful distinction which Deissmann has drawn between two types of mysticism, which he calls respectively " acting " and " reacting." " The one type "—the reacting—" is everywhere present where the mystic regards his communion with God as an experience in which the action of God upon him produces a reaction towards God. The other type of mysticism "—the acting—" is that in which the mystic regards his communion with God as his own action, from which a reaction follows on the part of Deity." [1] Much religion has been of the latter kind. Man's action has been regarded as the primary thing. The soul has endeavoured to ascend towards God. Spiritual exercises have been made the ladder for the ascent. But all this savours of the religion of works as contrasted with the religion of grace. Paul's attitude was different. His mysticism was essentially of the reacting kind. Christ, not Paul, held the initiative. Union with the eternal was not a human achievement : it was the gift of God. It came, not by any spiritual exercises, but by God's self-revelation, God's self-impartation. The words " It pleased God to reveal His Son in me," [2] which remind us that the Damascus experience itself was the foundation of the apostle's mysticism, are Paul's emphatic way of saying that God's action always holds the priority : His servant simply reacts to the action of God. Here, as everywhere in Paul, all is of grace ; and it is well to be thus reminded by the apostle that union with Christ is not something we have to achieve by effort, but something we have to accept by faith.

From what has now been said, it will be apparent why we cannot agree with the proposal to drop the term " *mystical* " *union*, and speak simply of a " *moral* " *union*. There is, of course, no such thing as a union with Christ which does not have the most far-reaching effects in the moral sphere. The man who comes to be " in Christ " has found the supreme ethical dynamic. But just as religion is something

---

[1] *The Religion of Jesus and the Faith of Paul*, 195.
[2] Gal. 1[15 f.]

more than a mere device for reinforcing conduct,[1] so union with Christ as Paul experienced it has more in it than can be described by the one word " moral." In this respect, it is like love. Love between human beings is morally creative. It is a master-force for character. It lets loose amazing energies for goodness. Superb ethical achievements are at its command. But no one imagines that to describe it thus is to say all that may be said. Love is moral *plus*, as it were : there is in it a whole range of glory and surprise which the single term cannot really convey. So with that divine union in which Paul's religion centres : it is ethical through and through, never for a moment is it anything but ethical ; and yet it is in simple justice to the facts that we press beyond the idea of a moral to that of a mystical union. Only so can we adequately depict the true inwardness and intimacy of this union, and the abiding wonder of those gifts—so lavish and undeserved and gracious and rich in beauty—which it brings with it from the side of God to man.

The analogy just used—that of the love of one person for another—lets in a flood of light on the whole matter of union with Christ. The notion which certain philosophies have almost taken for granted, that human personalities are mutually exclusive and impermeable, is disproved when the experience of love is taken into account. " Separateness " is not, in point of fact, the final truth about living souls. When we say of those to whom the gloriously enriching gift of love has come that they are " bound up " in each other, we are not indulging in empty metaphor : we are giving a strictly accurate description of what happens to their souls. Walls of partition go down, and self merges in self. Nor

[1] On this, see Oman, *Grace and Personality*, 107.

is the resultant union a lower state of being than the
rigid separation of the self-sufficient soul : on the contrary, it is definitely higher. Now it is this potential
permeation of one personality by another which makes
spiritual religion possible. It is this that promotes the
mystical union. But seeing that personality as it is in
Christ has far greater resources, both of self-impartation
and of receptiveness, than it has anywhere on the purely
human level, it follows that there can exist between
Christians and their Lord a degree of intimacy and unity
absolutely unparalleled and unique. Hence the analogy,
illuminating as it is, can never be more than an analogy ;
and we might indeed go the length of saying that the
union of believing souls with Christ is as far beyond any
merely human union as the union of the three Persons in
the Godhead is beyond them both.

We must guard, however, against conveying the
impression that such union implies virtual absorption
of a pantheistic kind. Nothing was further from Paul's
thoughts. Here again his doctrine runs along a different
line from that of Philo. " When the divine light blazes
forth," said Philo, " the human light sets ; and when
the former sets, the latter rises. The reason within us
leaves its abode at the arrival of the divine Spirit, but
when the Spirit departs the reason returns to its place." [1]
This suggests that what the divine immanence does is
to impair or even destroy the distinctness of the human
personality. But there is certainly no hint of any such
idea in Paul. He never thought of Christ as overriding
any man's individuality. Union with Christ, so far
from obliterating the believer's personal qualities and
characteristics, throws these into greater relief. How
far any thought of absorption was from the apostle's

---

[1] *Quis Rerum Divinarum Heres sit*, 249.

166

mind is evidenced by such statements as these: "As many as are led by the Spirit of God, they are the sons of God." "The Spirit itself beareth witness with our spirit, that we are the children of God." [1] The passage which, on a superficial view, comes nearest proclaiming the end of all personal identity—" I live, yet not I, but Christ liveth in me "—is followed immediately by the significant words, " the life which I now live in the flesh, I live by the faith of the Son of God," [2] in which, as Weiss has pointed out, Paul deliberately guards against the possible pantheistic interpretation by reasserting the religious attitude where " Thou " and " I " stand over against each other.[3] Clearly Paul's view is that the man whom Christ begins to possess does not thereby cease to be himself. On the contrary, like the younger son in Jesus' story, he then for the first time really " comes to himself." [4] Christian experience does not depersonalize men and reduce them to a monotonous uniformity : it heightens every individual power they have. " There are diversities of gifts, but the same Spirit. And there are differences of administrations, but the same Lord. And there are diversities of operations ; but it is the same God which worketh all in all." [5] More convincing than anything Paul ever said about this is the evidence of his own life. Study the record of that amazing career, mark the impact which this God-filled and Christ-mastered soul made upon the life of men and Churches and nations, and then declare if he was lacking in individuality ! No, it was anything but a blurring and obliterating of personality that resulted from the Damascus experience. Every quality of heart and brain

[1] Rom. 8[14,16].   [2] Gal. 2[20].
[3] J. Weiss, *Das Urchristentum*, 361 : " ganz im Geiste der Ich-und-Du-Religion."
[4] Luke 15[17].   [5] I Cor. 12[4 ff.]

and soul which the man possessed was lifted into sudden, new distinctness and vigour. This was what union with Christ meant to Paul, and what he believed it could mean to all the world.

Here it may be well to point out that Paul's mysticism, as we have now described it, constitutes *a very decisive challenge to that type of modern religion which is content to regard Jesus merely as example.* Writers like Harnack have offered the world a picture in which Jesus appears primarily as the ethical teacher, whose significance for humanity lies in the nobility of His prophetic utterances, and in the pattern of His sacrificial life and obedience unto death.[1] Now it is perfectly true that the noble ethic Jesus preached, and His own fulfilment of it in life and deed, have laid down the lines for all His friends to follow. Nor can there be any doubt that this was a real part of the divine plan by which the Word became flesh and dwelt among us—as indeed the New Testament apostle recognized who wrote, " Christ suffered for us, leaving us an example, that ye should follow His steps." [2] But what Paul's mysticism does is to remind us that the example of Christ is only a part, and not even the greatest part, of the redeeming Gospel. Were there no more than this, the contemplation of the perfect holiness of Jesus could only breed despair. No shining example, cold and remote as the stars, can cleanse the conscience that has been defiled, or break the octopus grip which sin gets upon the soul. The evangel of an ethical example is a devastating thing. It makes religion the most grievous of burdens. Perhaps this is the real reason why, even among professing Christians, there are so many strained faces and weary

[1] Harnack's *What is Christianity ?* may be taken as typical of this school of thought.　　[2] I Peter 2[21].

hearts and captive, unreleased spirits. They have listened to Jesus' teaching, they have meditated on Jesus' character ; and then they have risen up, and tried to drive their own lives along Jesus' royal way. Disappointment heaped on bitter disappointment has been the result. The great example has been a dead-weight beating them down, bearing them to the ground, bowing their hopeless souls in the dust. If Harnack's Christ is all, we are left without a Redeemer. But ever since Isaiah,[1] men have been aware that one of the vital distinctions between true religion and false is that, whereas the latter is a dead burden for the soul to carry, the former is a living power to carry the soul. Now Paul's mysticism grows lyrical with precisely this great discovery. " Christ in me " means something quite different from the weight of an impossible ideal, something far more glorious than the oppression of a pattern for ever beyond all imitation. " Christ in me " means Christ bearing me along from within, Christ the motive-power that carries me on, Christ giving my whole life a wonderful poise and lift, and turning every burden into wings. All this is in it when the apostle speaks of " Christ in you, the hope of glory." [2] Compared with this, the religion which bases everything on example is pitifully rudimentary. This, and this alone, is the true Christian religion. Call it mysticism or not—the name matters little : the thing, the experience, matters every-thing. To be " in Christ," to have Christ within, to realise your creed not as something you have to bear but as something by which you are borne, this is Chris-tianity. It is more : it is release and liberty, life with an endless song at its heart. It means feeling within you, as long as life here lasts, the carrying power of Love

[1] Isaiah 46[1-4].   [2] Col. 1[27].

Almighty ; and underneath you, when you come to die, the touch of everlasting arms.

One other question presents itself before we leave this part of our inquiry. *Is this union with Christ, which Paul makes central, something different from union with God ?* Not infrequently the opinion has been expressed that the apostle, in the fervour of his passion for Christ, has given to the Son a place that ought to belong to the Father alone. His Christ-enthusiasm is so great, it is said, that God retreats into the background. The particular mode in which he experienced redemption has tended to give him a false perspective and to throw his personal religion out of focus. Religion's goal must ever be, as the Westminster divines declared, " to glorify God and to enjoy Him for ever." But Paul would have answered the Catechism differently : he would have said " to glorify and to enjoy *Christ.*"

This criticism, however, is quite beside the mark. Union with Christ, as Paul conceives it, *is* union with God. He knows nothing of a mysticism which stops short of faith's final goal. Behind every expression of his intense intimacy with Jesus stands the great ultimate fact of God Himself. Indeed, as we have already seen,[1] the nature which can impart itself to believing souls in the way in which, by the plain testimony of experience, Christ's nature can and does impart itself, proves itself *ipso facto* to be divine. Hence the more any man comes to be " in Christ," the more is he " in God." There are not two experiences, but one.

Abundant evidence in support of this position can be found in the epistles. Everything in Paul's Gospel, even where his adoring gratitude to Christ seems to

[1] See p. 154.

banish every other thought, runs back to God, the
beginning of salvation and its end. How could God
be forgotten, when Christ Himself had been God's
gift ? " When the fulness of the time was come, God
sent forth His Son." [1] Behind the figure of the crucified Son, Paul always sees God the Father ; and behind the love that bled and died, the love that reigned
in the heart of the eternal. " *God* commendeth His
love toward us, in that . . . *Christ* died." [2] " All
things are of God, who hath reconciled us to Himself by
Jesus Christ." [3] " He that spared not His own Son,
but delivered Him up for us all, how shall He not with
Him also freely give us all things ? " [4] So, too, with
Christ's risen life. For Paul, to think of that was to
think of God : to be united with the risen Christ was
to be united with the God who raised Him. [5] The im-
possibility of distinguishing two types of union is
proved by such a statement as : " Ye are risen with
Him through the faith of the operation of God, who
hath raised Him from the dead." [6] At the heart of
Paul's fellowship with Christ lay the triumphant
certainty—" God was in Christ : " [7] so that he could
have said " Amen " to John's great declaration,
" Truly our fellowship is with the Father, and with His
Son Jesus Christ." [8] There was no hiatus, as though
fellowship with Christ were merely a stage on the road
to fellowship with God : they formed one indivisible
experience. In one of the most deeply mystical
passages in the epistles, Paul speaks about being
" hid with Christ " ; but here, what was always implicit in his mysticism is made explicit, when he writes

[1] Gal. 4[4].   [2] Rom. 5[8].   [3] II Cor. 5[18].
[4] Rom. 8[32].   [5] Rom. 8[11].   [6] Col. 2[12].
[7] II Cor. 5[19].   [8] I John 1[3].

" hid with Christ *in God*." [1] He recognizes that for
himself there would have been no fellowship with Christ
at all, had it not been for God's grace in electing him
to this glorious privilege : " It pleased God to reveal
His Son in me." [2] The indwelling Christ works in
the Church : yet the apostle writes to the Philippians,
" It is God which worketh in you." [3] Christianity's
aim in the world is " that every tongue should confess
that Jesus Christ is Lord," but this confession is " to
the glory of God the Father." [4] In the same breath in
which Paul announces that " the head of every man is
Christ," he also declares that " the head of Christ is
God." [5] There is also the great passage which looks
forward to the consummation : " Then cometh the
end, when He shall have delivered up the kingdom to
God, even the Father. . . . And when all things shall
be subdued unto Him, then shall the Son also Himself
be subject unto Him that put all things under Him,
that God may be all in all." [6]

Further evidence is unnecessary : enough has been
said to show how totally unfounded is the idea that the
apostle's Christ-passion resulted in a loss of perspective
in his religion. It is not true that God is thrust into
the background. God is everywhere. He is in every
thought of Paul's heart, and in every Christward
motion of Paul's will. When the apostle speaks of
being " in Christ," of having " Christ in me," it is
nothing other than union with God that he is experiencing. The title " Christocentric " justly describes his
religion ; but no mistake could be greater than to
suppose that this rules " Theocentric " out. Paul's
Christianity was both. Nor will this occasion difficulty

[1] Col. 3[3].   [2] Gal. 1[25 f.]   [3] Phil. 2[13].
[4] Phil. 2[11].   [5] I Cor. 11[3].   [6] I Cor. 15[24-28].

to any save to those who have had no experience of being apprehended by Christ. All whom Christ has truly possessed have known beyond a doubt that it was God who was possessing them. They have known that their Christ-experience was not a mere ante-chamber or outer court of the temple, beyond which more hallowed regions lay. That experience itself is the inmost sanctuary. That fellowship shines with the authentic light divine. For the soul which is united to Christ by faith is united to the living God.

III

Our next step must be to turn our attention to the great regulative fact which is always present to Paul's mind where union with Christ is the theme—*the fact of faith*. Before union can take place, two things must happen. On the one hand, there must be an outgoing of God to man. This is the divine initiative, and its name is " Grace." On the other hand, there must be an outgoing of man to God. This is the human response, and its name is " Faith." Paul has brought the two ideas very strikingly together in a phrase which presents, in condensed form, everything that matters in redemption : " By grace are ye saved through faith." [1] Let us examine this fact of faith, which is the principle of union between the Christian and his Lord.

The first point to notice is that *Paul did not create the term*. He found it lying ready to his hand. In the Authorized Version of the Old Testament, it is true, the word " faith " occurs only twice ; and in neither place is it a strictly accurate translation of the original.

[1] Eph. 2[8].

The song of Moses in Deuteronomy contains the words,
" They are a very froward generation, children in
whom is no faith ; " [1] but here the idea is " lacking in
fidelity." And in Habakkuk's famous declaration,
" The just shall live by his faith," [2] the rendering
" faithfulness " would better convey the meaning.
What the prophet is thinking of is the staunch and
stubborn strength of character by which God's people
would hold their own in face of the Chaldean menace ;
and it is clearly a different and deeper conception of
" faith " that Paul is working with in both places where
he quotes Habakkuk's words.[3] The term, then, is
singularly rare in the Old Testament. But this, after
all, is a minor matter, for the thing itself can be traced
everywhere from Genesis to Malachi ; as indeed the
writer of the epistle to the Hebrews reminds us, in the
great chapter where, with masterly insight, he has
shown the red thread of faith running right through
Israel's history.[4] Gunkel rightly warns us that if it is
a *doctrine* of faith we are seeking, we shall search
the Old Testament scriptures in vain.[5] But in the
Abraham story, where a soul rises up from the dark
night of heathenism and stakes everything on the
troth of the one and only God ; in the heroism of the
prophets, choosing disaster and death rather than disobedience to the call divine ; in the trust of the
psalmists, reposing with childlike confidence under the
shadow of a defending omnipotence ; in such im-
mortal words, shining like jewels on the finger of time,
as these : " In returning and rest shall ye be saved ;
in quietness and in confidence shall be your strength," [6]

[1] Deut. 32[20].   [2] Hab. 2[4].
[3] Rom. 1[17], Gal. 3[11].   [4] Heb. 11[1] ff.
[5] Art. " Glaube," in *RGG*, ii. 1425.   [6] Isaiah 30[15].

and " They that wait upon the Lord shall renew their strength ; they shall mount up with wings as eagles " [1] —in all this the fact of faith emerges, preparing the way of the Lord, and making straight through the desert a highway towards the culminating hour of Calvary's hazard and glory, when faith was to cry, " It is finished." In the Old Testament, says Schultz, " faith is everywhere the foundation of salvation." [2]

Both word and idea are frequent in the literature of later Judaism.[3] There is evidence to show that the statement in Genesis about Abraham, " He believed in the Lord, and He counted it to him for righteousness," which was the starting-point of one of Paul's most famous arguments, had become almost a standard text in the Rabbinic schools ; [4] nor was speculation on the question of faith and works unknown amongst Jewish theologians. It may well have been when sitting at the feet of Gamaliel that Paul had his first introduction to the idea of faith as a technical term of religion. In the apocalyptic literature, it is sometimes difficult, as Baillie has pointed out, " to know whether it is really *faith* in its true sense that is intended, or simply *faithfulness* " ; in times of persecution, such as those from which many of the apocalypses sprang, the two ideas naturally draw close together ; each tends to pass over into the other, and " faith and fidelity merge into one." [5] Philo, who wrote among other works the *De Abrahamo* and the *De Migratione Abrahami*, gave faith a dominating place

---

[1] Isaiah 40[31].   [2] *Old Testament Theology*, ii. 33.
[3] References are given by Lietzmann, on Rom. 4[25], in *HBNT*, 54 ; D. M. Baillie, *Faith in God*, 31 ff. ; Lightfoot, *Galatians*, 152 ff. ; Sanday and Headlam, *Romans*, 33 (*ICC*).
[4] Gen. 15[6], Rom. 4[3], Gal. 3[6].
[5] D. M. Baillie, *Faith in God*, 34.

at the heart of religion. He called it " the queen of the virtues." [1]

Can we define the conception, thus familiar to Jewish thought ? [2] Apart from the subsidiary sense of " faithfulness," two meanings—a general one, and a more particular one—seem to have been present. The general idea was *a conviction of the reality of things unseen*. This was the idea which the writer to the Hebrews put into memorable words : " Faith means we are confident of what we hope for, convinced of what we do not see." [3] It reappears in the epistle of James : " Thou believest that there is one God ; thou doest well." [4] More particularly, faith meant *a confidence that God would fulfil His promises*. This was the root idea of the Abraham story. And from a view of faith as something directed towards the promises of God it is but a single step—a step which at many points in Jewish literature you can actually see being taken—to the idea of faith as a practical force for life, an act and attitude of self-commitment to a God worthy of all trust.

From the moment when Jesus laid His hands upon this meaning of the word and baptised it into His own message to the world, its place in Christianity was secure. " Have faith in God "—this was the burden of His appeal.[5] The discovery of faith in unlikely places filled His soul with joy.[6] Faith, even in its weakness, was a mightier power than all the forces of the world.[7] Given faith on the side of man, He could do all manner

---

[1] *De Abrahamo*, 268.
[2] For the great variety of ideas included under the term πίστις, see Titius, *Der Paulinismus*, 209 ff., and Weiss, *Das Urchristentum*, 322 ff.
[3] Heb. 11[1] (Moffatt).
[4] James 2[19].
[5] Mark 11[22].
[6] Matt. 8[10].
[7] Matt. 17[20].

of mighty works.[1] By evoking faith in Himself, He sought to lead men into touch with God.[2] He made it perfectly clear that the gate of self-abandonment was the only way into the kingdom. He challenged men to an act of full surrender. He had no place for the man who would not commit himself.[3] The very essence of discipleship was faith. In short, Luther's dictum " God and Faith belong together " is entirely in the spirit of the Synoptic Gospels. And even Haering's bold assertion can be allowed to stand : " God produces Faith. Nothing else ? No ; for faith is everything."[4]

It is only natural, then, that Paul, seeking for some brief, pregnant expression which would describe his soul's deepest intimacy with God in Christ, should have chosen the word faith. Whatever the subject he might be writing about, the noun πίστις or the verb πιστεύειν was sure to appear before many lines had been penned. " To him," says Principal Cairns, " faith is the great fundamental human virtue, the indispensable condition of all salvation and life and blessing."[5] " Faith fills the New Testament," declares Denney, " as completely as Christ does : it is the correlative of Christ wherever Christ really touches the life of men. . . . It is just as truly the whole of Christianity subjectively as Christ is the whole of it objectively."[6] Now a word with a religious content so extraordinarily rich is not easy to define : and Paul attempts no definition. But some of

[1] Matt. 9[22], 15[28]. Contrast Matt. 13[58].
[2] Matt. 9[28], 18[6].
[3] Luke 9[57 ff.].   [4] *The Christian Faith*, ii. 801.
[5] *The Faith that Rebels*, 206.
[6] *The Christian Doctrine of Reconciliation*, 287 f., 291. Cf. Grafe, in *RGG*, ii. 1428 : " Kern und Stern seiner gesamten Verkündigung wie seiner persönlichen Frömmigkeit ist der Glaube."

the different shades of meaning which he gives to it must be noted here.

We may set aside the passages where the idea of " faithfulness " or " fidelity " reappears. It is probable that this is the sense which the word bears in the famous catalogue of virtues that are " the fruit of the Spirit." [1] And " faithfulness," not " faith," is obviously the thought conveyed by the adjective πιστός, as applied to God : " Faithful is He that calleth you, who also will do it." [2]

Nor need we linger on the passages where Paul's usage of " faith " is simply parallel to that of Jewish religion. We saw above that, outside Christianity altogether, two ideas were frequent—the general idea of conviction of the unseen, and the more specialized idea of confidence in the promises of God. The epistles offer instances of both these usages. As illustrating the former, there is the saying " We walk by faith, not by sight " ; [3] as illustrating the latter, there is the whole of the fourth chapter of Romans, with its great picture of a man " who against hope believed in hope . . . and being not weak in faith . . . staggered not at the promise of God through unbelief ; but was strong in faith, giving glory to God ; and being fully persuaded that, what He had promised, He was able also to perform." [4] If this idea of faith as something directed towards the promises of God is less frequent in Paul than might have been expected, the reason is not far to seek. For with Abraham and with Jewish religion generally, the centre of gravity lay in the future, and hope was directed towards the fulfilment of still outstanding

[1] Gal. 5²². So Moffatt, *Love in the New Testament*, 170.
[2] I Thess. 5²⁴. Cf. I Cor. 1⁹, II Cor. 1¹⁸, Rom. 3³.
[3] II Cor. 5⁷. Cf. I Thess. 1⁸, II Cor. 4¹³.
[4] Rom. 4¹⁸ ff.

prophecies ; whereas Paul had definitely passed beyond the sphere of hope and promise into that of realized fact.[1] Hence faith was not so much a confidence that God's word would some day be fulfilled, as a recognition that it had been fulfilled already, and fulfilled in a way that claimed the surrender of a man's life in love and gratitude and obedience. " For all the promises of God in Him are yea, and in Him Amen, unto the glory of God by us."[2]

Here we come in sight of another aspect of faith present in Paul's epistles, namely, faith as *a conviction of the Gospel facts*: " Tatsachenglauben," as Johannes Weiss denotes it.[3] This conception was already familiar in the primitive Christian community ; and a great part of the aim of the earliest mission preaching was to prove, by personal witness and Scripture reference, the facts of Jesus' resurrection and Messiahship, and thus to win for these facts a believing assent. Paul's own Damascus preaching, immediately after his conversion, seems to have followed this line. " He preached Christ in the synagogues, that He is the Son of God."[4] " He confounded the Jews which dwelt at Damascus, proving that this is very Christ."[5] Among the passages in the epistles where this idea of a believing acceptance of the Gospel facts is prominent, the following may be noted : " If we believe that Jesus died and rose again, even so them also which sleep in Jesus will God bring with Him."[6] " If thou shalt confess with thy mouth the Lord Jesus, and shalt believe in thine heart that God hath raised Him from the dead, thou shalt be saved."[7] " Faith cometh by hearing, and hearing by the word of

---

[1] So Weiss, *Das Urchristentum*, 323.   [2] II Cor. 1[20].

[3] *Das Urchristentum*, 324.   [4] Acts 9[20].

[5] Acts 9[22].   [6] I Thess. 4[14].   [7] Rom. 10[9].

God."[1] "Received ye the Spirit by the works of the law, or by the hearing of faith?"[2] Paul was far too clear-sighted, however, not to recognize that the idea of faith as the acceptance of certain historic facts was one which might easily, unless very carefully handled, land the Church in serious danger. How serious the inherent danger was, the subsequent development of Catholic Christianity, with its doctrine of "implicit faith"—believing what the Church believes—was to prove.[3] Saving faith, on this view of it, has ceased to be the response of a man's whole nature to the God who has revealed Himself through the facts of the Gospel: it has degenerated into a mechanical assent to propositions and dogmas. Faith itself has become a "work," acquiring merit. No blame for this corrupt view can be laid at the apostle's door. For even when he speaks of faith as the acceptance of certain facts, it is abundantly clear that what is meant is no mere intellectual assent, but a radical conviction influencing decisively and for ever the trend and direction of a man's life ; while as for the estimate of faith as a meritorious human achievement, any such idea is shattered once for all by Paul's great central declaration that God, and God only, is the author of salvation. The very faith which is the upward reach of man's soul comes from without, and is a gift of God. And if it be asked how that can be so, Paul's answer is that God, by revealing Himself in Christ, and in the life and death and resurrection of Christ, has shown Himself to be utterly worthy of all trust and devotion—which is equivalent to saying that God Himself is the creator and giver of faith. The human heart does not produce it :

---

[1] Rom. 10[17].   [2] Gal. 3[2].

[3] Perhaps this explains why Paul, who could write scarcely a page without some reference to faith, uses only rarely the construction πιστεύειν ὅτι with a relative clause.

God bestows it. No man can be convinced of the
Gospel facts in a saving way apart from the prior action
of God upon his soul. Or, as Paul himself puts it, " No
man can say that Jesus is the Lord, but by the Holy
Ghost." [1]

There is another set of passages where Paul uses
" faith " *almost as synonymous with " Christianity."*
Here again he is following in the steps of the primitive
community, which had begun to speak of the new
religion simply as " the faith." " A great company of
the priests were obedient to the faith." [2] " Exhorting
them to continue in the faith." [3] " So were the churches
established in the faith, and increased in number
daily." [4] It is in this sense that Paul is using the word
when he speaks about " obedience to the faith," [5] when
he urges the Galatians to " do good unto all men,
especially unto them who are of the household of faith," [6]
and when he sends to the Roman Church the counsel
" Him that is weak in the faith receive ye, but not to
doubtful disputations." [7] So, too, the adherents of the
new religion are sometimes in the epistles simply
designated " believers " (οἱ πιστεύοντες). " You that
believe," he calls the Thessalonians.[8] And when he tells
the Corinthians that " tongues are for a sign, not to
them that believe, but to them that believe not," [9] or
when he speaks about the unbelieving husband being
sanctified by the believing wife,[10] the distinction is
virtually identical with that between " Christian " and
" non-Christian." Nothing more forcibly illustrates the
vital place of faith in the Gospel as Paul conceives it
than the way in which he makes this word do duty for

[1] I Cor. 12[3].   [2] Acts 6[7].   [3] Acts 14[22].
[4] Acts 16[5].   [5] Rom. 1[5], 16[26].   [6] Gal. 6[10].
[7] Rom. 14[1].   [8] I Thess. 2[10.13].   [9] I Cor. 14[22].
[10] I Cor. 7[12 ff].

the Christian religion as a whole. That fact alone speaks volumes for faith's pre-eminence.

Faith as a conviction of the unseen, as a confidence in the promises of God, as an acceptance of the historic facts of the Gospel, and as an epitome of the Christian religion—such are some of the different shades of meaning which the word bears in Paul's epistles. But the characteristic Pauline conception comes into view only when faith is seen as *utter self-abandonment to the God revealed in Jesus Christ*. It is faith which begets that deepest and most intimate of all personal experiences—the mystical union of the believer and his Lord.

This is the sense in which all the great passages where Paul speaks of " the faith of Christ " are to be interpreted. " The life which I now live in the flesh, I live by the faith of the Son of God." [1] " Not having mine own righteousness, which is of the law, but that which is through the faith of Christ." [2] " A man is not justified by the works of the law, but by the faith of Jesus Christ." [3] It goes without saying that the genitive here is not to be taken subjectively, as in such a phrase as " the faith of Abraham," which Paul himself uses.[4] Quite certainly Paul was not thinking of the faith possessed by the Jesus of history, nor of the example set by that faith for future generations. There are real grounds for Deissmann's contention that all such passages are illustrations of what should be called a " mystic genitive ";[5] for it is the closest and most intensely personal of all life's relationships to which they refer. They are to be taken in conjunction with other passages where the apostle, speaking of faith,

[1] Gal. 2[20].   [2] Phil. 3[9]; cf. Rom. 3[22].
[3] Gal. 2[16].   [4] Rom. 4[12.16].
[5] *The Religion of Jesus and the Faith of Paul*, 177 f.

uses his favourite mystical expression " in Christ."
" Ye are all the children of God by faith in Christ
Jesus." [1] " I also, after I heard of your faith in the
Lord Jesus . . . cease not to give thanks for you." [2]
If we give the preposition here its due weight and value,
it becomes clear that to Paul Christ is not only the
object of faith, in the sense that faith directs itself
towards Christ as its goal : Christ is more than that—
He is the sphere in which faith lives and moves and
grows and operates. Occasionally Paul uses the preposition εἰς instead of ἐν, and in such cases it might
seem that the meaning is simply " believing *on* Christ,"
that is, being persuaded of His moral and spiritual
supremacy. " Unto you it is given in the behalf of
Christ, not only to believe on Him (τὸ εἰς αὐτὸν
πιστεύειν), but also to suffer for His sake." [3] But this
does less than justice to the original. For here, as in
all the other passages, what the apostle has in view is
nothing less than the human spirit encountering the
living God revealed in Christ, recognizing with endless
wonder the holy love that has been yearning for it from
the foundation of the world and has come forth to
meet it, and yielding itself to that seeking and implacable love, not grudgingly nor with many a reserva-
tion and doubt, but deliberately and vehemently and
for ever.

Nothing is finer in Matthew Arnold's *St. Paul and
Protestantism*—a treatise which still repays study—
than the description of the genesis of faith. " If
ever there was a case in which the wonder-working
power of attachment, in a man for whom the moral
sympathies and the desire of righteousness were all-
powerful, might employ itself and work its wonders,

---

[1] Gal. 3²⁶.   [2] Eph. 1¹⁵ᶠ.   [3] Phil. 1²⁸ ; cf. Gal. 2¹⁶.

it was here. Paul felt this power penetrate him ; and he felt, also, how by perfectly identifying himself through it with Jesus, by appropriating Jesus, and in no other way, could he ever get the confidence and the force to do as Jesus did. He thus found a point in which the mighty world outside man, and the weak world inside him, seemed to combine for his salvation. The struggling stream of duty, which had not volume enough to bear him to his goal, was suddenly rein- forced by the immense tidal wave of sympathy and emotion. To this new and potent influence Paul gave the name of *faith*." [1]

It is an important point that Paul's thought of faith as the principle of union between the Christian and Christ—" the wonder-working power of attach- ment "—is contained in germ in the Synoptic Gospels. There we see Jesus seeking to help men towards the higher life of sanctification by binding them to Himself in love and gratitude and devotion. Even while He was with them in the flesh, the disciples had a foretaste of that blessed sense of being one with Christ which was to possess them in its fullness in the days of His exalta- tion ; nor could Peter, James, and John have found a better summary of what their relationship to the Master meant than in such words as these—

> " O to grace how great a debtor
> Daily I'm constrained to be !
> Let that grace now, like a fetter,
> Bind my wandering heart to Thee."

" Like a fetter "—so strong was the bond that held them to His person, so indissoluble and enduring the

[1] *St. Paul and Protestantism*, 47.

inner union of heart with heart. It is the seed of this
idea, present already in the Gospel story, which bears
such a golden harvest in the epistles ; and the loyalty
which attached the first followers to the Leader whom
they loved prefigures the faith which now establishes a
living union between the members of the Church on
earth and their risen and exalted Head.

To Paul, who here as everywhere is building on his
own personal experience, faith-union means nothing
short of being overpowered by Christ.[1] It means the
making over of the whole man—thought and feeling
and will—to Christ in unconditional surrender. It
means an act, and then a life. " Now is our salvation
nearer," he writes, " than when we believed " : [2] there
is faith as an act, the original deed of self-committal
by which they had become Christians. " The life
which I now live, I live by faith " : [3] there is faith as
a life, the abiding condition of the consecrated soul.
Hence faith includes everything that enters into a vital
personal relationship to Jesus—trusting His guidance,
obeying His commandments, praying in His name,
giving Him our love. The fact is sometimes com-
mented on that Paul speaks far more frequently of
" believing in Christ " than of "loving Christ " ; and
it has even been suggested that this makes his religion
altogether colder than the religion of St. John. Such a
reading of the apostle is wholly superficial. Love to
Christ glows in every word he wrote. Faith, as Paul
conceives it, *is* love : it is the utter abandonment of
self which only an overpowering affection can generate.
And if Paul prefers to speak of " faith in Christ " rather

[1] According to E. Brunner, " faith *is* obedience—nothing else—
literally nothing else at all "(*The Mediator*, 592).
[2] Rom. 13[11].   [3] Gal. 2[20].

than of "love to Christ," he is simply marking the fact that while loving Jesus with all the burning passion of his heart, he still recognizes that Jesus is the Lord and himself the servant.[1] There have been saints in Christian history who have spoken of their fellowship with Jesus almost as if the believer and the Lord entered that union on equal terms : Paul was too great and too deep a spirit to fall into that familiarity. In any case, the real language of love is not words and phrases of endearment ; it does not talk much about itself ; it lives in deeds of sacrifice and surrender and devotion, and in the spirit that is ready, for the beloved's sake, to suffer and be silent. And all this enters into Paul's great cardinal conception of faith, as the willing, eager obedience of the bond-slave to the Lord, and the adoring, self-abandoning response of the redeemed to the Redeemer.

IV

The whole conception with which we have been dealing gains in vividness and precision when Paul goes on to show that it involves union with Christ *in His death and resurrection*. The exalted Saviour who takes believers into fellowship with Himself is no vague "Heavenly Being," but One who wears the very features of the Jesus who lived and died. It follows that all who are incorporated into Him by faith must in some way be identified with, and reproduce in their own spiritual history, the two overwhelming events by which He Himself passed into the power of His endless life. They must share here and now in the experiences of death and resurrection.

What, then, does it mean—to be *united with a*

[1] On this point, see Moffatt, *Love in the New Testament*, 160 ff.

dying Christ ? We have seen already [1] how Jesus, by being born " under the law," and by taking upon Himself at the cross the full weight of the law's curse, had drawn its sting and ended its tyranny. Hence the man who was " in Christ," the man who by faith identified himself with that victorious death, could feel that for him too the curse of the law was a thing of the past. It had no hold over him any longer. " Ye also," declares Paul to the Romans, " are become dead to the law by the body of Christ." [2] In the same way, the bondage of the flesh was vanquished. By taking upon Himself our human flesh, which is the seat and source of sin, Christ had brought Himself deliberately into closest touch with sin in all its force and despotism ; and by the death He had endured, He had settled the despot's fate and pronounced its doom for ever. Hence the man who was at one with Christ in that death could say with boldness that sin's ascendancy over him was broken. " Sin in the flesh," as a personal power, had dared to try conclusions with the Lord of glory, but it had lost its case, and at the cross God Himself had announced the evil thing's defeat. " God, sending His own Son in the likeness of sinful flesh, and for sin, condemned sin in the flesh." [3] Unite yourselves, then, with that death of Christ, says Paul, and with all that it means, and sin cannot lord it over your mortal flesh any more : " there is now no condemnation to them which are in Christ." [4]

The *locus classicus* for all this side of the apostle's thought is to be found in Romans 6. There Paul, with magnificent vigour and effect, drives home to heart and conscience the lesson that to be united with

---

[1] See pp. 116 f.   [2] Rom. 7⁴.
[3] Rom. 8³.   [4] Rom. 8¹.

Jesus in His death means for the believer a complete
and drastic break with sin. He pictures unregenerate
human nature being nailed down on to the cross with
Jesus. He begs his readers to remember that their
lives must reproduce towards sin the implacable
hostility which Jesus declared to it by His death. To
those who, after their conversion, are still conscious
of some clinging remnants of unrighteousness, his
blunt, emphatic word is this: "Die to them! Christ
did." [1] He bids them reflect on the finality of death.
Does death not end all entanglements, and cut the
knot of all hard problems, and bring release from all
binding obligations? And can the death to sin be
different? Must it not mean the utter disappearance
of sin's dominion and control? "Once dead," as
Paul puts it graphically, "a man is absolved from the
claims of sin." [2] Did Jesus have to die twice? Is it
not a fact that His death happened "once for all,"
and that henceforth He "dieth no more"? And must
there not be the same finality about the experience of
the man who, in union with Christ, dies to sin and all
its ways? You, who at your conversion have had
this great experience, says Paul in effect, live out your
life on the basis of it! Realise what has happened.
Tell yourselves that there is an impassable gulf—a gulf
as wide and deep as death—between you and what
once you were. "*Reckon* yourselves to be dead unto
sin."

Such is the trumpet-note that Romans 6 rings out;
and again and again through the epistles its echoes can

---

[1] So Matthew Arnold, in the passage where he deals with what
he calls "the doctrine of the *necrosis*, Paul's central doctrine."
St. Paul and Protestantism, 51 f.

[2] Rom. 6⁷ (Moffatt).

be heard. " Ye are dead, and your life is hid with Christ in God." [1] " If ye be dead with Christ . . . why, as though living in the world, are ye subject to ordinances ? " [2] " We thus judge, that if one died for all, then were all dead." [3] " They that are Christ's have crucified the flesh." [4] Belief in Christ means, for Paul, " being made conformable unto His death," having " my nature transformed to die as He died," [5] —a statement which reminds us that what Paul is speaking of in all these passages is no mere doctrine of *necrosis*, but the vividest of personal experiences. Here was a man who had a right to speak about union with the death of Christ. He had bought that right by a personal crucifixion. " I am crucified with Christ," he can say. [6] " God forbid that I should glory, save in the cross of our Lord Jesus Christ, by whom the world is crucified unto me, and I unto the world." [7] " Faith is a *suffering*," says Brunner, " comparable to the spark which flashes from the flint when struck by the steel." [8] If ever a man experienced the death to sin in all its pain and glory, Paul had experienced it. Hence the ringing assurance with which he bears his witness. " There is something bold, defiant, and jubilant in it," says Weinel truly. " He has not spent his life in burying that dead man who died on the road to Damascus, or in celebrating his memory with copious floods of tears. He boldly turned his back upon him once for all in order that the new life that had come to dwell in him might have room for growth and ultimate glory." [9] If you have died with Christ, he declares, then to sin reckon yourselves dead !

[1] Col. 3[3].   [2] Col. 2[20].   [3] II Cor. 5[14].
[4] Gal. 5[24].   [5] Phil. 3[10] (Moffatt).   [6] Gal. 2[20].
[7] Gal. 6[14].
[8] Emil Brunner, *The Word and the World*, 71.
[9] *St. Paul : the Man and his Work*, 97.

Werde das was Du bist—become what potentially you are ! [1]

It is more than likely that this thought of union with a crucified Saviour contains the clue to an understanding of the difficult passage where Paul speaks of " filling up that which is lacking of the afflictions of Christ." [2] This phrase might indeed suggest that what Jesus endured on Calvary was only a part of the sore travail required for the redemption of the world, and that it has been left to His followers to enter into the sacrificial work thus begun and to carry it forward to completion. Doubtless a deep truth lies in this picture of the sons of God helping Jesus to bear the sins of the world ; but it is not what Paul meant. Never for a moment would he allow any obscuring of his central conviction that Christ had finished the work God had given Him to do. His life and death were all-sufficient. No supplement was required. Redemption was achieved. Reconciliation was an accomplished fact. What Paul refers to as being still " lacking," or " imperfect," was not the sacrifice and suffering of Christ, but it was his own fellowship with that sacrifice and suffering. That this is the true interpretation is attested by the striking passage where he declares that the sole aim and object and ambition of his life is to know Christ better, and to enter more fully into " the fellowship of His sufferings, being made conformable unto His death." [3] It is as though he said, " With Christ I have died, with Him my former self has been crucified ; but every day I live I must seek to deepen my surrender, every day I would fain grow in conformity to Christ. For the ideal of complete Christ-likeness is far away beyond me still. I have not 'attained,'

---

[1] So Dodd, *Romans*, 93 (*MNTC*).   [2] Col. 1²⁴.
[3] Phil. 3¹⁰.

I am only ' pressing toward the mark.' There is much lacking in me yet, in many ways I still fall short of absolute identification with Christ in the death He died to sin. And what is lacking I must strive every day to fill up." In short, it is union with Christ the crucified that is here again the theme. Again the trumpet-note rings out, " Die to sin ! Reckon yourselves dead."

Returning to the passage in Romans 6, we find Paul speaking, not only of " dying with Christ," but also of being " *buried with Him* " ; [1] and the introduction of this further idea is clearly meant to bring out the absolute and final nature of the break which happens at conversion. Just as the Apostles' Creed uses the phrase " crucified, dead, and buried " to emphasize the awful depth and completeness of Christ's self-sacrifice, so Paul employs the image of burial to put the reality of the death to sin beyond dispute. And he has linked up the whole conception in a wonderfully illuminating way to the Christian Sacrament of Baptism. To the convert, going down into the water, the moment of immersion was like a burying of the old self which in union with Christ he had renounced. Not that baptism created a saving relationship to Christ : only by doing violence to Paul's teaching on salvation can such a position be deduced. But baptism was the seal set to faith's reality. Once and only once could it happen in the believer's life. There could be no going back upon it. On the one side of the line of baptism lay bondage to the old lusts and a life without God in the world ; on the other side of the line were joy and peace and membership in the community of Christ. Than the sacrament of baptism no more definite or decisive event could be imagined : to be baptized was to be committed publicly and for ever.

[1] Rom. 6⁴ ; cf. Col. 2¹².

And not less definite than the outward act, declares Paul, must be the inward change to which it sets its seal. " Reckon yourselves not only dead with Christ," he insists, " but *buried* with Him in baptism." For union to Jesus means an end and a beginning more absolute and clear-cut and radical than any other transformation in the world.

Beyond the reproduction in the believer's spiritual life of his Lord's death and burial lies the glorious fact of *union with Christ in His resurrection*. " Like as Christ was raised up from the dead by the glory of the Father, even so we also should walk in newness of life." [1] Everything that Paul associates with salvation—joy, and peace, and power, and progress, and moral victory—is gathered up in the one word he uses so constantly, " life." Only those who through Christ have entered into a vital relationship to God are really " alive." Existence outside of Christ is not worthy of the name at all ; for as compared with a soul that has seen everything in heaven and earth transfigured by a personal experience of redemption and has begun to live daily in the romance and wonder and thrilling stimulus of Jesus' fellowship, the man who lives for the world and the flesh and has no knowledge of God is virtually dead. He does not know it, he thinks he is " seeing life " ; he cannot guess the glory he is missing, nor realize the utter bankruptcy and wretchedness of everything in which he has put his trust. But the fact remains. " To be carnally minded is death ; but to be spiritually minded is life." [2]

For this usage of the word " life," Jesus Himself had given the warrant. It appears in such sayings as " Strait

[1] Rom. 6⁴.   [2] Rom. 8⁶.

is the gate which leadeth unto life," [1] " It is better for thee to enter into life maimed," [2] " This do, and thou shalt live." [3] But what Paul now saw with piercing clearness was that this life into possession of which souls entered by conversion was *nothing else than the life of Christ Himself*. He shared His very being with them. " Christ, who is our life," cries the apostle.[4] He speaks of " the life of Jesus " being " made manifest in our body." [5] Over against " the law of sin and death " stands " the law of the Spirit," which " brings the life which is in Christ Jesus." [6] This life which flows from Christ into man is something totally different from anything experienced on the merely natural plane. It is different, not only in degree, but also in kind. It is καινότης ζωῆς,[7] a new quality of life, a supernatural quality. As Paul puts it elsewhere, " There is a new creation "—not just an intensification of powers already possessed, but the sudden emergence of an entirely new and original element—" whenever a man comes to be in Christ." [8] He begins to live in the sphere of the post-resurrection life of Jesus. The life which he now lives bears the quality of eternity. McLeod Campbell, in his great work on the atonement, complains that " ordinary religion is so much a struggle to secure an unknown future happiness, instead of being the meditation on, and the welcoming of the present gift of eternal life." [9] This is Paul's glory and joy—life, with the stamp of eternity on it, a present possession ! Over the believer's true inward life, death has as little power as it has over the risen and exalted Saviour. " Ye are risen with Him

---

[1] Matt. 7[14].   [2] Mark 9[43].   [3] Luke 10[28].
[4] Col. 3[4].   [5] II Cor. 4[10].   [6] Rom. 8[2] (Moffatt).
[7] Rom. 6[4].   [8] II. Cor. 5[17] (Moffatt).
[9] *The Nature of the Atonement*, 13.

through the faith of the operation of God, who hath raised Him from the dead."[1] His life is yours, Paul means. You do not need to wait " until the day break and the shadows flee away " before beginning to live eternally. In union with Christ, that glorious privilege is yours here and now. Risen with Him, you have passed out of relation to sin, out of the hampering limitations of this present order, out of the domain of the world and the flesh, into the realm of the Spirit, and into life that is life indeed. In short, even here on the earth you are " a colony of heaven."[2] Never forget where your citizenship lies ! " Reckon yourselves alive unto God through Jesus Christ our Lord."[3]

It will now be apparent why we can regard the doctrine of union with Christ, not only as the mainstay of Paul's religion, but also as *the sheet-anchor of his ethics.* Critics of the apostle, from the days of the Judaizers downwards, have attacked him for the alleged antinomian tendencies of his Gospel. Their case against him might be put in some such words as these : " You preach a Gospel of free grace and un-merited forgiveness. But are you not thereby con-doning sin and encouraging moral laxity ? When you say that Christ is our substitute, bearing the penalty of our misdeeds so that we may go free, are you not cutting the nerve of all ethical endeavour ? If every sin of man provides God with a new opportunity of showing His sovereign grace in action, may not the sinner console himself with the reflection that his evil ways are actually promoting God's glory ? May he not say, ' Let us do evil, that good may come ; let us

---

[1] Col. 2¹².   [2] Phil. 3²⁰ (Moffatt).
[3] Rom. 6¹¹.

continue in sin, that grace may abound ' ? " [1] Paul, who was aware that such interpretations were being put upon his message, bluntly calls them calumnies ; [2] but others besides captious critics have raised the question. It is a real difficulty. Does the Pauline evangel have a strong enough hold on the primal moral duties ? Was it not a risky proceeding, to say the least of it, to eliminate the law and trust to the spirit, as the apostle did ? Those who originally challenged him on the point had practical evidence to support their case : for certainly there were antinomian Christians in the early Church, people to whom the new religion was mainly an emotional excitement, a little private luxury with no real reaction on life and conduct. Very probably it was against such a group that the striking words were written, " I tell you even weeping, that they are enemies of the cross of Christ ; " [3] and there were members of the Christian community at Corinth who regarded participation in the sacrament of the Lord's Supper as securing for them all the blessings of salvation both here and hereafter, and thus exempting them from a too scrupulous attention to moral duty and self-discipline.[4] Right through Christian history the workings of this spirit can be traced ; men have found it easy to shelter their sins beneath " the imputed righteousness of Christ," have used a phrase like " not under law, but under grace " [5] to blur the otherwise disturbing fact that God is holy and that there is such a thing as the moral stringency of Jesus, and have persuaded themselves that to an orthodoxy of creed, coupled with the cry " Lord, Lord," the gates of the Kingdom are bound to open. So the Christian faith has been

---

[1] Rom. 3[8], 6[1].   [2] Rom. 3[8].   [3] Phil. 3[18].
        [4] I Cor. 10[16] ff.   [5] Rom. 6[15].

wounded in the house of its friends, and the terribly damaging divorce between religion and ethics has cast a slur on the Church's name. " Religion without morality," says Otto Kirn very forcibly, " is emptied of its true content and value. Unless the Godhead is the source and safeguard of the moral life, it is not a reality to be reverenced at all, but merely the object of a mythical play-acting, and the worship that men offer descends to a selfish currying of favour or to superstitious magic." [1] Or, in the blunter words of Bishop Barnes, " religion without morality is a curse and snare." [2]

Plainly, then, the antinomian charge brought against Paul is a serious one. And yet, there is one factor in the apostolic Gospel which, even alone by itself and unaided, absolutely rebuts the charge and tears every criticism of the kind to shreds. That factor is union with Christ, union in His death and resurrection.

For to be united to Christ means to be *identified with Christ's attitude to sin*. It means seeing sin with Jesus' eyes, and opposing it with something of the same passion with which Jesus at Calvary opposed it. It means an assent of the whole man to the divine judgment proclaimed upon sin at the cross. It means, as the writer to the Hebrews saw, " resistance unto blood." [3] It means, as Paul put it tersely, death. In face of all this, to find antinomianism in Paul is simply to caricature his Gospel.

Moreover, it follows from everything that the apostle says about redemption and the Redeemer that the man whom Christ takes into fellowship with Himself

[1] *Grundriss der theologischen Ethik*, 27.
[2] *Should Such a Faith Offend ?* 176.
[3] Heb. 12[4].

is from that moment *possessed of an ethical motive of the first order*. Compromises and moral second-bests can no longer satisfy him. That blessed intimacy of Christ is daily putting him on his honour. Just as Zacchaeus found that he could not possibly remain in Jesus' company nor feel happy in that new and noble society unless he took steps immediately to straighten out the tangle of his life and to make restitution to those whom he had wronged,[1] so the man who enters into the living union with Christ which Paul has described finds it absolutely necessary, if that relationship is to continue, to bring all his other personal relationships on to a new footing of reality and sincerity and moral truth. It was therefore to the strongest of inward motives that Paul was appealing when he wrote, " If ye then be risen with Christ, seek those things which are above, where Christ sitteth on the right hand of God."[2] For, as Dr. Oman remarks, "to call Jesus Saviour is in the same breath to call Him Lord."[3] A great salvation begets a great love in the heart of the saved : and love's characteristic is that it would rather walk the narrow road of honour than any broad primrose path whatever. Love turns the discipline of life into romance, the cross into a shining splendour, and the cutting edge of Christ's morality into sheer glory and joy. Thus union with Christ supplies an unparalleled ethical motive.

But, declares Paul, it does more. Along with the motive, *it supplies the power*. To be " in Christ " means that Christ is the redeemed man's new environment. The human body, by the acts of eating and drinking and breathing, is continually drawing for its

---

[1] Luke 19⁸.   [2] Col. 3¹.
[3] J. Oman, *Grace and Personality*, 188.

strength upon the resources of its physical environment. So the Christian spirit, by prayer and worship and surrender, makes contact and keeps contact with its spiritual environment, which is Christ : thus the soul draws for its strength upon the supplies of power which in Christ are quite inexhaustible. " I can do all things," it says, " through Christ which strengtheneth me." [1] Faced with the strain and stress of the moral struggle, surrounded by stubborn hereditary foes, torn sometimes on the rack of almost unbearable temptation, if lifts its head and cries " Thanks be unto God which always causeth us to triumph in Christ." [2] Strange, surely, that such a Gospel, built on such an experience, should ever have been called indifferent to, or subversive of, morality! The wildest flights of parody could go no further. The fact is, the Gospel as Paul preached it holds a moral dynamic that is the one hope of the world.

It should be added, however, that the possession of this motive and this power in union with Christ *does not mean the end of the Christian's striving*. Rather is it a challenge to an effort as long as life itself. You are in Christ, Paul tells the Corinthians, but still you are only " babes in Christ." [3] By virtue of their conversion, they had entered the sphere of eternal life ; but material things, especially the body of the flesh, still hemmed them in. Only when this body had been exchanged for the spiritual body, waiting to be revealed beyond death, would their full liberty in Christ be realized. Hence Christian life in the present must be marked by watchfulness, strenuousness, and progress. " Mortify your members which are upon the earth." [4] The apostle wished none of his converts to

[1] Phil. 4[13].　　[2] II Cor. 2[14].　　[3] I Cor. 3[1].　　[4] Col. 3[5].

regard their initiation into the Christian community as a mechanical or automatic guarantee of salvation. Any such idea would savour far more of the pagan mystery religions than of the faith of the Gospel. Paul would have said that a Christian is a man who strives, every day he lives, to make more and more real and actual and visible and convincing that which he is ideally and potentially by his union with Jesus Christ. Dr. L. P. Jacks, speaking of religion in general, has drawn attention to the striking fact that " every truth that it (religion) announces passes insensibly into a command. Its indicatives are veiled imperatives." [1] The Christian's standing in Christ, according to Paul, is a great and glorious fact ; the man who has entered that union knows that what he is experiencing is beyond all challenge or denial—it is truth. But in the very moment of experiencing it, the truth passes over into a command. His relationship to Christ constrains him. It is a fact, but it is also a duty. It is a present reality, but also a beckoning ideal. It is a land of milk and honey, but also a desert where men go up for Christ's sake to do battle with their tempter. Its indicative is " Thy light is come, and the glory of the Lord is risen upon thee " : that is the glorious fact which nothing can shake or alter. But the indicative bears at its heart an imperative, strong, ringing, challenging : " Thy light is come. Then— *arise, shine* ! " " Are you in Christ ? " says Paul to the believer. " Then *be* a man in Christ indeed ! "

One further point remains to be noticed. The experience of union with Christ, as Paul describes it, *looks beyond the present to the future*. It is a

[1] *The Alchemy of Thought*, 315.

blessed and glorious experience here, but it points on to something still more wonderful to come. Never in this world can the believer know all that the fellowship of Christ may mean. Even while he is " a man in Christ," he is conscious of a yearning for a deeper intimacy, of a " Christus-Sehnsucht," as Weiss expresses it.[1] Even while he enjoys eternal life as a present possession, he dreams of the fullness of life that will be his when the shackles of the flesh and its frailty are gone for ever. Mystics, it is often said, have no use for eschatology : they are absorbed in what they have, and are not concerned with any future consummation. That such generalizations are unwise and misleading is made plain by the experience and teaching of Paul, whose mysticism has an eschatological colouring. Titius has brought this point out well. " The Spirit is but seal and earnest of the coming glory, sonship still awaits its perfecting, even communion with Christ is still an ' absence from the Lord ' ; and righteousness, peace, and joy, in which the Kingdom of God consists, become downright misery, if the resurrection hope is taken away." [2]

Here Paul and the fourth evangelist join hands. The keynote of the Johannine literature is eternal life. This life resides in Jesus,[3] who communicates it to men.[4] " He that believeth on the Son hath "—here and now— " eternal life." [5] But this does not rule out the conceptions of future resurrection and judgment and glory. " No man can come to Me," says the Johannine Christ, " except the Father which hath sent Me draw him : and I will raise him up at the last day." [6] Now accord-

---

[1] *Das Urchristentum*, 408.
[2] *Der Paulinismus*, 21.
[3] John 1⁴, 14⁶.
[4] John 10¹⁰.
[5] John 3³⁶.
[6] John 6⁴⁴.

ing to W. Bauer, these forward-looking passages in the
fourth Gospel are a mere concession to the strength
of popular ideas ; [1] and Heitmüller regrets that the
evangelist left unfinished his work of translating the
traditional eschatology into wholly inward and spiritual
forms ; [2] while Bousset goes the length of ascribing all
such passages to a redactor.[3] Explanations of this kind,
however, are thoroughly unsatisfactory. It would be
much nearer the truth to say that the references to the
future stand where they do, not in spite of the dominant
idea of eternal life in the present, but just because that
idea finds in them its complement and full significance.
Both Paul and John were convinced that a life so
glorious as that which in Christ they already enjoyed
must one day, in the mercy of Providence, break its
bands asunder and leap clear from all limiting conditions whatever, and be crowned by God in heaven.
For, as von Dobschütz has put it, " Christianity is—
and will ever be—the religion of sure salvation, brought
by Jesus and to be experienced by His believers already
during their present life. This does not exclude Christian hope. On the contrary, the more present salvation
is experienced in mankind, the stronger Christian hope
will be." [4]

What we are seeking to emphasize is that eschatology
does not begin where mysticism ends, nor does its
presence argue a defect in the mystic's position. In
point of fact, it proves the vitality and intensity of his
union. It is not because he has had so little of Christ

---

[1] *Johannesevangelium*, 38 (in *HBNT*) : " Spricht Joh gelegentlich
von dem Gericht am jüngsten Tag, so ist das als Anpassung an die
volkstümliche Anschauung zu werten."

[2] *Die Schriften des Neuen Testaments*, iv. 83.

[3] *Kyrios Christos*, 177.

[4] *Eschatology of the Gospels*, 205.

that he yearns for more. It is precisely because he has had so much of Christ that he is sure God intends him for the perfected experience. Hence the same man whose daily thanksgiving was that " it pleased God to reveal His Son " in him [1] could also hope for a day " when Christ, who is our life, shall appear." [2] The apostle whose faith centred in a Saviour, risen and alive and present, could also express " a desire to depart, and to be with Christ ; which is far better." [3] There is really nothing incongruous about this : vital Christianity, from the days when Jesus preached the Gospel of a Kingdom which was at once a present reality and a future hope, has always held the two positions together.[4] Paul knew that what had entered him, on the day of his conversion, was life of the eternal order. He possessed it : it was there. Yet Holtzmann is perfectly right when he says that " Biblical religion in general, Pauline in particular, is a *thirst* for life." [5] Conscious as the apostle was of Christ's real presence, not only in the sacraments but in all the joys and sorrows and vicissitudes of the common day, a presence that was an unfailing gleam of glory in his soul, he still could declare himself " willing rather to be absent from the body, and to be present with the Lord." [6] When he spoke of faith, which was the outgoing of the soul towards God, and of love, which was its outgoing towards men, he also spoke —to make the trinity of religious experience complete— of hope, which was its outgoing towards the final

[1] Gal. 1[15 f.]   [2] Col. 3[4].
[3] Phil. 1[23].
[4] It is significant that the idea of eternal life holds in the fourth Gospel and in Paul a place similar to that occupied by the idea of the Kingdom in the Synoptics.
[5] H. J. Holtzmann, *Neutestamentliche Theologie*, ii. 54.
[6] II Cor. 5[8].

redemption.[1] A day is coming, he declares, when the union, so wonderfully established here, will be flawless and unhampered and complete, when the last clinging relic of a material world's power to dim the vision and interrupt the harmony and spoil the sanctity will be blown away on the winds of death, and when the last veil of weak mortality, hiding the ultimate mystery, will be rent in twain by God's own hands from top to bottom. Then indeed, out of the cataclysm of that hour, there will arise a soul " in Christ " ! " So shall we ever be with the Lord." [2]

[1] E. F. Scott has drawn attention to the frequency with which Paul brings the three attitudes together. See *Colossians*, 15 (*MNTC*).

[2] I Thess. 4[17].

CHAPTER V

RECONCILIATION AND JUSTIFICATION

T HE greatest and most Christ-like service that one man can render another in this world is to help him towards rightness with God. Among the blessings of this life, peace with God stands supreme ; all other possessions are empty and unsatisfying, " vanity of vanities," if this is lacking. Hence the ministry to which Paul felt himself called by his conversion was, in his own phrase, a " ministry of reconciliation." [1] The word which he knew himself charged to deliver, the living word of God which—to use the great language of Jeremiah—" was in his heart as a burning fire shut up in his bones," was " the word of reconciliation." [2] As Christ's ambassador and spokesman, bearing a royal commission and authority, and charged with the vast responsibility of representing his Master to men, he made this his constant message and appeal—" Be ye reconciled to God." [3] Here, as everywhere, his own experience was decisive. On the day when Jesus met him, the peace for which through bitter years of battle he had yearned in vain came to him as a sudden, miraculous benediction : the man in Christ now knew himself to be right with God. And with the clearness of vision of a soul redeemed he saw that, if for him the estranging barriers had fallen, there was no reason why they should remain standing for any of the sons of men. If his own restless and distracted heart had found its

---

[1] II Cor. 5¹⁸.   [2] Jer. 20⁹ ; II Cor. 5¹⁹.   [3] II Cor. 5²⁰.

204

perfect rest, then on that same breast of God there must be rest for all the world. Reconciliation became his theme.

In the present chapter, then, we shall begin by discussing this great conception. This will lead on to an examination of the place which the death of Christ holds in the apostle's thought. Thereafter we must relate reconciliation to the cognate, but less personal, more forensic idea of justification. And finally, we must observe how here, as in his central doctrine of union with Christ, Paul looks beyond the present experience to a future consummation, when God's redeeming work in man will be complete and grace will merge into glory.

I

It has always been the fundamental postulate of religion that *man is made for fellowship with God*. To hold communion with his Creator—this is his nature and the very purpose of his existence. He bears God's image. He hungers and thirsts after righteousness. Deep calls to deep, and the eternity within the soul reaches out hands of faith and kinship to the eternity that is in God. It is man's glory to live in this world as a child in his Father's house. It is God's glory to declare "When Israel was a child, then I loved him." [1] "Can a woman forget her child ? Yea, they may forget, yet will I not forget thee." [2] Man fulfils his destiny when he is at one with God and lives in the light and love of that high fellowship.

But religion has always recognized that there is one factor in human experience which has the fatal power of disturbing this fellowship. That factor is sin. Of all

[1] Hosea 11[1].　　　[2] Is. 49[15].

sin's consequences—and they are many and varied, including outward penalties, and suffering to self and others, stings of conscience, hearts hardened and wills enslaved and " a certain fearful looking for of judgment " [1]—by far the most serious is the loss of fellowship with God which sin involves. It brings a cloud across the sun. It interrupts the family relationship. Purity of heart sees God ; and anything which smirches the purity necessarily spoils the vision. What makes sin an essentially lonely thing is not the separation of the sinner from his brother men or even from his own best self : it is his isolation from God. This is what Paul calls " alienation." " You that were sometime alienated (ἀπηλλοτριωμένους), and enemies in your mind by wicked works, yet now hath He reconciled." [2] He charges his converts that they " walk not as other Gentiles walk . . . alienated from the life of God." [3]

This condition of alienation has various stages and degrees. It begins with a vague feeling of estrangement. The soul becomes aware of a barrier which has mysteriously arisen between itself and God. It realizes that although in the actual sin there may have been no intention of wounding God, indeed no conscious thought of God at all, still the relationship has subtly changed. " Against Thee, Thee only, have I sinned, and done this evil in Thy sight." [4] Unless the evil is dealt with, the sense of fellowship is going to be radically impaired, perhaps even ruined for ever. In Jesus' greatest parable, home and love and a happy welcome are the returning prodigal's portion ; but the story makes no effort to conceal the fact that the soul in the far country

---

[1] Heb. 10[27].   [2] Col. 1[21].
[3] Eph. 4[18]. Cf. Eph. 2[13] : " aliens from the commonwealth of Israel . . . without God in the world."   [4] Psalm 51[4].

has lost, for the time being at least, the Father's fellowship.[1] The Old Testament prophet who declared, " Your iniquities have separated between you and your God,"[2] and Paul with his blunt demand " What fellowship hath righteousness with unrighteousness, and what communion hath light with darkness ? "[3] are both proclaiming the one plain, emphatic truth, that sin and God cannot go together. Inevitably the barrier rises, and the fellowship is broken. The soul is alienated.

In Paul's own case, the sense of alienation was connected with his experience under the law. He had failed to fulfil the law's requirements. Conscience told him that he would never succeed. And yet the law was the will of God. How, then, could he hope to escape the divine displeasure ? Must not God be angry with him ? Was not this stinging sense of guilt itself a symptom of God's wrath ? And would not that wrath consume him utterly on the great day of final judgment ? Had he not sinned too often and too deeply ever to be forgiven ? Had not the friendly relationship vanished too completely to be restored ? Fellowship with God—were not the very words a mockery ? When Paul described the bitter experience of estrangement he was describing what he knew.

Now it often happens that alienation of this kind hardens into resentment. The soul in its bitterness turns and accuses God. It lays the blame for the estranging barrier at God's door. Has it failed to observe the law ? Then the fault is God's, who has pitched His demands so unreasonably high. Is God almighty, and the soul itself but feeble ? That only serves to increase the resentment. Thus failure breeds hopelessness, and hopelessness begets recklessness, and

---

[1] Luke 15[18].   [2] Is. 59[2].   [3] II Cor. 6[14].

recklessness becomes downright hostility. The man who was made for the highest fellowship now stands over against his Creator as an enemy. " We were enemies " (ἐχθροί), says Paul, describing the general attitude to God before conversion.[1] By this disturbance of life's central relationship, all its other relationships are deranged and thrown out of gear. To be wrong at this one point is to be wrong all along the line. For, as Dr. Oman has cogently expressed it, " reality is not one thing and God another ; and if we are at enmity with God, we are at enmity with reality, past and present, as well as to come. . . . Enmity against God is enmity with the lives He appoints." [2] Clearly it is here that any redemption which claims universal validity must be tested. Can it deal with this alienation ? Can it remove the enmity ? Can it achieve at-one-ment ? This is the decisive test. Paul perceived that a Gospel which broke the bondage of legalism, and ended the tyrant sway of principalities and powers, and remitted sin's fearsome penalties, and brought up reinforcements for cowed and beaten human wills, *and then stopped there*, was no Gospel worthy of the name. Great and marvellous achievements these all might be ; but over and above them all, one thing was needful, one thing without which all the other glories of redemption must remain sterile and unavailing—the restoration of the lost fellowship with God. Man wants more than the remission of his sins, more than an escape from inward accusations, more than the crossing of his Red Sea and the vision of his Egyptians lying dead, more than a ransom from the wrath to come. He wants to be right with God. He

---

[1] Rom. 5[10]. Cf. Col. 1[21], Rom. 11[28].
[2] *Grace and Personality*, 115, 118.

wants to be back in the family again. He wants, in a word, reconciliation. Any Gospel that offers itself to a sinning, suffering world must stand and be tested here. This is the real test. It is, quite literally, the " crucial " test : for at the heart of it lies a cross.

The word which Paul uses to describe the peace with God into which his union with Christ ushered him is καταλλαγή. In later ecclesiastical usage this term denotes the admission or readmission of penitents to Church fellowship and to the Lord's Supper ; [1] but in classical Greek it is simply a variant of the more frequent διαλλαγή and συναλλαγή, and means the establishing of friendly relations between parties engaged in a quarrel. Now clearly there are more ways than one in which such a peace-making may happen. Much depends on the nature of the estrangement. If the resentment has been mutual, then fellowship can be re-established only when both parties agree to put their angry feelings away. If the enmity has been on one side, harmony may be restored either by a deliberate change of feeling in the hostile mind, or by a friendly approach from the other side which disarms antagonism. Reconciliation, when it is between man and man, can and does take place along these different lines. It is of the utmost importance to determine the line along which it comes when it is between man and God. Other religions there are, apart from Judaism and Christianity, which make use of the idea : and it is significant that all of them take it for granted that God is the one who requires to be reconciled. Ritual acts and offerings are prescribed through which the offended deity may be placated. Is this, then, the conception

[1] Cremer, *Biblico-Theological Lexicon of NT Greek*, 93.

with which Paul is working ? When he speaks of reconciliation, is he thinking of a change in the attitude of God ? Or is it a mutual process which he has in view ? Or is it man—not God at all—who needs to be reconciled ?

Let no one imagine that these are merely academic questions. They are anything but that. Practical issues of the profoundest kind are raised by them— our belief in atonement, our attitude to the work of Christ, our very idea of God. It is not easy to reckon the damage that the Church of Christ has suffered down the centuries by some of the theories of salvation which the Church itself has sponsored, and not easy even to-day to disabuse men's minds completely of the suspicions fostered by the long reign and pressure and prestige of doctrines now recognized to have been, at the best, repulsively mechanical, at the worst, flagrantly immoral. Not yet has Christianity lived down—not perhaps for years to come will it wholly live down— the misunderstandings from the world outside which have been the inevitable nemesis of some of its own unfortunate pronouncements on the centralities of the faith. Certain it is that a truer and more spiritual handling of the great concept of reconciliation would have made some of the more disastrous interpretations impossible. Hence our questions are by no means unreal. They are decisively important. In reconciliation, is man the subject and God the object ? Or *vice versa* ? Or is the process mutual ?

If we allow the consensus of other religions to influence us, the first position is the one we must accept. But if we do accept it, we shall most certainly be wrong. This is one of the points where the danger of parallelism comes out very clearly. Christianity is not to be understood by the analogy of any other faith whatever : if we think to understand it so, we are sure to blunder badly. It is much too independent and original. With one voice the pagan creeds declare that man must take steps to reconcile his God, and so restore himself to favour. Christianity cuts clean across this, and declares the exact opposite. *God is the Reconciler.* God, in His changeless and unwearying love, has taken the initiative, has broken into the atmosphere of man's hostility, and has thrown down every estranging barrier that guilt and hopelessness and dull resentment can erect. " That the willing God seeks to bring unwilling men to His holy fellowship is the uniform teaching of the Scriptures, and the heart of the Gospel." [1] The answer to our question about subject and object stands out clear : it is God who reconciles, man who is reconciled.

This undoubtedly is Paul's position.[2] His own words are plain and unequivocal. " All things are of God, who hath reconciled us ($\tau o\hat{v}$ $\kappa\alpha\tau\alpha\lambda\lambda\acute{\alpha}\xi\alpha\nu\tau os$ $\dot{\eta}\mu\hat{a}s$) to Himself by Jesus Christ." [3] " God was in Christ, reconciling the world unto Himself." [4] " If, when we were enemies, we were reconciled ($\kappa\alpha\tau\eta\lambda\lambda\acute{\alpha}-\gamma\eta\mu\epsilon\nu$) to God by the death of His Son, much more, being reconciled, we shall be saved by His life." [5] If we are to take the apostle's language at its face value, we can only say that of the notion that God requires to be reconciled there is not a trace. Had Paul held any such belief, it is certain that he would have felt it as his bounden duty, for the sake of the souls of men, to declare it in season and out of season.

---

[1] W. N. Clarke, *An Outline of Christian Theology*, 325.
[2] Kaftan, *Dogmatik*, 494 f.   [3] II Cor. 5[18].
[4] II Cor. 5[19].   [5] Rom. 5[10].

But in point of fact, he was far more concerned to rebut the idea than to propagate it. A God who needs to be reconciled, who stands over against offending man and waits till satisfaction is forthcoming and His hostility is appeased, is not the apostolic God of grace. He is certainly not the God and Father of Jesus Christ.

Those who hold the contrary view—that reconciliation is mutual, and that God is the object of it as much as man—rely mainly upon three arguments.

The first concerns the apostle's use of the word "enemies" (ἐχθροί) as applied to sinners. Reference is made to the passage in the epistle to the Romans where Paul declares—"As concerning the gospel, they are enemies for your sakes : but as touching the election, they are beloved for the fathers' sakes."[1] Here, it is said, the clearly intended antithesis between "enemies" and "beloved" denotes that ἐχθροί, like ἀγαπητοί, is being used in a passive sense, and that it means, not "hostile," but "hated" or "hateful"— hateful, that is, to God ;[2] and if God thus views men with hostility, there must be a change of attitude on His side, as well as on the other, before redemption can be achieved. But this, surely, is putting upon a single passage a weight greater than it can bear. Moreover, in the sentence in question, it is by no means as certain as is generally assumed that the passive interpretation of ἐχθρός is the right one : if an antithesis is required by the construction, may we not say that stronger

---

[1] Rom. 11²⁸.
[2] So Sanday and Headlam, *Romans*, 130, 337 (*ICC*) ; Denney, *EGT*, ii. 684 ; Cremer, *Biblico-Theological Lexicon of NT Greek*, 91 ; H. J. Holtzmann, *Neutestamentliche Theologie*, ii. 106.

and more vivid than the accepted antithesis between
" hated " and " beloved " would be that between
" hating " and " beloved "—hating on man's side, and
yet beloved on God's—and that this contrast would not
only be more radical, but also have much more of the
evangel in it ? [1] In any case, the other passages where
Paul speaks of " enemies " put his meaning beyond
doubt. " You, that were sometime alienated," he
writes, " and enemies in your mind by wicked works,
yet now hath He reconciled." [2] That expresses, as
plainly as words can do it, the truth that it is man's
hostility, not God's, which is the problem with which
the Gospel has to deal. " While we were yet sinners,
Christ died for us," declares the apostle, and then
expands his own statement by adding—" if, when we
were enemies, we were reconciled " ; [3] clearly what is
present to his mind is man's rebellion, that opposition of
self to God which is the very essence of sin. Man, not
God, is the rebel ; man's, not God's, the enmity. The
words that Ahab, in the day of his sin's discovery, flung
out at the prophet are still sinful man's cry to his God,
" Hast thou found me, O mine enemy ? " [4] The haunted
spirit, troubled by a presence from which there is no
escaping, hurls at God the stinging, angry epithet. But
always he is wrong. Always Jacob discovers, when
morning breaks, that he has been wrestling with the
lover of his soul.[5] Paul himself, at one period of his life,
had been almost sure that God's face was set implacably
against him ; but there came a day when he learned
how wide of the mark and how untrue to the facts this
deeply rooted notion of a hostile God had been. From

---

[1] So Anderson Scott, *Christianity according to St. Paul*, 78.
[2] Col. 1[21].
[3] Rom. 5[8, 10].
[4] I Kings 21[20].
[5] Gen. 32[26].

Damascus onwards, " Thou hast found me, O my friend," was the burden of his grateful thoughts. In Dr. Oman's words, " It is only the shadow of our misunderstanding, as if, fleeing from a friend in the dark, we meet disaster as though he were a foe ; and, as our friend only needs to show his face, we need only truly to see God's face to be succoured." [1] It is the very nerve of Paul's Gospel, that while we are yet sinners, " enemies," openly hostile and downright rebellious, " God commendeth His love toward us," [2] proves His love by doing what One animated by feelings of antagonism could never do, and sacrificing what One who was hostile could never sacrifice. Ours, says the apostle, is the enmity ; and therefore ours—not God's —the need to be reconciled.

The second fact to which those who hold the opposite view are wont to appeal is Paul's use of the idea of " *propitiation*." His words, as translated in the Authorized Version, are these : " Being justified freely by His grace, through the redemption that is in Christ Jesus ; whom God hath set forth to be a propitiation through faith in His blood." [3] This certainly seems to open the door to the conception against which we have been arguing. But what does the apostle mean here by ἱλαστήριον ? There is only one other occurrence of the word in the New Testament, namely, in the epistle to the Hebrews, where " mercy-seat " is clearly the meaning.[4] This follows the usage of the Septuagint.[5] In the Romans passage, however, the word can hardly bear

[1] *Grace and Personality*, 216 f.
[2] Rom. 5[8].   [3] Rom. 3[24 f.]
[4] Heb. 9[5], " the cherubims of glory shadowing the mercy-seat."
[5] Exod. 25[17].

this sense.[1] The cognate term ἱλασμός occurs twice in the first epistle of St. John. " He is the propitiation for our sins : and not for ours only, but also for the sins of the whole world." [2] " Herein is love, not that we loved God, but that He loved us, and sent His Son to be the propitiation for our sins." [3] In the parable of the Pharisee and the publican, the verbal form ἱλάσθητι is found—"God be merciful"; [4] and in Hebrews 2[17] εἰς τὸ ἱλάσκεσθαι is translated " to make propitiation for the sins of the people." Little light is cast on this circle of ideas by classical Greek : there, from Homer downwards, the verb is found with the accusative and means to placate an offended individual or an angry god, but this construction is quite foreign to biblical usage.[5] It is now coming to be generally accepted that ἱλαστήριον, as used by Paul in Romans 3[25], is not a noun at all, but a masculine adjective agreeing with ὅν—" whom God hath set forth with propitiatory power." [6]

If this is the correct rendering, important results follow. One of the most important is that the crude view of the atonement as a sacrifice by which an angry God was appeased (which for long was the orthodox view) immediately loses what it has always regarded as its main scriptural warrant and support. Among all the divergent theories of atonement, one dominant line of thought can be seen reaching back from recent times right across the centuries, through the Reformers to Anselm, and beyond him to Augustine. According to

[1] Luther keeps the literal meaning in his translation " Gnadenstuhl." So also Cremer, Biblico-Theological Lexicon of NT Greek, 305.
[2] I John 2[2].   [3] I John 4[10].   [4] Luke 18[13].
[5] On this point, see F. Platt, art. " Propitiation," in HDAC, ii. 281.
[6] So Denney, EGT, ii. 611: H. A. A. Kennedy, Theology of the Epistles, 130 ; Sanday and Headlam, Romans, 88 (ICC).

this line of thought, man's sin has offended God's holiness and dignity, and merits infinite punishment. The absolute destruction of the human race would not be punishment too great. Can God be induced to let men off their punishment ? Not until satisfaction has been given Him, and the debt has been paid. To offer such payment is quite beyond man's powers. And yet God demands—and, because He is God, is bound to demand—a full requital. Only when such requital is forthcoming will He be prevailed upon to lay aside His just displeasure and to exercise His clemency towards the offenders. Where, then, can the necessary satisfaction be found ? The difficulty, declares Anselm, is that man *must* make the payment : yet, because it is infinite, only God *can* make it.[1] It is to meet this difficulty that the God-man has appeared. Christ by His sacrifice has offered infinite compensation for the infinite wrong. The cross has persuaded the Father to relent towards man, and to grant him pardon. It has satisfied and appeased the offended dignity of heaven. It has placated the divine antagonism. It has propitiated God.

Such was the orthodox position. Its greatest merit was the serious view it took of sin. Its greatest defect was its disastrous view of God. The adjective is not too strong. " When the Atonement is presented in that form," says the Master of Balliol pointedly, " it seems as though the redeeming love of Christ could save men, but not God, as though God was the one person who was beyond redemption." [2] That is what many in our generation are feeling, as they contemplate the theory of Christ's propitiating work which was once almost taken for granted. The orthodox position has always

[1] *Cur Deus Homo*, ii. vi.
[2] A. D. Lindsay, *The Nature of Religious Truth*, 80 f.

claimed to have apostolic authority behind it. To-day, however, it is growingly apparent that at many points that claim cannot be substantiated. It cannot be too firmly emphasized that the whole idea of propitiating God is radically unscriptural. It plays havoc with the Bible's fundamental tenet, which is the divine initiative. When Paul affirms that Christ possesses " propitiatory power," he is careful to remark that it is God Himself who has " set Christ forth " in this character ; and it is simply flying straight in the face of such a statement to suggest (as so many theories of atonement do) a difference of attitude towards men on the part of the Father and the Son. Indeed, it might be well to drop the term " propitiation " altogether. The English word has a shade of meaning which Paul, in using ἱλαστήριον, had no wish to convey. What he is declaring here is simply that God was in Christ, working for the removal of the estranging barrier which man's sin had interposed.[1] And this is in direct line with what we have seen to be Paul's main teaching on reconciliation.

The third and final argument in favour of the view which we are opposing—namely, that God as well as man needs to be reconciled—is drawn from certain statements in the epistles about the " *wrath of God*." " The wrath of God is revealed from heaven against all ungodliness and unrighteousness of men." [2] " Because of these things cometh the wrath of God upon the children of disobedience." [3] Does this not mean, it is asked, that God, having been wronged, cherishes a resentment against the wrongdoer ? Surely, then, God has to be pacified before fellowship can be restored.

---

[1] So Westcott, *The Epistles of St. John*, 87.
[2] Rom. 1¹⁸.   [3] Eph. 5⁶ ; cf. Col. 3⁶.

Our answer is that this is precisely what Paul did *not* mean. Let us look at his words more closely.

We notice, to begin with, that in the majority of the passages where ἡ ὀργὴ τοῦ Θεοῦ appears the reference is eschatological. It is the conception of " the day of the Lord "—familiar alike to Jewish and Christian ears —with which he is working. He speaks of " Jesus, which delivered us from the wrath to come." [1] " God hath not appointed us to wrath, but to obtain salvation by our Lord Jesus Christ." [2] " Being justified by His blood, we shall be saved from wrath through Him." [3] " The day of wrath " is the " revelation of the righteous judgment of God." [4] In all this, it is the prophetic strain in Paul that we are hearing. Amos and Malachi and the apocalyptists provide the background. Now this is really a different circle of ideas altogether from that in which our present discussion is moving. What we are concerned with is God's existing relation to men. Passages plainly eschatological are therefore not relevant here. And when these are excluded, Paul's remaining references to the wrath of God are few and far between. To build on them an argument that God must be the object, not the subject, of reconciliation is surely—to say the least—highly precarious.

Another fruitful source of error has been the unduly anthropomorphic way in which the concept of the divine wrath has been regarded. " It is often taken summarily for granted that Paul is here contemplating an attitude in which God for the time lays aside His love and acts like a man who has lost his temper. We may be quite sure that Paul the Apostle never thought of God after this fashion." [5] " Wrath " is a word

---

[1] I Thess. 1[10].   [2] I Thess. 5[9].   [3] Rom. 5[9].   [4] Rom. 2[5].
[5] D. Lamont, *The Creative Work of Jesus*, 152.

which very readily suggests angry, vindictive feelings : but surely it ought to be as clear as day that the resentment which one man who has been offended frequently bears towards another who has offended him has no analogy in God whatever. Unfortunately, this most obvious of truths has all too often been obscured ; and of some at least of those who have sought to elucidate the thought of the divine wrath, Jesus' words to Peter might not inaptly be used, " Thou savourest not the things that be of God, but those that be of men "— " Your outlook is not God's but man's." [1] Between the wrath of God and most of what this world calls wrath, no parallel exists. Between them there is no connection, no faintest resemblance at all. Beware, then, of anthropomorphic interpretations here : they cannot but mislead.

What Paul means by the wrath of God—in its present, non-eschatological sense—is the totality of the divine reaction to sin. Everything that man's rebellion against the moral order brings upon him— suffering for his body, hardening for his heart, blinding for his faculty of inward vision—is included in that reaction. Is this punishment ? Yes, certainly ; but it is not God's outraged dignity retaliating by a direct, penal act. Rather is it the sinner who punishes himself. Charles Kingsley's vivid way of putting it was that men " punish themselves by getting into disharmony with their own constitution and that of the universe ; just as a wheel in a piece of machinery punishes itself when it gets out of gear " ; [2] and if the imagery there is modern, the spirit is entirely Pauline. " Sin is the attempt to get out of life what God has not

---

[1] Matt. 16[23] (Moffatt).
[2] *Charles Kingsley : his Letters and Memories of his Life*, 204.

put into it. Necessarily it is a hopeless and calamitous warfare, in which the blows are not light and the falls not soft. . . . The experience of God's wrath is overwhelmingly calamitous, not as anger, outside of the moral order, but as the essential nature of its working." [1] To think of God as growing angry and inventing punishments for the offender is to misconceive the situation entirely. Paul's thought, like that of the New Testament in general, is much nobler, much simpler, much more solemnizing. " This is the judgment, that light is come." [2]

In this interpretation of Paul's meaning, there is no intention of minimizing the seriousness of the divine attitude to sin, or of regarding it as anything other than life's sternest reality. God's will has expressed itself in the very constitution of the universe ; and therefore it is inevitable that evil, wherever and in whatever shape it appears, should feel the full weight of the divine reaction. The stars in their courses fight against Sisera. But this is not " wrath," as we commonly conceive it. Had anyone suggested to Paul that God's wrath alternates with His love, that where the one begins the other ends, that sometimes God acts out of character and needs to be won round from punishment to mercy, he would certainly have branded the idea as a deadly heresy : he would have declared that God's wrath is not understood until it is seen as the obverse of His grace. " It is inevitable in the moral order ; it is the negative aspect of an order which has a positive purpose of good in it." [3] " The Will of God must be thought of as the embodiment of a single

---

[1] Oman, *Grace and Personality*, 216.
[2] John 3[19].
[3] W. F. Halliday, *Reconciliation and Reality*, 132.

principle—the Will to Good." [1]   God's wrath is God's
grace. It is His grace smitten with dreadful sorrow.
It is His love in agony. It is the passion of His heart
going forth to redeem. Of God no less than of man it
is true that " He that goeth forth and weepeth, bearing precious seed, shall doubtless come again with rejoicing, bringing His sheaves with Him." [2]

Thus our investigation of the three Pauline expressions—" enemies," " propitiation," " wrath "—con-
firms our original conviction, that there is no question of reconciling God. Paul speaks always of man,
not God, being reconciled. Doubtless when the reconciliation is accepted and the estranging barrier dis-
appears, a new situation arises for God as well as for
man. If the experience makes a difference to the forgiven, it must also make a difference to the Forgiver.
" There is joy in the presence of the angels of God over
one sinner that repenteth." [3]   It is true that something
happens on the divine side, no less than on the human.
It is also true that the redeeming death of Christ, which
means so gloriously much for man, means more than
mortal mind can ever fathom for God. But we cannot
agree with Denney's contention that because there is
this changed situation for God as well as for man, we
should go beyond the New Testament usage and speak
of God being reconciled. " He is not reconciled in the
sense that something is won from Him for us against
His will, but in the sense that His will to bless us is
realized, as it was not before." [4]   But is this not using
the language of reconciliation in two distinct meanings ?

---

[1] B. H. Streeter, *Reality*, 229.
[2] Psalm 126[6].   [3] Luke 15[10].
[4] *The Christian Doctrine of Reconciliation*, 238.

Surely what happens on God's side is so essentially
different from what happens on man's side that to
apply the one term to both can only cause confusion.
Far wiser is it to follow the explicit guidance of the
New Testament, which recognized the danger and was
careful to avoid it.   Where reconciling has to be done,
God is always the subject, never the object. This is
Christianity's distinctive glory.   And " be ye reconciled to God " is its challenge.

No other position was indeed possible for a man like
Paul in whose thinking grace—that is to say, the
divine initiative—was fundamental. Everything in
religion that matters starts from God's side. Even
faith and penitence and prayer, three attitudes of
soul which might appear to originate in man and to be
human virtues, are, if we believe Paul, nothing of the
kind : they are God's creation, God's gift — faith
because it is evoked by the action of God in revealing
Himself as worthy of all trust, penitence because it is
produced by that divine reaction to sin of which the
cross is the culmination, prayer because when " we
know not what we should pray for as we ought . . . the
Spirit itself maketh intercession for us." [1]   In the
words of Baron von Hügel, " The passion and hunger
for God comes *from* God, and God answers it with
Christ." [2]   Man's intelligence and will and heart and
conscience never initiate anything in religion ; and
over the best moral and spiritual triumphs of this life
the saints can only cry, " Not unto us, O Lord, not
unto us, but unto Thy name give glory." [3]   In this
sense at least, Schleiermacher was right when he de-

---

[1] Rom. 8[26].
[2] Greene, *Letters from Baron von Hügel to a Niece*, xxxi.
[3] Psalm 115[1].

fined religion as an absolute dependence.[1] Of ourselves we can do nothing : there is no Creator but God.

> " And every virtue we possess,
>   And every victory won,
>   And every thought of holiness,
>   Are His alone."

This is the meaning of grace, and this is the inmost
secret of reconciliation.[2] It is hardly likely that a
Gospel so annihilating to human pride will ever be
popular with an age conscious of its own enlightenment
and trusting to its own initiative for world-redemption
and the building of the New Jerusalem upon earth.
Nor will Paul ever be *persona grata* with those—and
there are many of them—who seek, by a punctilious
observance of religious ordinances, to screen from their
own souls and from others the stern and disturbing
fact that their first necessity is to have God change
radically their whole attitude to Himself. If Paul's
doctrine of reconciliation means anything, then the
religion that is tinged with self-satisfaction is, even
when it bears the Christian name, a thing downright
heathen, and the man who thinks that his own deeds
and character are doing God credit and that they have
a claim on God's regard and favour is the victim of a
disastrous delusion. To spiritual pride of every degree
nothing more devastating than Paul's evangelicalism
could be conceived ; and where religion walks clothed
in the garments of moral unreality his Gospel will
always be anathema. But what matter ? It is the
Gospel of God, and there is no other. It is the very
Gospel of Jesus, who proclaimed God's initiative first

[1] *The Christian Faith*, 12.

[2] χάρις, says Moffatt, is "one of the shining words that serve
the world " (*Grace in the New Testament*, 21).

and last, who was Himself God's initiative become flesh, whose eyes were like a flame of fire to those who would propitiate God by their gifts and offerings and character, whose face smiled the welcome of heaven to those who confessed they had no standing before God at all, who did not wait till sinners sought Him but went forth to seek them first, who lived to bring the gift of reconciliation near to men, who died to put it in their hands. No man who is too proud to be infinitely in debt will ever be a Christian. God gives for ever : for ever man receives. Is it incomprehensible that the holy God should thus deal with unworthy man ? But, as Barth pointedly remarks, " only when grace is recognized to be incomprehensible is it grace." [1] For me, Paul would say, religion began on the day when I ceased straining and striving and struggling for heaven's favour, and was content to bow my head and accept the gift I could never win. " It is all the doing of the God who has reconciled me to Himself through Christ." [2]

It remains to be added that wherever the primary experience of reconciliation to God is realized, two secondary experiences immediately follow—*reconciliation to life*, and *reconciliation to the brethren*; and both these aspects of the Gospel are stressed by Paul. No man can be at war with God without being at war with everything in his environment which is of God's appointing. When there is disharmony at the centre, there cannot be peace at the circumference. Life and its conditions look unfriendly. There is a perpetual sense of irksomeness and maladjustment and strain. The

[1] *Romans*, 31.
[2] II Cor. 5[18] (Moffatt).

world is a " sorry scheme of things," and man dreams of being able to

> " Shatter it to bits—and then
> Remould it nearer to the heart's desire."

Meanwhile, he is a rebel. It may never occur to him that this attitude to life and outward circumstance is an infallible symptom of a wrong relationship to God. He may indignantly repudiate any such suggestion. But none the less, it is a fact. The first thing that reconciliation with God does is to adjust the soul to life and its vicissitudes. Rebellion and strain become acceptance and peace. When Paul speaks of this, his words ring with the triumph of a personal discovery : " All things work together for good to them that love God." [1] " If God be for us, who can be against us ? " [2] " I have learned, in whatsoever state I am, therewith to be content." [3]

Reconciliation with God also means reconciliation to the brethren. Nothing amazed Paul more than the way in which the age-long feud between Jew and Gentile vanished before the name of Christ. Utterly insurmountable the age-long barrier had always seemed ; but those who had entered on the new life found that, for them at least, it existed no longer. " He is our peace, who hath made both one, and hath broken down the middle wall of partition between us." [4] Hence Paul would have said that a failure in love, no less than a rebellious attitude to life, is a sure sign of a defective spiritual religion. The man who, while accepting the Gospel, is capable of censoriousness and resentment and uncharity, is unconsciously announcing to all and sundry, as plainly as if he stated it aloud in words, that

---

[1] Rom. 8²⁸.   [2] Rom. 8³¹.
[3] Phil. 4¹¹.   [4] Eph. 2¹⁴.

he is inwardly wrong with God. That is why all human alienations are serious. Invariably they betoken an alienation, at some point, between man and God. Reconciliation, when it is real, changes all this. To be genuinely reconciled to God is to see all mankind with new eyes. It is to have " the love of God shed abroad in our hearts by the Holy Ghost." [1] It is to have the living Christ within, which means to feel towards others as Christ would feel towards them. It is to be raised above all dividing barriers and all the pettiness of spirits unredeemed, into a realm of wider horizons and ampler air, where " there is neither Jew nor Greek, bond nor free, male nor female : for ye are all one in Christ Jesus." [2]

II

It is an outstanding characteristic of Paul's religion that when he thinks of reconciliation and peace with God *the thought of the cross is never far away*. He speaks of Jesus " reconciling men unto God by the cross," [3] " making peace through the blood of His cross." [4] Why this continual emphasis ? Wherein did the reconciling power of the cross lie ? What were Paul's main convictions about the death of Christ ? These are the questions to which we must now attempt an answer.

At the outset, however, it will be well to remind ourselves of a fact already noted, namely, that to isolate the death of Christ from His resurrection, as some theologies have done, is definitely un-Pauline.[5] Too often there has been a tendency to regard the cross as in itself the assurance of salvation, apart altogether

[1] Rom. 5[5].   [2] Gal. 3[28]   [3] Eph. 2[16].
[4] Col. 1[20].   [5] See pp. 135 f.

from the earthly ministry that went before it and the resurrection that came after. This is not the point of view of the New Testament. Everything depends on a man's union with a living, present Saviour. In the absence of that union, even the Gospel of the cross loses its saving efficacy. " If Christ be not raised, your faith is vain ; ye are yet in your sins." [1] Atonement remains impersonal and largely irrelevant until we make contact with the One who atones : and contact of a vital kind is possible only if Jesus is risen and living now. Hence the New Testament writers refuse to treat either the death or the resurrection of Christ in isolation. When they speak of the cross, they see it ever in the light of the Easter glory ; and when they speak of the resurrection, they set it against the dark background of the cross. Paul's words are typical : " If, when we were enemies, we were reconciled to God by the death of His Son, much more, being reconciled, we shall be saved by His life." [2] " Who is he that condemneth ? It is Christ that died, yea rather, that is risen again." [3]

Another note of warning should be sounded here. Do not let us try to reduce to a formula or co-ordinate into a single system Paul's many-sided interpretations of the cross.[4] Efforts of this kind have been the bane of theology. Could such a formula or system be found, it would only mean that Paul was a less towering spiritual genius than we had imagined him. The essential greatness of the man enabled him to see now one aspect of the cross, now another, and now another. Such flashes of insight are not to be regimented into any formula. The history of dogma has shown conclusively that whenever one solving word or phrase is sought, to epitomize and

[1] I Cor. 15[17].   [2] Rom. 5[10].
[3] Rom. 8[34].   [4] See p. 3.

explain the meaning of the death of Christ, truth is in danger of passing into heresy. The cross is too great and glorious for such treatment. Everything has been different since the Son of God climbed Calvary. Life has been different, death has been different, sin has been different, faith and hope and love have been different. Round the wide universe the arms of the cross have reached ; its head has touched the heavens ; its shaft has gone down as deep as hell. How should all this be formulated ? Paul knew better than to make the attempt. It was much more than one solitary word that God had spoken to him at Calvary : it was a message of quite inexhaustible significance. Hence the varied interpretations that meet us in the epistles. Each is part of the total truth. Each is an attempt to share with others something which Paul himself had seen as he stood face to face with the Crucified. Let us, putting theories away, listen to his own words.

The important passage in which the apostle has summed up the main themes of his mission-preaching begins with the statement, " I delivered unto you first of all that which I also received, how that Christ died for our sins according to the scriptures." [1] Here we discover the basal belief which he shared with the primitive community. Here was the Church's message from the very day of its birth. *Christ died for our sins.*

The narratives at the beginning of the Book of Acts suggest that in the earliest Christian thinking and preaching on the death of Christ there were three notes. First, the cross was *man's most flagrant crime*. It was sin's crowning horror. " It originated in the very slums of the human heart." [2] " Ye denied the Holy One and the Just," declared Peter to the people of Jerusalem,

[1] I Cor. 15³.   [2] D. S. Cairns, *The Faith that Rebels*, 199.

" and desired a murderer to be granted unto you ; and killed the Prince of life." [1] " Which of the prophets," demanded Stephen, " have not your fathers persecuted ? and they have slain them which shewed before of the coming of the Just One ; of whom ye have been now the betrayers and murderers." [2] Never could the Church forget that it was human minds that had planned the cross, human hands that had erected it on Calvary.

But there was far more than this in the earliest thinking on the death of Christ. From the very first, *the hand of God was seen.* Behind the apparent tragedy, a divine purpose had been at work. All that had happened had been " by the determinate counsel and foreknowledge of God." [3] Exploring afresh their Old Testament scriptures, the Christians found passage after passage in which the cross was shadowed forth. The great description of the Suffering Servant in Isaiah 53, on which Jesus in the days of His flesh had meditated long, now sprang to sudden life and meaning in the minds of Jesus' followers ; and Philip, in his conversation with the Ethiopian eunuch, was only doing what any other member of the primitive community would have done when he " began at the same scripture, and preached unto him Jesus." [4] Resolutely they held to the conviction that had gripped them : the cross had been, not God's defeat, but God's purpose and God's victory. Human, historic forces had doubtless played their part. Pharisaic blindness and intolerance, priestly exclusiveness and self-seeking, imperial policy and power, popular disappointment and resentment—all had a share in Calvary. But none of these had been the

[1] Acts $3^{14 f.}$.
[2] Acts 7^{52}.
[3] Acts 2^{23}.
[4] Acts 8^{35}.

229

final, determining factor. Jesus had gone to death, not
driven like a slave, but marching in the freedom of His
own unconquered soul. Necessity had been laid upon
Him—" the Son of man *must* suffer and be slain " [1]—
but it had been the necessity, not of mortal tyranny
and violence, but of His own love for the souls of men.
In the cross of Jesus, the divine purposes had been, not
thwarted and broken, but embodied and proclaimed.
This was the second note in the earliest Christian
preaching.

The third note connected the death of Christ with
the forgiveness of sins. The way in which the cross
brings pardon was left largely undefined ; but as to
the fact itself, there was never any doubt whatever.
Jesus died and rose, declared Peter, " to give repentance
to Israel, and forgiveness of sins." [2] " Through His
name whosoever believeth in Him shall receive remission of sins." [3] To find a warrant for this conviction,
it was not necessary for the primitive community to
hark back to ancient prophecy, although there (and
very notably in the Isaiah passage already referred to)
strong support was forthcoming. There were words of
Jesus Himself which gave all the warrant that was
needed. " The Son of man came not to be ministered
unto, but to minister, and to give His life a ransom for
many." [4] " This is My blood of the new testament,
which is shed for many." [5] Hence the earliest Christian
proclamation, " He died for our sins," carried the
Master's own authority with it. *How* the death of the
cross mediates forgiveness may be hard enough to define :
that it *does* mediate forgiveness is as sure as the word of

---

[1] Luke 9[22].
[3] Acts 10[43].
[5] Mark 14[24].
[2] Acts 5[31].
[4] Mark 10[45].

Christ Himself, as unshakable as the deepest instinct of the human heart.

This, then, was the fundamental conviction with which Paul began. " Christ died for the ungodly." [1] He " gave Himself for our sins." [2] Man by his sin had involved himself in chaos and death ; and Christ, in His passion to extricate man from his self-made ruin, did the one thing that could effectively deal with sin and with the desperate situation sin had caused— He made our doom His own, and gave His life for our redemption. In all this Paul was saying no more than the Christian conscience had been saying since Pentecost. But he went further than this. He advanced to new conclusions. Truths still latent he drew out and made explicit. It is to these we must now turn. What were the deeper insights that were granted to the apostle as he pondered the mystery of the cross ?

Some of them have already occupied our attention in connection with other features of Paul's religion : these we shall not dwell upon here. Thus, for example, our study of the conversion showed us how the cross ceased to be a stumbling-block and a " scandal," and became a messenger of grace and truth.[3] We have seen, too, what Paul means when he declares that the death of Christ has brought deliverance from the curse of the law, on the one hand, and escape from the power of the flesh, on the other. By being made " under the law," and by wearing human flesh, Christ accepted deliberately the full, dread consequences of both these conditions ; in His death He allowed the double tyranny to work its uttermost will upon Him,

[1] Rom. 5⁶.   [2] Gal. 1⁴.
[3] See pp. 138 ff.

231

so that its force was spent, its sting drawn, and its domination broken.[1]   Again, on the negative side, we have marked the fact that Paul never regards the cross as an offering by which Christ sought to placate an angry God or to turn Him from hostility to love.[2] These points have already engaged our thoughts, and call for no further comment now.   But there are other directions which Paul's mind follows.   In particular, three great realities come home to him as he views the cross—the condemnation of sin, the revelation of love, and the gift of salvation.   Let us briefly examine his teaching on these three cardinal facts.

It was one of the apostle's most radical convictions, that at the cross *sin stood condemned once for all.* The law had made sin hateful enough : but how infinitely more hateful it appeared when its true handiwork thus stood revealed !   And conscience told Paul —as indeed conscience tells every soul still in the hour of its awaking—that his was the sin that had compassed the death of the Son of God, and his the guilt of that terrible betrayal.   Others besides Pilate and Caiaphas and the rulers of the Jews were involved : the cross was a mirror held up to the sins of all the world.   " This is what sin means always and everywhere," it seemed to say.   Paul, in his pre-Christian days, had persecuted the Christians madly ; but the first words that broke across his trembling soul in the turmoil of the Damascus hour were " Why persecutest thou *Me* ? "[3]   Then there dawned upon him a truth which he never afterwards forgot, a truth which sooner or later dawns upon every soul that is moving on

---

[1] See pp. 116 ff.   [2] See pp. 214 ff.

[3] Acts 9⁴.

towards salvation—" My hand inflicted Jesus' wounds. My deeds drove in the cruel nails."

> " Lo ! Every soul is Calvary,
> And every sin a Rood."

But the condemnation of sin at the cross goes deeper even than this. The death of Christ, according to Paul, not only shows what sin is : it also declares what God thinks of it. Absolutely uncompromising Jesus was, when sin appeared on the field : He opposed it with His life. To His last drop of blood He resisted it. Here, then, the mind and judgment of God stand revealed. Sin cannot be tolerated. Righteousness cannot come to terms with it. If love is to deal with sin, then it must deal with it in a way that will not minimize its gravity. There must be no blurring of the eternal difference between right and wrong. Forgiveness, if forgiveness there is to be, must vindicate the moral law that sin has outraged. The very act that mediates pardon must also proclaim judgment. Mercy cannot replace justice : it must itself be justice. Is this possible ? Does the problem admit of any solution ? Can such a forgiveness be found ? It was Paul's burning conviction that he had found it at the cross. Pardon was there, pardon full and free : but the stern moral realities of life were also there, and the very mode of God's pardoning grace was sin's downright condemnation for ever.

It is in this sense that the difficult passage in Romans 3²³ ᶠᶠ· is usually understood. Dr. Moffatt's translation runs as follows : " All have sinned, all come short of the Glory of God, but they are justified for nothing by His grace through the ransom provided in Christ Jesus, whom God put forward as the means of propitiation by His blood, to be received by faith. This was to demonstrate the justice of God in view of the fact that sins previously committed during the time of God's forbearance had been passed over ; it was to demonstrate His justice at the present epoch, showing that God is just Himself and that He justifies man on the score of faith in Jesus." [1] After Calvary, Paul seems to say, no man can possibly imagine that sin does not matter to God. To some minds, the fact of the divine patience and long-suffering might lend colour to the view that the sins of men are of little account. Earlier in this same epistle, reference is made to the attitude of those who make light of evil and presume upon the forbearance of God ; [2] and it is worth recalling how in his Athenian speech, as reported in Acts, Paul characterizes pre-Christian history with the words, " The times of this ignorance God winked at." [3] Judaism, too, had become awake to the fact that through man's defective moral values God's righteous-

---

[1] Cf. Denney, *EGT*, ii. 612 ; Sanday and Headlam, *Romans*, 89 f. ; Dodd, *Romans*, 59 f. ; R. H. Strachan, *The Individuality of St. Paul*, 159 ; Gore, *Belief in Christ*, 291, 302 ; Pfleiderer, *Paulinism*, i. 93 ; Weinel, *St. Paul*, 305 ; Weizsäcker, *Das Apostolische Zeitalter*, 144. Dr. Moffatt, whose translation of the passage we have given, points out that the Greek admits another interpretation. If, as is possible, πάρεσις is taken as equivalent to ἄφεσις, and if δικαιοσύνη is regarded as God's " saving favour," the idea of a misunderstanding of God's attitude to sin, which the cross was designed to remove, vanishes (*Grace in the New Testament*, 217 f.). Dr. Anderson Scott (*Christianity according to St. Paul*, 60 ff.) argues strongly against the traditional interpretation. But the idea underlying that interpretation, namely, that men see at the cross how real and terrible is the problem with which sin confronts God, is one which runs through Paul's thinking. Quite apart from the present passage, it is present when he speaks of Christ as being " made sin for us " (II Cor. 5[21]), " made a curse for us " (Gal. 3[13]), and indeed whenever the costliness of redemption is stressed (*e.g.* I Cor. 6[20], 7[23], Rom. 8[32]).

[2] Rom. 2[3 f.]   [3] Acts 17[30].

ness was in serious danger of being compromised. This was the situation that called forth the significant warning of the Mishna which declared, " If anyone says to himself, ' I will sin, and the Day of Atonement will expiate it,' the Day of Atonement does not expiate it." [1] The same disastrous delusion as to God's true estimate of sin evidenced itself in the spurious Christianity which cried " Let us continue in sin that grace may abound." [2] " Open your eyes to the cross," is Paul's command. " Do not think that, because former sins have been passed over in the divine forbearance, you are entitled to conclude that God is lax and indulgent to evil. If you can think that, you have never been at Calvary. For there the shadow cast upon the divine righteousness by man's misconception God Himself has dispelled for ever. There the thought that there can be in God any trifling with moral realities is finally shattered. There the divine passion for truth and holiness is vindicated. And there, in the very act of forgiving, God has judged sin with His uttermost judgment."

Beyond this supreme condemnation of sin, Paul saw in the cross *a supreme revelation of love.* The marvel of it was overwhelming, that the sinless One should have been ready and glad, for the sake of miserable sinners, to endure such shame and agony. Words were poor inadequate things to describe a love so glorious and subduing. It " passeth knowledge," he wrote to the Ephesians. [3] " I am controlled by the love of Christ," he told the Corinthians. [4] It is not theology, it is the adoration of a breathless wonder,

---

[1] Yoma 8, 8 : quoted Moore, *Judaism*, i. 508.   [2] Rom. 6[1].
[3] Eph. 3[19].   [4] II Cor. 5[14] (Moffatt).

that we hear in the greatest words he wrote to the Galatians : " The life which I now live in the flesh, I live by the faith of the Son of God, who loved me, and gave Himself for me." [1] There speaks the individual soul alone with its crucified Redeemer ; but Paul could also see the arms that had been stretched wide on Calvary reaching far out beyond himself and embracing the whole beloved community. " Christ loved the Church, and gave Himself for it." [2] He begs the brethren to make Christ's spirit of sacrificial love the ideal and inspiration of their own corporate life. " Walk in love, as Christ also hath loved us, and hath given Himself for us, an offering and sacrifice to God." [3]

Love and sacrifice—the two ideas belong together. Now we know what Paul meant when he spoke of the cross as the deed of an infinite love. But what did he mean when he thought of it as a sacrifice ? Here we must exercise caution. To read some of the older commentaries is to receive the impression that sacrifice, in the Levitical sense of the word, was the apostle's regulative conception. Nothing could be more misleading. In point of fact, he scarcely ever uses the technical language of sacrifice with reference to Christ's death at all.[4] This ought to warn us that to find a clue to Paul's doctrine of the cross in the supposed analogy of ancient sacrifices, Levitical or other, is precarious exegesis. We must guard against ascribing to Paul positions and points of view with which the

[1] Gal. 2[20].   [2] Eph. 5[25].   [3] Eph. 5[2].
[4] Christ as sacrifice ($\theta\upsilon\sigma\iota a$) is mentioned in Eph. 5[2] ; but the usage here, as E. F. Scott points out (*Ephesians*, 225. *MNTC*) is purely metaphorical. Christ as Passover occurs in I Cor. 5[7] : this also, as the context shows, is a metaphor (H. A. A. Kennedy, *Theology of the Epistles*, 130).

epistle to the Hebrews has familiarized the mind of later generations. Moreover, our study of his teaching on reconciliation disclosed the fact that any idea of an offering made to God for the purpose of securing the divine favour was thoroughly alien to Paul's whole outlook. He does indeed speak quite frequently of " the blood of Christ " (αἷμα), and it has been suggested that here at least the thought of the sacrificial blood-offering must be in his mind. Sinners were " made nigh by the blood of Christ." [1] For them Jesus " made peace through the blood of His cross." [2] " We have redemption through His blood." [3] We are " justified by His blood." [4] All this has seemed to many to point to ideas of sacrifice similar to those present in the Old Testament. [5] But is this the case ? Surely such an interpretation blunders by its very literalism, and reads into Paul's use of αἷμα more than he intended to convey. It is far more likely that the phrase " the blood of Christ " stood simply as a synonym for the death of Christ, a synonym expressing in a peculiarly vivid and emphatic way the awfulness of the price at which redemption was purchased, and the absoluteness of the devotion with which the Redeemer gave Himself for men. We are not, of course, arguing that thoughts of sacrifice were absent from Paul's mind as he meditated on the death of Christ : that would be patently untrue. [6] The *fact* that Paul regarded the

---

[1] Eph. 2[13].   [2] Col. 1[20].
[3] Eph. 1[7].   [4] Rom. 5[9].

[5] Mackinnon, *The Gospel in the Early Church*, 92 : " From the frequency with which he uses the phrase ' the blood of Christ,' he evidently had in mind the Jewish idea of blood sacrifice for sin."

[6] Deissmann definitely goes beyond the mark when he says, " The idea of sacrifice in Paul has not even remotely the importance which is usually attached to it " (*St. Paul*, 177).

cross as a sacrifice is not in dispute : the *sense* in which
he so regarded it is the vital question. And the conclusion to which we are brought is this, that by sacrifice
Paul means the utter self-abandonment and self-
consecration of love. " I beseech you," he writes to the
Romans, " that ye present your bodies a living sacrifice ; "[1] the principle there enunciated held good for
all the sons of men, but in Christ alone had it been seen
at work in full perfection. The obedience of His life,
crowned by the self-oblation of His death—this was
Christ's offering to God. This was His tribute of
uttermost devotion. This was His " sacrifice." And
to all who identified themselves with it, in faith and
vital union, the blessedness of salvation was sure.

But the love of Calvary which had laid its spell on
Paul's mind and heart was more than the love of Jesus :
it was the love of God the Father. Once he had thought
of God as remote and inexorably stern, setting His face
against weak, sinful man, dealing out the awards of
retributive justice, and visiting the iniquity of the
fathers upon the children unto the third and fourth
generation. Now he saw a Being of infinite grace and
mercy, who from the foundation of the world had been
yearning for the wayward sons of men, and had come
forth to seek and to save. " God commendeth *His* love
toward us."[2] " He that spared not His own Son, but
delivered Him up for us all, how shall He not with Him
also freely give us all things ? "[3] The statement to
which a dull, myopic type of religion sometimes com-
mits itself, that the cross proves Jesus' love but not
God's, that indeed a God who could look on while such
a tragedy was happening and do nothing to avert it
cannot be love at all, would to Paul have been simply

[1] Rom. 12[1].   [2] Rom. 5[8].   [3] Rom. 8[32].

meaningless. "God was *in* Christ, reconciling the world." [1] Just as the flame which flashes out from a volcano momentarily reveals the elemental, unceasing fires burning at the earth's heart, so the love that leapt out on one crowning day of history in the sheer flame of the cross disclosed what God's inmost nature is for ever. Jesus, as we have seen, made Himself a sacrifice when He poured out His soul unto death : but in the deepest sense, the sacrifice was God's. It was God who made the offering, God who paid the price, God who "having loved His own which were in the world, loved them unto the end." [2]

Awe and wonder fill Paul's mind as he dwells on the cost of man's redemption to the divine love. "Ye are bought with a price," he says ; [3] and the quiet words convey more of the terror and the glory of the sacrifice, more of the love's majestic heights and awful depths, than any rhetoric could have done. Bushnell was not misreading Paul when he fixed on the fact of the cost of forgiveness to God as the very heart of the atonement. A God who deals with sin by divine fiat, by a mere announcement of pardon, is not the God that the apostle knows and worships. Could forgiveness have come that way, how much less moving it would have been to those who received it, how much less morally creative and spiritually vitalizing in its results ! Paul's own life exemplifies the truth that incomparably the greatest power in this world for stirring the human deeps of gratitude and devotion is a forgiveness achieved by the sacrifice of the Father and the Son. To know oneself forgiven at a cost so terrible is first to be brought to one's knees in utter penitence, and thereafter to be set upon one's feet, ready for God's command. The view

[1] II Cor. 5[19].   [2] John 13[1].   [3] I Cor. 6[20], 7[23].

of the death of Christ which Abelard in the twelfth century held may not cover all the facts : but so far as it goes, his conception of the sacrifice of the cross as the way which divine love took to awaken an answering love in the hearts of men, and so to influence them for righteousness and turn their faces from the earth to the skies, is entirely valid and true to the spirit of the Gospel which Paul proclaimed. " He died for all," declares the apostle, " in order to have the living live no longer for themselves but for Him who died and rose for them." [1] After Calvary, God has a claim on men. To refuse what meets us there is to proclaim ourselves devoid of feeling and honour. Bought with such a price, we are no longer our own. We are bound to Him who bought us with fetters stronger than steel. Jesus Himself saw that His death would have this result. He saw it, and He intended it ; and in the lifelong devotion of His bond-slave Paul and of an uncounted multitude of others, the dream of His heart came true. He " died for us, that, whether we wake or sleep, we should live together with Him." [2]

> " Love so amazing, so divine,
> Demands my soul, my life, my all."

These two great realities which confronted Paul at the cross—the condemnation of sin, and the revelation of love—held in their arms a third, *the gift of salvation*. Not only had Christ by dying disclosed the sinner's guilt, not only had He revealed the Father's love : He had actually taken the sinner's place. And this meant, since " God was in Christ," that *God* had taken that place. When destruction and death were rushing up to

---

[1] II Cor. 5[15] (Moffatt).   [2] I Thess. 5[10].

claim the sinner as their prey, Christ had stepped in and had accepted the full weight of the inevitable doom in His own body and soul. Thus the cross " represents an actual *objective* transaction, in which God actually *does* something, and something which is absolutely necessary." [1] Paul could never stand in thought before the cross without hearing an inward voice which said, " He died instead of me." To endeavour, as some theologies have done, to eliminate all substitutionary ideas from Paul's presentation of the faith is quite arbitrary and unreal. " One died for all," he writes.[2] Jesus was " made sin " for us, " that we might be made the righteousness of God in Him." [3] If words mean anything, this means that Christ did something for Paul which Paul *could* not do for himself, something which —now that Christ had done it—Paul did not *need* to do. As Denney puts it, " In His death everything was made His that sin had made ours—everything in sin except its sinfulness." [4] There are modern students of the Gospel who profess to be repelled by the bold, unhesitating use Christianity makes of the vicarious principle, and would fain construct a creed in which an idea which they complain to be so dangerous or even immoral would have no place. They do not see that to surrender this is to make an end of the Gospel : if God in Christ has not borne our sins, there is no good news to preach.[5] Nor do they see that it means giving up love and life itself : for life is built on those lines, and on the day when love ceases to be vicarious it will cease to be love. It is a sure instinct of the soul that sees the

[1] E. Brunner, *The Mediator*, 439.

[2] II Cor. 5^{14}. [3] II Cor. 5^{21}.

[4] *The Death of Christ*, 160.

[5] The essential correlate of the substitutionary idea is that " *God was in Christ* " : many critics of the idea have forgotten this.

crucified Christ standing in the sinner's place, taking all the guilt and shame and horror upon His own great loving heart, and allowing sin's direst consequences to have their way with Him in grief and agony—until, in that death of Christ on Calvary, the curse of sin has worked itself out to an end and is finished once for all. This is Paul's Gospel ; and Christian experience in every age will repeat, humbly and wonderingly but with unassailable conviction, the words of the apostle's great confession, " The Son of God gave Himself for me." [1]

But this thought of Christ as our substitute always for Paul went hand-in-hand with another which safeguarded and completed it—the thought of Christ as our representative. " One died for all "—that is the one aspect of salvation : " then were all dead "—that is the other.[2] In Athanasius' words, " The death of all was fulfilled in the Lord's body." [3] Jesus, travelling the road of the cross in the greatness of His sacrificial love, has become " the second Adam," the head of a new humanity. " As by one man's disobedience many were made sinners, so by the obedience of one shall many be made righteous." [4] " As in Adam all die, even so in Christ shall all be made alive." [5] It is here that the full force of Paul's great conception of union with Christ appears. Christ unites Himself with us, and takes our place and bears our sins : we then identify ourselves with Him by surrendering up to Him our life. Thereby His attitude to sin becomes our attitude, His love for the Father our love, His passion for holiness our passion. " They that are Christ's have crucified the flesh." [6] United with Christ in His death, they die to sin. By

[1] Gal. 2[20].　　　　　　　　[2] II Cor. 5[14].
[3] *De Incarnatione*, xx. 5.　　[4] Rom. 5[19].
[5] I Cor. 15[22].　　　　　　　[6] Gal. 5[24].

the cross on which Jesus poured out His soul, the world
is crucified to them and they to the world.[1] In His
resurrection, they also rise, and live henceforward in
newness of life. Their prayer now is this :

> "Look, Father, look on His anointed face,
> And only look on us as found in Him."

He is their representative. They are " in Christ." And
in virtue of that identification, God receives them. They
are accepted " for Jesus' sake." As Denney said finely,
looking at Charles Wesley's familiar words from a suddenly new angle, " It is the voice of God, no less than
that of the sinner, which says, ' Thou, O Christ, art all
I want ; more than all in Thee I find.' "[2] The man
who is in Christ is right with God. He may be far from
perfection yet, but that union is the seed which contains
within itself all the promise of the future. In the face
and in the soul of Christ, God sees what the man yet
may be ; and He asks nothing more. " This is My
beloved," He says, " and this is My friend." Nothing
in life or death, no voice of earthly criticism, no accusing
challenge of sin, can shake that verdict or " lay anything to the charge of God's elect." [3] It is the word of
atonement. And the mouth of the Lord hath spoken it.

III

The extraordinary paradox which lies at the heart
of the Christian experience of reconciliation was never
more succinctly or startlingly expressed than in Paul's
phrase—" *God who justifies the ungodly.*" [4] " Justification," says Emil Brunner finely, " is the most incomprehensible thing that exists. All other marvels

---

[1] Gal. 6[14]. [2] *The Christian Doctrine of Reconciliation*, 162.
[3] Rom. 8[33]. [4] Rom. 4[5].

are miracles on the circumference of being, but this is the miracle in the centre of being, in the personal centre." [1]

There is, indeed, a tendency to-day, in reaction from theologies which made justification the quintessence of Paulinism, to regard this whole aspect of the apostle's thought and teaching as purely ephemeral, the product of controversies which have long been dead and irrelevant. " That the so-called doctrine of justification," writes Deissmann, " is so prominent in Paul's letters, which have come down to us, has less an inner, than an outer, cause. The hard fight against the Judaizers and the Law compelled the Apostle thereto." [2] This doctrine, declares Titius, " has an almost exclusively polemical character." [3] Wernle goes even further. " Whoever examines St. Paul's doctrine of justification," he says, " laying aside all Protestant prejudices, is bound to reckon it one of his most disastrous creations." [4] One can only wonder at the recklessness of this last statement. Strange, surely, that this " disastrous creation," this child of controversy, should have possessed such vitalizing power throughout the centuries ! Luther's discovery of the apostolic doctrine of justification was like Milton's discovery of the sonnet :

> " In his hand
> The thing became a trumpet ; whence he blew
> Soul-animating strains."

And every revival of religion has evidenced the stirring and bracing and energizing influence of this great

---

[1] *The Mediator*, 524.
[2] *The Religion of Jesus and the Faith of Paul*, 271.
[3] *Der Paulinismus*, 270.
[4] *The Beginnings of Christianity*, i. 309.

article of the faith. No doubt the Judaistic debate of the first century gave it a special significance in Paul's writings. No doubt the forensic colour still clings to it. But to regard it as a mere weapon brought into being to meet the exigencies of a passing controversy is entirely gratuitous. It would be better to turn the argument round and say, not that the controversy produced the doctrine of justification, but that the revolutionary religious position implicit in the doctrine produced the controversy.[1] That position, put quite simply, is this : no man can save himself, for " salvation is of the Lord." And he must be blind indeed who denies the relevance of this to an age like our own, in which so many modern substitutes for the Gospel—secularism and humanitarianism and moralism and legalism—have appeared on the field, and so many voices are declaring that Abana and Pharpar are better than all the waters of Israel. Even among Christians the attempt to develop Christian graces (which are the circumference of religion) without having first faced up to the question of self-surrender and rightness with God (which is religion's centre) is not unknown ; and as long as this is so, Paul's doctrine of justification, so far from being an obsolete survival of merely historical and antiquarian interest, will remain a living word of God, challenging and convincing and convicting, and mighty to save.

Behind Paul's doctrine lies the Old Testament conception of *righteousness*. This cardinal idea of Hebrew religion defies definition. It includes more than justice or holiness. " Succour is included under

[1] Moffatt holds that this is true of Paul's teaching on grace. *Grace in the New Testament*, 131.

it ; the deliverance of the weak from their oppressions ; and also disciplinary correction. Ultimately ' righteousness ' and ' grace ' become almost indistinguishable." [1] " It is the quality in God, which divides His Godhead with His power, something intellectual as well as moral, the possession of a reasonable purpose as well as fidelity towards it." [2] Barth explains it as " the consistency of God with Himself," [3] and this is perhaps the nearest approach that can be made to a satisfactory definition. The important point is that God's righteousness, as the Old Testament conceives it, is dynamic, not static. It manifests itself in God's active vindication of His purposes with mankind, and particularly of His purpose with Israel. In times of His people's distress and defeat, it is the saving favour that champions their cause, and the retribution that descends on their enemies. This explains the frequent collocation of the ideas of " righteousness " and " salvation." " My righteousness is near ; My salvation is gone forth." [4] " My salvation shall be for ever, and My righteousness shall not be abolished." [5] " My salvation is near to come, and My righteousness to be revealed." [6] " There is no God else beside Me ; a righteous God and a Saviour." [7] Now this idea points beyond itself to another. For when God, in His capacity as righteous, vindicates His afflicted people's cause, He proves that they, not their enemies, are in the right : in other words, He is demonstrating their righteousness as well as His own. This is the sense of the word in such a saying as " The Gentiles shall see

---

[1] A. Martin, *The Finality of Jesus for Faith,* 184.
[2] G. A. Smith, *Isaiah,* ii. 227.
[3] *Romans,* 40.   [4] Isaiah 51[5].
[5] Isaiah 51[6].   [6] Isaiah 56[1].   [7] Isaiah 45[21].

thy righteousness, and all kings thy glory." [1] But here there rises a crucial problem for Hebrew faith. Not always is God's vindication forthcoming : sometimes Israel appeals in vain. Does this mean that God has ceased to be righteous ? The answer of the prophets is, No : it means that Israel itself must be in the wrong. It means that God cannot vindicate wickedness. Thus we see the two ideas of righteousness in the sense of a divine pronouncement and righteousness in the sense of integrity of character merging into each other.

Later Judaism, with its profound emphasis on the law, carried this process a stage further. God's righteousness now becomes the consistency of the divine character and action with the revealed law. Man's righteousness is everything involved in conformity to the law of God. Pharisaism found its watchword in such sayings as this of Deuteronomy— " It shall be our righteousness, if we observe to do all these commandments before the Lord our God, as He hath commanded us." [2] But only God Himself can tell whether a man's conformity reaches the requisite standard. To God alone belongs the final verdict, and each man must appear before the bar of God to hear that verdict pronounced. Hence in the last resort, righteousness is not something a man attains by himself : it is something " reckoned " to him by God.[3] The great question confronting every soul is— " Shall I be counted righteous or unrighteous ? What will God's verdict be—' Guilty ' or ' Not Guilty ' ? " Fidelity to the law would no doubt influence that

[1] Isaiah 62[2].
[2] Deut. 6[25] ; cf. Deut. 24[13].
[3] Cf. Gen. 15[6] : " and He counted it to him for righteousness."

247

verdict : hence the painstaking devotion with which all the minutiae of the law must be observed. God's fiat would be absolute, and God's judgment none could forecast ; but always there was the lurking thought that sheer unremitting faithfulness might establish a claim upon God, and that a record of unbroken obedience would decide the fateful balance and secure a favourable verdict. God would acquit, or pronounce righteous, or " justify," the man whose good works merited salvation.

Such was the background to the apostolic thought of righteousness. The term, as Paul uses it, covers a wide range of meaning. It stands both for the divine nature itself, and for a status given to men. It " exists already in God as an attribute and active force ; it is transferred to man, and realized in him by the action of Divine grace." [1] In the former sense, it is used occasionally as an equivalent of the more sombre aspect of justice, and stresses the fact that there is no laxity with God ; [2] but generally it denotes that energy of the divine character by which men are delivered from the power of sin, while at the same time moral realities are upheld. A good instance of this occurs in Romans I [16 f.], where the phrases " the power of God unto salvation " and " the righteousness of God " are virtually synonymous. There is thus no cleft between God's righteousness and His love : it is in the love which goes forth to save men from the tyranny of evil that the divine righteousness most clearly appears. On the other side, Paul speaks of righteousness as passing over from God to man. Here, too, there is a double meaning. Occasionally it is righteousness as an ethical quality which is in

---

[1] A. Sabatier, *The Apostle Paul*, 298. [2] Rom. 3[5].

the apostle's mind, as in the saying, " Neither yield ye your members as instruments of unrighteousness unto sin : but yield . . . your members as instruments of righteousness unto God." [1] But in the main, Paul treats of righteousness as a status conferred on men by God. When God accepts a man " for Christ's sake," He vindicates him ; He declares him to be acquitted ; He pronounces him righteous. " Just as the touch of the royal sword," says Brunner, " transforms a burgher into a noble, so the divine declaration of forgiveness raises the sinner into the state of righteousness." [2] The Old Testament conception here shines clearly through. This is the underlying idea of the words, " He hath made Him to be sin for us, who knew no sin ; that we might be made the righteousness of God in Him." [3] Paul's great ambition—so he tells the Philippians—was to be found in Christ, " not having mine own righteousness, which is of the law, but that which is through the faith of Christ, the righteousness which is of God by faith." [4] The very form of the words ($\tau\grave{\eta}\nu$ $\grave{\epsilon}\kappa$ $\Theta\epsilon o\hat{u}$ $\delta\iota\kappa\alpha\iota o\sigma\acute{u}\nu\eta\nu$) emphasizes the fact that man's acceptance has its source, not in any human achievement, but in the character of God. In short, the only righteousness which is valid before God is one of God's own conferring. It consists in a radically new relationship to God, and a consequent participation in the life which is life indeed.

The gift of this new status Paul calls " *justification* " ($\delta\iota\kappa\alpha\acute{\iota}\omega\sigma\iota s$). Resemblances there are to Jewish doctrine, but the difference is momentous and decisive. Pious Jews could only peer into a dim, mysterious future,

---

[1] Rom. 6¹³ ; cf. Rom. 14¹⁷. [2] *The Mediator*, 523.
[3] II Cor. 5²¹. [4] Phil. 3⁹.

hoping against hope that God would pronounce a sentence of acquittal at the last. But it was Paul's glorious certainty that for himself, and for all who had faith in Christ, the liberating sentence had already been pronounced. What else could the peace and joy which had come to him at Damascus mean ? Judaism toiled and hoped and struggled and doubted : Paul possessed. The new life surging in his heart could betoken only one thing—God had accepted him. " Not guilty," had been the verdict. What, then, had become of his sins, that bitter and grievous burden which had been the problem of long, haunted years ? God, in accepting him, had blotted them out. They were annulled. Hence justification and forgiveness went hand-in-hand. Daily forgivenesses might still be necessary for daily sins, as Jesus in the great prayer He taught His followers implied ; [1] but the initial act was complete. The alien had been proclaimed a member of the household. The defeated devotee of an elusive righteousness had been clothed in a righteousness of a higher and diviner order. The sinner had been " justified."

At point after point in our survey of the apostle's thought, we have observed the extraordinary prominence he gives to the fact of the divine initiative ; and nowhere does this receive greater emphasis than in his teaching on justification. It is the cardinal fact of religion, and here it is asserted in its most naked, challenging, and even paradoxical form. This alone would ensure that the doctrine of justification will never become obsolete. Human nature has an inveterate tendency to work with ideas of merit ; and the doctrine which, more than any other, flatly negates such notions

---

[1] Matt. 6[12] ; cf. I John 1[7], where καθαρίζει bears the sense of " goes on cleansing."

will always have a salutary and indispensable message
for mankind. Pedantry has often buried Paul's doctrine
beneath a mass of words and lost the living soul of it in
a haze of argument ; and many have been repelled.
But justification, when truly seen, is nothing less than
Christianity at its grandest and most daring. Brunner's
words go to the heart of the matter : " It is just in this
way that Christian faith is distinguished from all religion.
No religion ever had the courage thus to go to the bitter
end in giving man up, as the Christian faith does. All
religions make an attempt at the self-justification of
man—at least of man as a religious subject. It is
exclusively the faith in justification by grace alone
which sacrifices not only the rational man, or the moral
man, but the religious man as well." [1] That is well and
truly said. The " last infirmity of noble mind " is to
think that the virtuous soul deserves something of God.
In the Egyptian Book of the Dead, thousands of years
older than Christianity, the soul of the departed enters
Osiris' hall of judgment, reciting its own righteous acts ;
and Bunyan's Mr. Honest made arrangements with
" one Good-conscience " to meet him at the end and
help him over the river. Outside Romanist theology
altogether, the thought of merit still clings to the moral
and spiritual life of multitudes. But when Paul came
preaching his Gospel of justification by faith alone, that
clean-looking, high-principled thought had the searchlight of God turned upon it, and was branded for ever
as a lie. Pharisaism, then and now, may boast its
religious devotion, its exemplary morality, its visiting of
the fatherless and widows in their affliction, its unspot-
tedness from the world ; but when justification drives
its real message home, then—in Paul's words—" boast-

[1] *The Word and the World*, 80 f.

ing is excluded." [1] How can anyone boast who realizes that everything he has—forgiveness, and a place in the family of God, and eternal life—comes from sheer un-merited grace ? That is the negative aspect of the doctrine. On the positive side, it conveys the glorious truth that the redeeming welcome of God awaits all who, weary of futile quest and fruitless effort, cast themselves in simple faith on Christ.

> " Just as I am, and waiting not
>   To rid my soul of one dark blot "—

that is the secret of acceptance. That is justification.

Is this consonant with Jesus' teaching ? The charge is frequently heard that Paul overlaid the simple thoughts of the Gospels with complexities of doctrine which were unwarranted in their origin and ruinous in their effect. Nowhere, it is said, did this happen more disastrously than in his argument on justification. This criticism is more plausible than profound. When justification is understood, it is seen to be an unfolding of the central truths of Jesus' message. It is clear, for example, that our Lord's purpose in telling the parable of the labourers in the vineyard [2] was to convey to those who had ears to hear the truth that the man who thinks to bargain about final reward will always be wrong, and that God's sovereign loving-kindness will always have the last unchallengeable word : and what is this but Paul's thought of a God who " justifies the ungodly " ? Another parable depicts a servant coming in from the field at the close of day, and making ready his master's evening meal before thinking of anything for himself.[3] Is he seeking to acquire merit ? Is he looking for thanks ? Is he putting his master under an obligation ?

---

[1] Rom. 3[27].   [2] Matt. 20[1-16].   [3] Luke 17[7-10].

No, declares Jesus, the question of obligation never enters : he is merely doing his duty. Here again the germ of Paul's doctrine is clear. The actual term " justified " (δεδικαιωμένος) occurs in the story of the Pharisee and the Publican,[1] a story which, as the evangelist points out, was specifically directed against certain people who " trusted in themselves that they were righteous (δίκαιοι) and despised others." [2] In the greatest of all the parables, the father accords the returned prodigal a lavish welcome : there is no question of a period of probation, no " forgiveness by degrees," no dwelling upon the shame and rebellion of the past.[3] " Father, I have sinned "—that is enough. The wanderer's face is homeward, and the father restores him there and then to the full status of sonship. " He brought me to the banqueting-house, and his banner over me was love." [4] It is the elder brother, whose merit-philosophy is more deeply rooted than his love, who stands condemned. Jesus did more than teach all this in words : He expressed it in His life. His whole attitude to sinners embodied it. He sought them out. He overturned all human verdicts. He would observe no canons of merit. He made the last first. He was the divine initiative incarnate. Men suddenly knew, looking at Jesus, that God had accepted them. His fellowship gave them a new standing. For this end He was born ; for this, in word and deed, He laboured ; for this He laid down His life. Here is the true root of Paul's conception of justification. It is no invention of his own. It is no mere legacy of Jewish scholasticism. It springs

[1] Luke 18⁹⁻¹⁴.

[2] " Christ's reflection on the two men is equivalent in drift to Paul's doctrine of justification by grace through faith " (A. B. Bruce, *The Parabolic Teaching of Christ*, 314).

[3] Luke 15¹¹⁻³².   [4] Song Sol. 2⁴.

from Gospel soil. It bears the stamp of Paul's deep, evangelical experience. It mirrors the life and death and teaching of his Lord.

What happens in justification Paul sometimes describes by the term " *adoption* " (υἱοθεσία). The justified man is now aware that his relationship to God is that of a son to a Father. No longer is he an outcast or a hired servant : his place is in the family. " Ye have not received the spirit of bondage again to fear ; but ye have received the Spirit of adoption, whereby we cry, Abba, Father." [1] God " predestinated us unto the adoption of children by Jesus Christ." [2] " God sent forth His Son . . . that we might receive the adoption of sons." [3] Behind such statements lies Paul's own radical change of attitude, when he passed out of bitterness and slavish fear into peace and liberty. The vivid poignancy and the deep, thankful joy present in the apostolic idea of adoption have perhaps never been better expressed than in these words of McLeod Campbell : " Let us think of Christ as the Son who reveals the Father, that we may know the Father's heart against which we have sinned, that we may see how sin, in making us godless, has made us orphans, and understand that the grace of God, which is at once the remission of past sin and the gift of eternal life, restores to our orphan spirits their Father and to the Father of spirits His lost children." [4] The keynote of the life of adoption is freedom. On the other side of the line lies bondage, the unconfessed but sore and melancholy servitude of the man who has no strong controlling purpose, whose path is lit by no guiding light more reliable

[1] Rom. 8[15].　　　[2] Eph. 1[5].　　　[3] Gal. 4[5].
[4] *The Nature of the Atonement*, 147.

than his own reason and desires, whose inner life is one of inglorious moral defeat. But adoption into the family carries with it " the glorious liberty of the children of God." [1] Personality, once disintegrated, is now unified ; repression gives way to release ; the tone of the moral life becomes victorious. It is life " in the Spirit," says Paul. " As many as are led by the Spirit of God, they are the sons of God." [2] And it is a life of wonderful assurance. It does not spend its days anxiously debating the question, " Am I saved or am I not ? " Its cry is—" Heirs of God, and joint-heirs with Christ." [3] This confidence, of course, is based on nothing in the man himself. It has its source in God, and in the troth of God, who " never goes back upon His call." [4] If God has accepted a man into His family, who is to shut him out ? As Paul himself puts it bluntly, " When God acquits, who shall condemn ? " [5] Come the whole universe against him, the man who knows his sonship of God can remain untroubled and unshaken. One word of the living God means more than a thousand loud hectoring voices of this earth. " Faithful is He that calleth you " [6]—that is the adopted soul's high confidence ; and it stands against the world.

Paul's critics have sometimes urged that his main argument on justification and adoption involves a " legal fiction." Moral interests, it is claimed, are inadequately safeguarded by a doctrine which can speak of God looking upon a guilty soul and pronouncing it " Not guilty." And if God " imputes " to the sinner something the man does not possess—the righteousness of Christ—is not the unreality of the whole transaction

[1] Rom. 8²¹.
[2] Rom. 8¹⁴.
[3] Rom. 8¹⁷.
[4] Rom. 11²⁹ (Moffatt).
[5] Rom. 8³³ (Moffatt).
[6] I Thess. 5²⁴.

thereby increased and made still more flagrant ? Is there not a risk that the absolute emphasis on divine grace, and the depreciation of every idea of human work and merit, may destroy all incentive to ethical strenuousness and self-discipline ?

But this criticism, cogent as it may appear, is really quite beside the point. There is no such thing in Paul's epistles as a mechanical imputing of the righteousness of Christ to sinners. Everything turns upon faith. Justification does not happen in a vacuum. It happens in a faith-pervaded atmosphere. Paul's faith-conception we have already examined, in our discussion on union with Christ.[1] The sinful soul, confronted with God's wonderful self-disclosure in Christ, and with the tremendous and subduing fact of the cross where the whole world's sins were borne, responds to that divine appeal and abandons itself to the love that stands revealed : and that response, that abandonment, Paul calls faith. This is what God sees when He justifies the ungodly. Far from holiness and truth and all that makes a son of God, the sinner may yet be : but at least his face is now turned in a new direction. He may still, like Abraham, be in the midst of paganism, but his heart is in the land of promise. He may still dwell, like Daniel, in Babylon, but his windows are " open toward Jerusalem." This is what God sees ; and on the basis of this, God acts. It may be that the sinner is still woefully entangled in his sins; it may be that there is a long, weary road to travel before he can finally escape from the far country which he has made his home. But that matters comparatively little. What matters supremely is that his life has found a new orientation. He is now " in

[1] See pp. 173 ff.

Christ." He is "looking unto Jesus." [1] And that means three things. It means, first, that the sinner is now looking, not inwards, but outwards—trusting not to any merit in himself, but to something outside of himself altogether, the grace and love of an entirely trustworthy God. It means, second, that he is looking not downwards, but upwards, not down to sin's alluring shame, but up to the beauty and purity of Christ. It means, third, that he is looking, not backwards, but forwards, "forgetting those things which are behind, and reaching forth unto those things which are before." [2] His position may not have altered much, but his direction has been changed completely ; and it is by direction, not position, that God judges. Once the sinner had his back to Christ : now his face is Christward. This is faith, and it holds the potency of a glorious future. This is what God sees; and seeing it, God declares the man righteous. God "justifies" him. Is this a "legal fiction" ? The question answers itself. There is nothing fictitious about it whatever. It is the deepest and most genuine of realities.

The same result appears when we examine the connection between justification and its cognate idea, *sanctification*.[3] It is safe to say that if Paul's commentators had followed the apostle's example and bound these two great conceptions indissolubly together, instead of sundering them and endeavouring to treat them apart, no talk of "fictions" or "antinomianism" would ever have been heard. Too often sanctification has been spoken of as a secondary work of the Spirit of God, superimposed on the original

[1] Heb. 12[2].   [2] Phil. 3[13].
[3] Rom. 15[14], I Cor. 1[30], 6[11], I Thess. 4[3], II Thess. 2[13].

act of justification as a kind of extra. In reality, of
course, there is no such hiatus. When Paul uses the
verb δικαιοῦν he means, as we have seen, " to pronounce righteous," not " to make righteous " ; but
the very pronouncement does, in point of fact, have the
effect of making a man something he was not before.
Justification carries life with it. It puts life into the
man who receives it. It *is* life.[1] " Had there been
any law," writes Paul to the Galatians, " which had the
power of producing life, righteousness would really
have been due to law " [2]—an illuminating sentence
which shows that justification and the producing of
life were, in the apostle's mind, virtually synonymous.[3]
" Justification is not a mere precondition of the
blessing : the whole blessing is given with it." [4] It
is a dynamic, creative act. Dr. Oman brings this point
out well when he emphasizes the fact that the " righteousness of God " into which by faith the Christian
enters is not merely a righteousness God demands or
confers, but " a righteousness God looks after." [5] In
other words, sanctification is not a new thing, but
simply the unfolding, by the operation of the Spirit,
of something already present. It is God's justifying
verdict itself which sanctifies, for it makes a new
creature, with a new heart, in a new world. It translates the soul from the domain of the flesh and all evil
spirits into the control of the Spirit of Christ. To be
justified means that a man stands up and lives, really

[1] Cf. the phrase " justification of life " (δικαίωσις ζωῆς) in Rom.
5[18].

[2] Gal. 3[21] (Moffatt).

[3] " In Paul's terminology δικαίωσις is ζωοποίησις " (Moffatt, *Grace
in the New Testament*, 220).

[4] Titius, *Der Paulinismus*, 166.

[5] *Grace and Personality*, 230.

lives at last, erect and clean and in his right mind before God.   And this is sanctification.

No doubt the Gospel of justifying grace and free forgiveness as Paul preached it involves, not only faith on the part of man, but also a risk on the side of God.   Guarantees of any kind the sinner cannot give ; nor does God demand them.   He deals with sinful men as Jesus dealt with Zacchaeus and many another, accepting them without any security of accumulated merit, or any period of probation, long or short.   Is there any risk greater than that which God takes, when in sheer grace He forgives ?   But perhaps the idea of a faith which " creates its own verification " goes deeper than even William James, the great exponent of the idea, suspected.[1]   Perhaps in that idea there is a truth which holds good on the divine even more than on the human level.   Perhaps the very faith which God has in the future of a poor defeated sinner who has nothing to offer but a cry, the faith by which God accepts the risk for Jesus' sake and justifies the ungodly, creates its own verification and brings that apparently impossible future into actual existence. Certainly this was what happened when Jesus brought all His love and trust to bear upon the publicans and sinners who felt that they had forfeited all love and trust for ever :   His forgiveness not only cancelled the past, but regenerated them in the present, and made them saints for the future.   And this is the Pauline nexus between justification and sanctification.   The divine love which takes life's greatest risks creates life's most glorious results.   It is precisely because God waits for no guarantees but pardons out-and-out, because He dares to trust a man who has no claim or

[1] *The Will to Believe,* 24 f.

right to trust at all—it is because of this that forgiveness regenerates, and justification sanctifies. It is not only or mainly that the man so forgiven feels bound in honour to put forth greater moral efforts than before, though this, of course (as indeed Paul is careful to point out),[1] is involved in the redeeming experience : the determining fact is that the forgiven man is now possessed by a power greater than his own. The leaven of Christ has begun its work of leavening the whole lump. So completely has the whole atmosphere and climate of his life been changed that graces, hitherto unheard-of and impossible, begin to grow. Henceforward it is simply not true to say that " failure is the fate allotted." [2] Moral problems with which he could hardly cope unaided lose their terror when Christ is dwelling within. The new relation to God produces results which once would have seemed incredible ; the new spiritual status bears fruit in daily miracles ; the new identification with Christ means " being changed into the same image from glory to glory, even as by the Spirit of the Lord." [3] Where once there lay the shadows of sin, now shines the steady light of holiness ; and where once there was an ever-deepening despair, now rises the victor's cry, " I can do all things through Christ which strengtheneth me." [4]

IV

It is characteristic of Paul that, while rejoicing in the assured possession of a real and present salvation,

[1] Eph. 4[22 f.], Phil. 2[12], Col. 3[9 f.]

[2] " Whatever else we are intended to do, we are not intended to succeed ; failure is the fate allotted " (R. L. Stevenson).

[3] II Cor. 3[18]. [4] Phil. 4[13].

he can also gaze away into the future and see visions and dream dreams of a culminating and glorious day of the Lord. Faith, by its very nature, is paradoxical ; and Paul's Christianity glories in paradox. " Although Christ is already present, His coming is still expected ; although Christians are already redeemed, still must they wait for the full redemption ; sonship is theirs now, and yet they have still to obtain it ; they are already glorified, and yet hope for glory ; they possess life, but life they must yet receive." [1] Justification, according to Paul, has an eschatological side ; and this we must now consider.

Let us guard, however, against exaggeration here. There is a school of writers who hold that it was in eschatology that Paul's main religious interest lay. This, they believe, is the master-key to unlock all the secrets of the apostle's mind. Such a position is radically unsound. If fails entirely to do justice to Paul's dominating conviction, that in Christ the promised Redeemer had appeared and the Messianic age had projected itself out of the future into the present. Jewish prophecy and apocalypse foretold a time when the Spirit of God would be poured forth with sudden power : but the revolutionary belief which Paul shared with the primitive Christian community declared that the great day had actually dawned. " This is that which was spoken by the prophet Joel." [2] The new order of things, the age of the Spirit, had broken in upon them. They were living in it every day. And their daily fellowship with the risen Christ was the proof of it. " As ye have received Christ, so walk ye in Him," [3] writes Paul, reminding his readers that God's

[1] J. Weiss, *Das Urchristentum*, 421.
[2] Acts 2[16].   [3] Col. 2[6].

unspeakable gift of grace was a realized fact. " Such were some of you," he declares to the Corinthians, after a sombre catalogue of the vicious ways of paganism, " but ye are washed, but ye are sanctified, but ye are justified in the name of the Lord Jesus, and by the Spirit of our God." [1] The great transaction had happened. They had entered the Kingdom. They had " received the atonement." [2] They had passed into a new realm of being. Things which prophets and kings of olden time had yearned in vain to see and hear were now happening all around them. Eternity had broken through into time. Christ was with them. The Spirit was in control. Their own lives were eternal. It is absurd, in the face of all this, to maintain that Paul was primarily an apocalyptist, or that his main concern with religion was eschatological.

But hope did occupy an important place in his thoughts. In our study of his fundamental doctrine of union with Christ, we saw that the very wonder of the intimacy with his risen Lord which he now enjoyed constrained him to look forward to a still closer intimacy to come.[3] In the same way, his thought of justification glows with the rapture of the forward view. " Our salvation," he writes, " has a great hope in view." [4] " We rejoice in hope of the glory of God." [5] Very striking is his expression to the Galatians, " We through the Spirit wait for the hope of righteousness by faith." [6] Here God's justifying decree, which has already been heard in the hour of a man's conversion, is regarded as anticipating the verdict of the final judgment : as there is " no condemnation " now, so there will be none in the

[1] I Cor. 6[11].
[2] Rom. 5[11].
[3] See pp. 199 ff.
[4] Rom. 8[24].
[5] Rom. 5[2].
[6] Gal. 5[5].

last great hour of decision. The age of the Spirit has begun, and believers inhabit a new world of joy and freedom ; but the gift of the Spirit is a " foretaste " (ἀπαρχή),[1] an " earnest " (ἀρραβών),[2] of a still deeper joy and a still ampler freedom. This will happen when Christ, now present with them but unseen, returns in the fullness of His splendour and power. "When Christ, who is our life, shall appear, then shall ye also appear with Him in glory." [3] " Our citizenship is in heaven ; from whence also we look for the Saviour." [4] To be a Christian means " to serve the living and true God ; and to wait for His Son from heaven." [5] With all the early Church, Paul could raise the cry " Maranatha " [6] —Lord, come !

Various causes suggest themselves for this feature of the apostle's thought.

First, it is important to observe that Paul here stands in direct line with *the teaching of Jesus Himself.* Oral tradition, in the days before the Gospels as we have them were written, preserved not a few sayings of the Master in which the thought of a rapidly approaching consummation was enshrined. These were no doubt Paul's background when in prophetic mood he wrote of Christ's return and of the certainty of the victory of God.

Second, *Paul's personal religious experience* pointed in the same direction. That experience was emphatically a growing thing. There was nothing static about it. Great as the revolution of Damascus had been, it was but the prelude to a life of ever-increasing wonder and ever-deepening knowledge of the grace of God in Christ.

---

[1] Rom. 8[23].   [2] II Cor. 1[22].   [3] Col. 3[4].
[4] Phil. 3[20].   [5] I Thess. 1[9 f.]   [6] I Cor. 16[22].

A piety to which "being saved" is the goal of all ambition, the climax beyond which it is unnecessary and impossible to go, is totally unlike that of Paul. Conversion, he found, was not an end, but only a beginning. He knew something of what Jesus meant for the world and for himself when he looked up from the dust to which the flashing vision had abased him, and cried "Lord, what wilt Thou have me to do?"[1]—but he knew far more when, years afterwards, he wrote from prison, "To me to live is Christ."[2] However much he discovered, there was always more beyond. "O Lord God," prayed Moses, when his life on earth was almost done, "Thou hast *begun* to shew Thy greatness";[3] and it is the same note we hear in Paul's words to the Philippians—"Not as though I had already attained, either were already perfect: but I follow after, if that I may apprehend that for which also I am apprehended of Christ Jesus."[4] God's riches were unsearchable, and to the very end of the day there would remain much land to be possessed. Hence personal experience, no less than the teaching of Jesus, added hope to faith, and turned his eyes towards the day of consummation.

Third, there was *the problem of the body*. Terribly hampering, even to a man in Christ, the burden of the flesh remained. Against the limitations of the flesh, the spirit had to fight incessantly; and sometimes it had to acknowledge defeat. Perfect attainment could scarcely be hoped for, until "the body that belongs to our low estate," as Paul describes it,[5] had been radically and for ever changed and transformed. For the flesh, while not itself sinful, gave sin its material to work upon,

---

[1] Acts 9⁶. [2] Phil. 1²¹. [3] Deut. 3²⁴.
[4] Phil. 3¹². [5] Phil. 3²¹ (Moffatt).

and hence was an element of weakness and a constant menace to the soul. " We sigh to ourselves," declares Paul, " as we wait for the redemption of the body that means our full sonship." [1]

Fourth, there was *the fact of death*. To the Hebrew mind, death was more than a mere physical change : it was an event of profound spiritual significance. Brought into the world by sin, it meant separation from God. Hence the horror with which every spiritually minded Jew regarded it. Paul shared that horror. Death is " the wages of sin." [2] It is " the last enemy that shall be destroyed." [3] But destroyed it must be : else Christ's work remains incomplete. The very principle of death, by which sin's dire hold over the human race has from the beginning of time been signalized, shall be eliminated and cease to be.

Finally, Paul could not but yearn for a day *when the struggles of the present would be crowned with glorious victory*. Rank upon rank of hostile forces stood confronting the Church of God ; and the unseen forces were the deadliest. " We have to struggle, not with blood and flesh but with the angelic Rulers, the angelic Authorities, the potentates of the dark present, the spirit-forces of evil in the heavenly sphere." [4] Was this state of things to endure indefinitely ? Was Christ committed to a perpetually indecisive warfare ? Was an uneasy balance of power between Christ and Antichrist the best that could ever be hoped for ? Paul could not believe it. The day was sure to come when God would break in irresistibly and gather His kingdom to Himself. Then at last the stubborn spirits of evil would be beaten from the field. Then not an enemy

---

[1] Rom. 8²³ (Moffatt).   [2] Rom. 6²³.
[3] I Cor. 15²⁶.   [4] Eph. 6¹² (Moffatt)

would be left to trouble the endless peace or to challenge Jesus' sway. Then the universe itself would be remade, nature as well as human nature would be redeemed, and God would " sum up all things in Christ." [1]

Such were some of the factors that inspired Paul's religion with an eternal hope. To frame a fully articulated scheme of eschatology, however, was certainly not his intention. Commentators with a passion for carefully elaborated schemes will no doubt continue to " systematize " Paul's doctrine of the things to come : but it is a mistaken endeavour.[2] The apostle's dreams of the future, his sudden insights, his flashes of vision, his long deep ponderings and meditations, are not patient of such treatment. But let us, for the sake of convenience, take three great eschatological concerns of early Christianity—the Resurrection, the Judgment, and the Parousia—and examine briefly his teaching about each.

It is clear that when Paul speaks of *a coming resurrection*, he is thinking mainly of the destiny of believers. The words " As in Adam all die, even so in Christ shall all be made alive," [3] have sometimes been interpreted in a universalist sense, implying that all shall rise and that all must in the end enjoy salvation. But that this was the apostle's meaning cannot be conclusively proved. It would be truer to say that on this matter he deliberately refrained from dogmatic statements and preserved a reverent agnosticism. His belief in future judgment does indeed suggest that, in his view, there would be resurrection for all. But it is the Christian's future with which he is primarily concerned, and speculations on the ultimate doom or salvation of men

---

[1] Eph. 1[10].   [2] See pp. 27 f.   [3] I Cor. 15[22].

outside of Christianity are conspicuous by their absence. The Christian has already been raised with Christ ; already he has passed from death to life ; even now he is living eternally. Hence the resurrection of the hereafter is simply God's seal set upon the life in Christ which the believer now possesses. Here Paul's thought comes very close to that of the fourth evangelist, to whom the possession of eternal life is not the consequence of a future resurrection, but its presupposition.[1]

Now to Greek minds, the whole conception of a resurrection was strange and novel and puzzling. The first natural reaction of a Greek to the new idea would be to ask, " With what body do they come ? "[2] Philosophy had taught the Greek to believe in a purely spiritual immortality, without a body of any kind. Wise men regarded the body as a tomb in which the living spirit lay buried : $\sigma\hat{\omega}\mu\alpha$ $\sigma\hat{\eta}\mu\alpha$, they used to say.[3] Death was the imprisoned soul's escape.[4] But Paul could not thus conceive a realm of disembodied spirits. To him, the very idea would have been repugnant : witness the earnestness of his desire that he should " not be found naked " after death, but " clothed upon with our house which is from heaven."[5] The real point at issue, of course, as Paul saw very clearly, was the continuance of personal identity. Some sort of body there must be, if the soul's essential individuality was to survive. But if Paul differed from the Greek conception of immortality, he differed equally from the Jewish. Resurrection was a familiar enough idea to the Jew, but it was marked by a crass materialism. The very body which had died was to rise again. Even if its elements

---

[1] John 6[40.54].   [2] I Cor. 15[35].
[3] Plato, *Gorgias*, 493A : τὸ μὲν σῶμα ἐστιν ἡμῖν σῆμα.
[4] Plato, *Phaedo*, 64C : τῆς ψυχῆς ἀπὸ τοῦ σώματος ἀπαλλαγή.
[5] II Cor. 5[2 f.].

had been dissolved and its particles scattered, they would be reassembled and made to live by a miraculous act of God. This, too, Paul rejected. His own position was one midway between the Greek and the Jewish. And it seems to have been the direct consequence of the vision that came to him at his conversion. There Christ had appeared to him with His resurrection body. It was the same Jesus who had died. On the question of identity, there could be no doubt whatever. And yet there was a difference. A change had happened. " The body of humiliation " had become " the body of glory."[1] In it the very essence of God's nature was revealed. Thus when Paul, after speaking of the resurrection of believers, was faced with the inevitable question " With what body do they come ? "—he had not to seek far for his answer, no further indeed than the Damascus road where his Lord had met him. " They come with a spiritual body like Christ's," was his answer. Just as the ψυχή, the natural life-principle, has a body corresponding to itself, the σῶμα ψυχικόν, so the πνεῦμα, the divine life of the " new creation," has a body corresponding to itself, the σῶμα πνευματικόν.[2] The Greek view of immortality safeguarded spirituality, but endangered personal identity. The Jewish view safeguarded identity, but endangered spirituality. Paul's view preserves both spirituality and personal identity. And this is what gives it its surpassing influence and appeal.

A second factor which held a place in Paul's thinking about the hereafter was *the day of judgment*. Most of the passages in which he speaks about " the wrath of God " have, as was pointed out above, an eschatological reference.[3] Impenitent sinners are " treasuring

---

[1] Phil. 3[20].　　[2] I Cor. 15[44].　　[3] See p. 218.

unto themselves wrath, against the day of wrath and revelation of the righteous judgment of God." [1] Apocalyptic literature had depicted the terrors of judgment in lurid colours and with an excessive wealth of detail. Very different is Paul's treatment, which is characterized throughout by a noble dignity and restraint. It is noteworthy that judgment, in his view, is universal. Christians, as well as unbelievers, have to meet it. " We must all appear before the judgment seat of Christ." [2] God " will render to every man according to his deeds." [3] When Paul appeals to Christian people to refrain from censoriousness and criticism of their neighbours, it is on the ground that " the hour of reckoning has still to come, when the Lord will come to bring dark secrets to the light and to reveal life's inner aims and motives." [4] Apostolic preaching owed much of its urgency and passion to the conviction that life in the present, for every soul without exception, was charged with eternal issues, and that everything depended on men's relation to God here and now. But if the Christian, no less than the non-Christian, had to appear before the divine tribunal, he could contemplate that hour of decision without fear or trembling. For God's justifying verdict had already been spoken. The sentence of full acquittal had been pronounced. The indwelling, present Christ was the believer's security. United with Christ by faith, he could face the future with confidence and courage. The great words of Thomas à Kempis are thoroughly Pauline in their tone and meaning : " The sign of the cross shall be in heaven when the Lord cometh to judgment." [5] There could be no terror in

---

[1] Rom. 2[5].   [2] II Cor. 5[10].   [3] Rom. 2[6].
[4] I Cor. 4[5] (Moffatt).   [5] *The Imitation of Christ*, II. xii.

judgment to those whom the Son of God had sealed. Having died with Him in His death and risen with Him in His resurrection, sharing now His attitude to sin and to holiness, belonging to Him by virtue of God's grace and their own full, willing surrender, and growing up daily into His likeness by the operation of His Spirit in their hearts, they knew that even in the last crisis they would stand unshaken. "There is no condemnation to them which are in Christ." [1]

The third great hope which filled Paul's thoughts as he looked forward to the future was that of *the Parousia*. In God's good time, Jesus would return. We "wait for His Son from heaven." [2] "The Lord Himself shall descend from heaven with a shout, with the voice of the archangel, and with the trump of God."[3] It is sometimes argued that such expressions are characteristic of a comparatively early stage of the apostle's Christian thinking, and that as time went on he grew away from them and sought to modify them. If the epistles are taken in their chronological order, it is said, a distinct process of development can be traced. Now it is certainly possible that, on the question of the time of Christ's return, Paul's views may have been subject to change with the passage of the years. More than this we cannot say. It was Bernhard Weiss who set the fashion of discovering intricate processes of theological development as between the earlier epistles and the later.[4] Of course Paul's was a living mind and a growing religion ; but none the less, most of the

---

[1] Rom. 8[1].　　　　[2] I Thess. 1[10].
[3] I Thess. 4[16].
[4] E.g. in his *Biblical Theology of the New Testament*.

schemes of development are precarious and artificial.[1] Apart from the fact that the true sequence of the epistles is by no means finally settled,[2] there are two important considerations which the development theorists have somewhat surprisingly ignored : namely, that Paul had been preaching and meditating on the Christian Gospel for about twenty years before our earliest epistle appeared ; and that thereafter all the epistles, from the earliest to the latest, fell within one decade.[3] To speak as if I Thessalonians represented an early and comparatively undeveloped stage of the apostle's religious thought is therefore quite unwarranted. Does the expectation of the Parousia, prominent in one epistle, recede in another ? That does not mean that it has been lost. Sooner or later it reappears. " It is high time," Paul tells the Romans, " to awake out of sleep. The night is far spent, the day is at hand." [4] " We are a colony of heaven," he writes to the Philippians, " and we wait for the Saviour who comes from heaven." [5] Here the note of his earliest epistles is reproduced. If that note rings out more clearly at some points than at others, we need not be surprised. It is only natural that " at certain moments in his career the vista of the kingdom of God would lengthen out for him, at others it would

---

[1] " He is described as sitting down, like a philosopher, and producing a ' first draft ' of his theory in one of his epistles and a considerably different version of the theory in another " (Gore, *The Philosophy of the Good Life*, 293).

[2] The generally accepted position as to the dates and places of origin of the " captivity epistles " may have to be radically revised in view of Professor G. S. Duncan's important book, *St. Paul's Ephesian Ministry*.

[3] Moffatt, *Grace in the New Testament*, 157 ; Inge, *Christian Ethics and Modern Problems*, 72.

[4] Rom. 13[11 f.]   [5] Phil. 3[20] (Moffatt).

seem to contract." [1] The important point is that Paul, realizing that eternity had now broken through into time and that the long prophesied age of the Spirit had begun, felt—as did all his fellow-believers—a wonderful thrill of hope and expectation. Nothing now could defeat Jesus or bring His cause to confusion. The coming consummation was faith's most radiant certainty.

In hours of vision, Paul already saw it near. He saw the day of God breaking like dawn in the eastern sky. He saw the same mighty Lord, who once at Damascus had stirred his own soul from its slumber, now awakening the whole wide world. Two crowning blessings Christ's return would bring. For the individual believer, there would be the life of glory. " This corruptible must put on incorruption, and this mortal must put on immortality." [2] And for the cause of God, there would be victory, final and complete. " Then cometh the end, when He shall have delivered up the Kingdom to God, even the Father." [3]

This high faith, conceived in Paul's heart by the Holy Ghost, born of his conversion experience, nourished by daily communion with Christ, never left him, never wavered. It is the faith of a reconciled and justified soul. Over it, the world and the assaults of the enemy and the slow years' disillusions have no power nor sway. Courage and confidence and zest and meaning are its gifts to life, while life endures ; and it greets death as glorious gain.

[1] H. A. A. Kennedy, *St. Paul's Conceptions of the Last Things*, 162.
[2] I Cor. 15^{53}.
[3] I Cor. 15^{24}.

CHAPTER VI

HISTORIC JESUS AND EXALTED CHRIST

FROM our study of Paul's religion, one fact has emerged predominantly—the man's overwhelming devotion to the person of his Lord. Paul felt he had nothing which Christ had not given him. Forgiveness, a fresh start, a new relation to God, guidance for each day's need, reserves of moral power, glad fearlessness in the face of life's vicissitudes, an eternal hope that mastered death—all were the Redeemer's gift. He was immeasurably Christ's debtor. In view of this, the question naturally arises, What was his final estimate of the One to whom he owed it all? What place does he give Christ in relation to God and man and the universe? And this question involves another. How does his Christ-religion stand related to the historic Jesus? Is it consonant with the picture offered in the Gospels? These are the questions which must engage our attention in this concluding chapter.

I

The idea has gained wide currency that Paul was responsible for changing the whole character of Christianity. In Paul's cosmic Christ, it is said, the Jesus of the Gospels is barely recognizable. The evangelic tradition shows us a village carpenter who becomes a preacher and prophet. He moves from place to place, preaching and teaching and doing good. He makes friends of a group of fishermen and others. He lives in their company. He washes their feet. He teaches them to pray to God as Father. He gets into trouble with the authorities. He is arrested and condemned as a public danger. He dies on Calvary between two thieves. He is buried in a garden grave. He returns from the dead, and shows Himself to His followers. This is the one side of the picture. Over against it—so runs the argument—stands the Christ of Paul. The carpenter-preacher has now become the Judge of all mankind. The voice which taught simple lessons from the lilies of the field and the birds of the air now awakens the world like a trumpet. The homeless wanderer of Galilee is enthroned above the kings of the earth, all creation sings His praise, and the whole universe finds in Him its meaning and its goal.

What conclusion can be drawn from this, it is asked, but that the New Testament itself contains, not one Gospel, but two ? And of these two, which are we to accept ? Which strikes the authentic note ? Must we not conclude that Paul has been to blame, that he has led Christianity along a track which its own Founder never intended for it ? The simplicities of Galilee have been overlaid with ideas—theological, metaphysical, and mystical—which are quite unwarranted, and burdened with Christological speculations foreign to their nature. The religion *of* Jesus —a creed of simple trust in the heavenly Father—has been turned into a religion *about* Jesus. He who was faith's pattern and example has become faith's object. Surely Paul has been supremely indifferent to history ! The human life of Jesus he has simply ignored. He was not interested in it. He took no trouble to acquaint himself with the facts of it. Do not his own words about " not knowing Christ after the flesh " suggest that he actually gloried in his ignorance ? Between the Jesus of history and the Pauline Christ a great gulf is fixed.

Such is the argument. Wrede, in his *Paulus*, made himself its champion.[1] Harnack, who subordinated everything else in the Gospel to Jesus' ethical teaching and revelation of the Fatherhood of God, gave it modified support. " The Gospel, as Jesus proclaimed it," he declared, " has to do with the Father only and not with the Son." [2] The position is stated emphatically by Morgan. " In Paul we meet with a fully elaborated doctrine of redemption of which Jesus can scarcely be said to know anything at all. . . . So far from sharing Paul's pessimistic estimate of the natural man, He appeals to him with a confidence that is rooted in a splendid optimism. . . . Jesus has no doctrine of adoption. . . . There is nothing in Jesus' teaching to correspond with the Pauline doctrine of the Spirit. Human goodness is traced not to the Spirit's supernatural operations, but to the human heart and will." [3] " The God of the Jews and of Jesus," according to Professor Kirsopp Lake, " is a very beautiful figure—much more beautiful than the God of Paul " : a statement whose effect is scarce likely to be enhanced by the words that immediately follow, " But for us, as for educated Greeks of the first century, it is a beautiful picture which we cannot fully accept." [4] Again, Pfleiderer, to take another representative of the view we are discussing, asserts that

[1] *Paulus*, 90-97.

[2] *What is Christianity ?* 144. For a criticism of Harnack's position, see E. Brunner, *The Mediator*, 65 ff.

[3] *The Religion and Theology of Paul*, 252 ff.

[4] *Paul : his Heritage and Legacy*, 76.

Paul's " dogmatic indifference to the historical life of Jesus really presupposes a lack of historical knowledge of that life, and was only possible at all on this ground." [1] The argument, however, by which Pfleiderer seeks to support this statement is far from convincing. He points out that when Paul wishes to impress upon his converts the duty of a mutual, self-sacrificing love, he adduces as an example of this virtue, not any of the events of Jesus' public ministry, which ought surely to have occurred to his mind as illustrating it, but either the incarnation or the death. " It is more than probable," says Pfleiderer, " that one who had so far to seek for an example of self-sacrificing love, had no precise information regarding the circumstances of the historical life of Jesus which lay much nearer to hand." [2] This, surely, is strange reasoning. If Paul, wishing to set before his readers' eyes a pattern of sacrifice and love, refers to the incarnation and death of Christ rather than to any of the other incidents of sacrifice and love with which the Gospel narrative abounds, it is not because these incidents are unknown to him, but simply because he wishes, quite naturally and rightly, to select the supreme and most heart-subduing illustrations available. Many of the assumptions on which the theory of a hiatus between Jesus and Paul rests can only be called precarious in the extreme.

But let us examine the matter more closely. There is certainly less reference in the epistles to the events of Jesus' earthly life than might have been expected. Moreover, the apostle himself draws attention to the independence of his Gospel. This is a point of which those who regard Paul as " the second founder " of Christianity make much. And undoubtedly it is

[1] *Paulinism*, i. 124. [2] *Ib*. i. 123.

important. " I certify you, brethren," he writes, " that the gospel which was preached of me is not after man. For I neither received it of man, neither was I taught it, but by the revelation of Jesus Christ."[1] Paul disclaims all intermediaries. " I conferred not with flesh and blood," he says.[2] Nothing will he preach except what he calls " *my* Gospel."[3] Direct revelation is its source. When Paul, writing out of the fullness of an intensely individual experience, declares to the Corinthians, " No man can say that Jesus is the Lord, but by the Holy Ghost,"[4] he is virtually reproducing the great words of the Master to Peter, " Flesh and blood hath not revealed it unto thee, but My Father which is in heaven."[5] And Paul not only claims independence. Quite obviously he *is* independent. The personal equation is everywhere. At no time has the Christian Church contained a more original or creative mind. To Paul, a plagiarized creed would have been intolerable. A humanly derived religion would have appeared little better than agnosticism. Hearsay and report were no basis for a working faith. God alone could give that. But to recognize all this quite frankly is certainly not to say that Paul turned the stream of Christianity out of the channel that Jesus made for it : that does not necessarily follow by any means. For after all, independence such as Paul showed in his religion is only what every Christian must be able to claim, if his Christianity is to be real and vital and significant. Second-hand piety has always been the Church's bane and a lamentable source of weakness to the Christian cause. Indeed, we might put it in the form of a paradox

[1] Gal. 1[11f.]   [2] Gal. 1[16].
[3] Rom. 2[16], II Cor. 4[3].   Cf. I Thess. 1[5], II Thess. 2[14], Gal. 2[2].
[4] I Cor. 12[3].   [5] Matt. 16[17].

and say that the more original a man's Christianity is, and the more the personal equation enters with it, the more likely is it to be true to Christ. This is what we see in Paul. It is " my Gospel," as he says ; and just in the degree in which it is his own, it is more than his own—it is Christ's. To separate Paul from Jesus, to explain Paul's Gospel without reference to the life that Jesus lived and the message Jesus taught and the Gospel Jesus brought to light, is, as Raven has well expressed it, " as absurd as to explain the movements of the planets without reference to the sun." [1]

On the question of Paul's acquaintance with the facts of the life of the historic Jesus, one or two points call for notice. We may be sure, as was pointed out in our discussion of the pre-conversion period,[2] that Paul already at that time had taken trouble to acquaint himself with the beliefs of the men and women he persecuted. Who was this Jesus to whom they were so extraordinarily devoted ? How had He lived ? What had He taught ? What was there in His character to explain an influence so remarkable ? For information on these matters, Paul had obviously two sources at his disposal—fellow-Pharisees who had been eye-witnesses of Jesus' ministry, and members of the Church with whom the persecutor's activities brought him into contact. But the question rises here, Was there perhaps a third source available ? *Is it possible that Paul himself had seen Jesus ?*

This is one of the unsolved questions of the New

[1] *Jesus and the Gospel of Love*, 46. H. J. Holtzmann (*Neu-testamentliche Theologie*, ii. 238) says that if Paul was the founder of a religion, it was only in the relative sense in which Luther also has been called the founder of a religion (Religionsstifter).

[2] See p. 120.

Testament. On the negative side, there is the fact that the epistles contain no explicit reference to any such meeting. Is there not a high degree of probability, it may be asked, that if Paul had encountered Jesus or listened to His voice, some mention of the fact would have been made ? On the positive side, there is the consideration that Paul may well have been in Jerusalem at the time of Jesus' trial and death. If so, is it not likely that their paths would cross ?

Many commentators have claimed that II Corinthians 5[16] settles the matter, and points to a positive answer.[1] It is doubtful, however, if this passage can be admitted as evidence. The crucial words are these : " Wherefore henceforth know we no man after the flesh : yea, though we have known Christ after the flesh, yet now henceforth know we Him no more." This statement presents a number of difficulties.[2] When Paul uses the plural " we," is he speaking of himself alone, or of the apostles in general ? Is " Christ " here an official title, equivalent to Messiah, or is it a name purely personal ? Does the phrase " after the flesh " indicate the method of " knowing," or does it stand closely conjoined to the word Christ ? Gore suggests that Paul is speaking for the Christian messengers generally, with no specific personal reference at all.[3] But the whole context seems to indicate quite definitely that it is his own name in which he is speaking, and his own experience which he is recording.[4] Again, it is only very rarely indeed in the epistles that " Christ " bears

[1] W. Sanday, art. Paul, in *HDCG*, ii. 887 ; J. Weiss, *Das Urchristentum*, 137 ; J. H. Moulton, *From Egyptian Rubbish Heaps*, 72.

[2] Even H. J. Holtzmann confesses, " Die Stelle 5[16] widerstrebt jeder sicheren Auslegung " (*Neutestamentliche Theologie*, ii. 68, n.).

[3] *Belief in Christ*, 105.

[4] Moffatt so translates it throughout.

the official sense of Messiah : [1] if we are to be guided by
Paul's predominating usage, we shall certainly be inclined to take the term personally here. As to the words
" after the flesh," we must go to the first part of the
verse for the necessary clue.[2] When Paul declares,
" Henceforth know we no man after the flesh," he means
that whereas before his conversion such distinctions as
those between Jew and Gentile, rich and poor, learned
and illiterate, slave and free, were of paramount importance to him, now they have practically ceased to exist :
the only distinctions he now recognizes are spiritual. No
longer will he take any man for granted. Even Jewish
birth and piety guarantee nothing. All such differences
among men are purely fortuitous and external. Once
they impressed him mightily : now, in the light of the
Gospel, they are nothing. " Henceforth know we no
man after the flesh. We refuse to have our estimate of
any man dictated to us by externals." Then he goes
on, " Yea, though we have known Christ after the
flesh "—as though to say, " If my estimate of Christ
was once similarly superficial, if as a Pharisee I thought
of Christ in terms of His attitude to the law, if as a
Roman citizen I regarded Him simply as a strange
phenomenon in history, if my view of Him was obscured
by prejudice and misunderstanding and all the criticisms
natural to an unsurrendered will, if, in short, I knew
Him in any way but the redeeming and reconciling way
—all that is over. In that way I know Christ no longer.
Henceforth and for ever He is to me the power of God unto
salvation. It is thus—and thus alone—I know Him."

It is possible that Paul intends this as a veiled rebuke

---

[1] Rom. 9⁵ is one such occurrence ; possibly Rom. 10⁶⋅⁷ is another.
[2] Notice that Paul says κατὰ σάρκα, not ἐν σαρκί, which would
give a very different meaning.

to the Judaizing Christians. These men seemed bent on carrying over into Christianity the very formalism and externalism which the new religion had been born to destroy. They were emphasizing secondary things out of all proportion : their real interest was not in Christ the personal and universal Saviour, but in Christ as embodied in the framework of Jewish history and piety.[1] Whether this was in the back of the apostle's mind or not when he wrote the words, it is clear that they cannot be adduced as evidence for the belief that he had actually seen Jesus before the crucifixion.

But neither do they in any way negate that possibility. And indeed the pupil of Gamaliel in Jerusalem, the witness of the death of Stephen, was hardly likely to miss the opportunity, if opportunity occurred, of looking upon One whose words and ways had given the religious leaders of the land so much food for thought. " It is no unsupported phantasy," says Principal W. M. Macgregor, "that Paul, though with jaundiced eyes, had seen Jesus, thinking of Him only as a disturber of the worship of God, and that the memory of the encounter had remained with him, like a fragrance, subtly influencing thought and memory and feeling." [2]

If the answer to the problem we have been investi-

---

[1] So J. Weiss, *Das Urchristentum*, 347. The words in II Cor. 5[16] mean, according to Weiss, "dass er auf irgend welche natürlich-menschlichen Beziehungen zu ihm, deren die Judaisten sich rühmen, keinerlei Gewicht mehr legen kann." R. H. Strachan, *The Historic Jesus in the New Testament*, 28 : " aimed at his legalistically-minded Christian opponents, who quoted the example and teaching of Jesus regarding the Law and His general attitude towards Jewish institutional religion against Paul himself." Lietzmann, *I und II Korinther*, 191 (*HBNT*) : " Dass er eine polemische Spitze hat, ist unverkennbar."

[2] *Christian Freedom*, 108. Dr. Anderson Scott (*Living Issues in the New Testament*, 15) says it is " not only possible but probable."

gating must remain in doubt, there can be no uncertainty about the larger question. Whether Paul had seen Jesus with his own eyes or not, *he was thoroughly cognizant of the facts of Jesus' life.* Apart from the information which he was able to gather in his persecuting days, his contacts with the apostles after his conversion would certainly be turned to good account. From the lips of Peter and others he would learn the full story in all its intimacy and wonder and beauty.[1] When critics, arguing from the reticence of the epistles, commit themselves to the statement that " Paul was not interested in the human Jesus," one can only express amazement at the underlying psychology. The " argument from silence " is proverbially risky : it is completely fallacious here. Is it conceivable that this incomparably loyal, passionately devoted servant of Christ could have been indifferent to anything that concerned his Lord ? Does not the theory of a purely nominal interest on Paul's part in the Jesus of history bear its refutation on its face ?

Indeed, it is unlikely that this charge would ever have been brought against the apostle if due stress had been laid upon the obvious fact that what we have in Paul's New Testament writings is not his preaching to the unconverted but his letters to Christian brethren. He was writing to people who had already been instructed in the evangelic history and presumably knew it well. In preaching, the conditions were different. As long as the Christian mission was confined to Palestine, the missionaries could doubtless count on a certain knowledge of the facts among their hearers ; but when they faced the Gentile world, they had to build from the very foundation. For here no common

[1] Gal. 1[18].

ground existed : the very name of Jesus was unknown.
Who was this Jesus of whom so great things were told ?
Some answer to this question was essential.[1] Hence
the apostolic preaching involved more than a proclamation of the redeeming death and resurrection :
it consisted largely of an account of the life and character and sayings and miracles of the One who had
died and risen.   It was κήρυγμα, a heralding of Jesus.[2]
The best evidence of the importance which the early
Church attached to the story of the historic Jesus lies
before us in the Gospels.[3] Behind a Gospel like Mark
stand the sermons of the Christian preachers, who felt
themselves charged, wherever they went, to hold up
Christ, to " placard " Christ, as Paul puts it.[4] It
was the gathering together of the themes on which
they discoursed, and of the subsequent instruction
they gave their converts, which formed the basis of
the Gospel tradition. If Paul's epistles say little
about the earthly ministry of Jesus, it is certain that
his preaching was full of it.   And the suggestion that
Paul may have confined himself to proclaiming the
heavenly Christ, and have left his subordinates Barnabas and Silas to fill in the details of the human story,
is—as Johannes Weiss has shown—patently absurd.[5]
Is Christ divided ?   No Christian, least of all an apostle,
can hold the two aspects apart, as though there were
two Redeemers.   The Gospel is a unity, or it is nothing.

Here we come in sight of another important consideration. The epistles were written to men and
women who not only had been instructed in the historic

---

[1] J. Weiss, *Das Urchristentum*, 166.
[2] Rom. 16²⁵ ; I Cor. 1²¹, 2⁴, 15¹⁴.
[3] *Das Urchristentum*, 544.
[4] Gal. 3¹.   [5] *Das Urchristentum*, 167.

facts but were actually in touch with the living Christ every day. That is what Christianity meant for them. If they were not always looking towards the past or dwelling in the memory of the Galilean and Judean days, it was not because the earthly ministry of Jesus meant little to them : it was because He had become a vivid and abiding presence. They did not need to hark back continually to the experiences of the original disciples : they themselves were now disciples, learning daily from their Lord. Through dangers and per-plexities and sufferings their road might often lead them ; but always He was there, " closer than breath-ing, nearer than hands and feet," guiding them, speaking to them, flooding them with His own risen life and power. But this does not mean that the knowledge of the historic facts ceased to be a treasured possession. It was with joy and wonder that they realized that the exalted Christ with whom they held daily communion was none other than the Jesus who had walked the earth. They could not think of their eternal Lord without thinking of the life He had lived and the death He had died. On this point, Paul's own language is full of significance. We naturally expect him to use the name " Christ "where the exalted Lord is intended, and " Jesus " where he is thinking of the earthly story ; and, in point of fact, this is often what we find. But what is important to observe is that sometimes this rule is reversed. Sometimes Paul uses " Jesus " of the heavenly One, and " Christ " of the human figure.[1] This is another witness to the truth we are maintaining, namely, that for Paul's mind and heart and conscience there was no hiatus between

---

[1] *E.g.* " Jesus " in I Cor. 9[1], II Cor. 4[11] ; " Christ " in Rom. 5[6], II Cor. 10[1].

Christ in glory and the Jesus who had " lived on earth abased." [1] That the man who knew the former so well deliberately ignored the latter is clearly incredible, alike to psychology and to religion.

No doubt there have been Christians who have sat loose to history ; but Paul was not one of them. He had the genius to see that in a world full of fantasies and myths and cults and mysteries, it was precisely in its historic basis that the new religion's strength and promise of victory lay. Abstract questions—such, for example, as the famous one which Anselm was later to propound, *Cur Deus Homo?*— were never his principal concern : his real interest was a Person. Salvation, in his view, did not mean being initiated into a Logos Philosophy : it meant, as he said himself, " being conformed to the likeness of God's Son." [2] It is not a divine idea of Incarnation which redeems, nor is it a vague principle of Atonement that is the sinner's hope. It is through the personality of Jesus that men for nineteen centuries have seen the Father. To say that history meant little or nothing to Paul is simply not true : it meant everything to him. As Denney put it : " Paul could not in his work as an evangelist preach salvation through the death and resurrection of an unknown person ; the story which was the common property of the Church, and with which her catechists everywhere indoctrinated the new disciples, must have been as familiar to him, in substance, as it is to us." [3] As familiar ? Far more so. Sayings of our Lord and incidents of His life now unknown to us may well have been in the

---

[1] On this whole matter, see J. Weiss, *Das Urchristentum*, 349 f. " Dieselbe Persönlichkeit in zwei Phasen " is Weiss's phrase.

[2] Rom. 8[29].   [3] *II Corinthians* (Expositor's Bible), 203.

knowledge of His great apostle. The earthly and heavenly Christ were one ; and never while Paul gloried in his daily fellowship with the eternally living Redeemer did he cease to ponder on the life and walk and character of One who by entering history had changed all history for ever.

II

It is commonly assumed and stated that in Paul's writings reminiscences of the historic Jesus are extremely meagre. But is this the case ? Let us take the fact of Jesus under the three aspects of His life, His character, and His teaching ; and let us see whether Paul's references are really as scanty as the critics of the Tübingen school and others have declared them to be.

Looking back to the story of *the earthly life*, Paul dwells in one of his most impressive passages on the fact that Jesus entered history " born in human guise, and appearing in human form." [1] He was " made of a woman, made under the law." [2] By natural descent He stood in the direct lineage of David.[3] His primary ministry was among the Jews of His own nation.[4] He set a great example of self-sacrifice and bravery under persecution.[5] Ere He died, He instituted, by His words in the upper room, the great Sacrament of the Lord's Supper.[6] He was arrested by treachery.[7] He was killed upon the cross—" crucified in His weakness." [8] He was buried.[9] He rose from the dead.[10]

[1] Phil. 2[7 f.] (Moffatt).   [2] Gal. 4[4].
[3] Rom. 1[3].   [4] Rom. 15[8].   [5] Rom. 15[3].
[6] I Cor. 11[23 ff.]   [7] I Cor. 11[23].
[8] II Cor. 13[4].   [9] I Cor. 15[4].   [10] I Cor. 15[4].

He appeared after His resurrection to many of the brethren.[1]

Turning to *the character of Jesus*, we must give due weight to the passage where Paul declares it as God's purpose that Christians should be " conformed to the image of His Son, that He might be the first-born among many brethren," or, as Dr. Moffatt translates it, " the first-born of a great brotherhood."[2] Clearly this pre-supposes, as Professor C. H. Dodd has pointed out, that both writer and readers have a fairly accurate under-standing of Jesus' character.[3] Elsewhere Paul speaks of " the meekness and gentleness of Christ,"[4] thus stressing the very qualities enshrined in our Lord's own words "I am meek and lowly in heart."[5] More than once he dwells on the obedience of Jesus to the Father's will.[6] He prays God that his readers' hearts may be directed towards the patient endurance ($\dot{v}\pi o\mu o\nu\acute{\eta}$) of Christ.[7] It would probably not be too much to say that, in all his delineations of Christian life and character, Paul has Jesus before his eyes as the norm and the ideal. Professor John Baillie has suggestively remarked that what we have in the great description of the nature of love in I Corinthians 13: " Love is very patient, very kind. Love knows no jealousy ; love makes no parade. Love is never glad when others go wrong, love is glad-dened by goodness, always slow to expose, always eager to believe the best, always hopeful, always patient "[8] —is not so much a philosopher discoursing on an abstract virtue as a Christian saint meditating on the character of Jesus. " Can we have any doubt who it was who sat

[1] I Cor. 15[5] ff.
[2] Rom. 8[29].
[3] *Romans*, 142 (*MNTC*).
[4] II Cor. 10[1].
[5] Matt. 11[29].
[6] Rom. 5[19], Phil. 2[8].
[7] II Thess. 3[5]. But this may be " the patience Christ inspires."
[8] I Cor. 13[4, 6, 7] (Moffatt).

in the studio of Paul's imagination for that famous little
vignette of the ideal man ? " [1]

But it is when we turn to *the teaching of the historic
Jesus* that the real range and extent of Paul's knowledge stands revealed. There are, first of all, certain
passages where Paul expressly quotes sayings of Jesus.
In treating of marriage and divorce, for example, he
is careful to distinguish between primary rulings
which have Christ's direct authority behind them, and
secondary rulings which carry only apostolic sanction.
Of the former, he says " these are the Lord's instruc-
tions, not mine " ; of the latter, " these are my instruc-
tions, not the Lord's." [2] Dealing at a subsequent point
in the same chapter with another problem of social
ethics, he introduces his advice with the words, " I have
no orders from the Lord, but I will give you the opinion
of one whom you can trust, after all the Lord's mercy to
him." [3] Here we have a clear indication of the decisive
importance Paul attached to authentic words of Jesus.
Another direct reference to Jesus' teaching is present in
the words, " Even so hath the Lord ordained, that they
which preach the gospel should live of the gospel." [4]
Again, Paul quotes Jesus' picture of the coming consummation. " This we say unto you *by the word of the
Lord* . . . the Lord Himself shall descend from heaven
with a shout, with the voice of the archangel, and with
the trump of God." [5] There is also the " unwritten
saying " quoted in Paul's address to the elders at
Miletus : " Remember the word of the Lord Jesus, how
He said, It is more blessed to give than to receive." [6]

---

[1] *The Place of Jesus Christ in Modern Christianity*, 81.
[2] I Cor. 7[10-12]. Cf. Matt. 19[6-9]. [3] I Cor. 7[25] (Moffatt).
[4] I Cor. 9[14]. Cf. Luke 10[7]. [5] I Thess. 4[15 f.]. Cf. Matt. 24[30 f.]
[6] Acts 20[35]. This has no Gospel parallel ; but the same thought
is presented in Luke 14[12-14].

In addition to these direct citations, there are numerous passages in Paul where indirect reminiscences of Jesus' teaching are very apparent.[1] Thus the instruction to " render to all their dues, tribute to whom tribute is due, custom to whom custom," [2] clearly presupposes Jesus' famous declaration about Caesar's rights and God's.[3] When Paul, in the course of a summary of the Christian's ethical duties, writes " Bless them which persecute you. Recompense to no man evil for evil. If thine enemy hunger, feed him ; if he thirst, give him drink," [4] we are at once reminded of the words in the sermon on the mount, " Love your enemies, bless them that curse you, do good to them that hate you." [5] It is from Jesus that Paul has taken his dramatic picture of the thief in the night.[6] Jesus spoke of a faith which could move the mountains, and Paul reproduces the image in his great hymn to love.[7] The apostle's repeated warnings against an unchristian use of the critical faculty point back to the Gospel passage beginning " Judge not, that ye be not judged." [8] " Be careful for nothing," writes Paul to the Philippians, using the same word ($\mu\epsilon\rho\iota\mu\nu\hat{\alpha}\tau\epsilon$) which occurs in Jesus' injunction, " Take no thought for your life." [9] The true inwardness of the new religion was stressed by Jesus when He affirmed that nothing outside of a man could defile him : this has a parallel in Paul's declaration, " I know, *and am persuaded by the Lord Jesus* " (a significant phrase in this connection) " that there is nothing unclean of itself :

[1] A. Titius, *Der Paulinismus*, 11 ff., has a very careful and elaborate investigation of this question.   [2] Rom. 13[7].

[3] Matt. 22[21].   [4] Rom. 12[14.17.20].   [5] Matt. 5[44].

[6] I Thess. 5[2 ff.]. Cf. Matt. 24[36.43 f.]

[7] I Cor. 13[2]. Cf. Matt. 17[20].

[8] Rom. 14[4.10.13]. Cf. Matt. 7[1 ff.]

[9] Phil. 4[6]. Cf. Matt. 6[25].

but to him that esteemeth any thing to be unclean, to him it is unclean." [1] In the prayer which He taught His disciples and in the words expounding it, Jesus revealed the essential connection which exists between human forgiveness and divine : Paul reproduces this idea in a way which makes it almost certain that he knew the Lord's Prayer well, although there is no explicit allusion to it in his epistles.[2] On the primary duty of loving one's neighbour, Paul speaks almost in the very words of his Master.[3] When the apostle, at the opening of his hymn to love, repudiates certain forms of religion which make a brave outward show and are eloquent in words, we seem to be hearing an echo of Jesus' warning, " Not every one that saith to Me, Lord, Lord, shall enter into the kingdom of heaven." [4] The strong statement, " Ye cannot drink the cup of the Lord, and the cup of devils," points back to one equally uncompromising, " No man can serve two masters. Ye cannot serve God and mammon." [5] Further illustrations could be given ; but enough has been said to show how wide and accurate was Paul's knowledge of the sayings of Jesus.[6] Resch has argued that Paul (whose epistles, of course, were written before our Gospels in their present form appeared) had at his disposal some earlier docu-

[1] Rom. 14[14]. Cf. Mark 7[15].

[2] Col. 3[13]. Cf. Matt. 6[12.14 f.]. E. F. Scott argues, on the basis of this text in Colossians, for a knowledge of the Lord's Prayer. *Colossians*, 72 (*MNTC*).

[3] Rom. 13[9]. Cf. Matt. 22[39 f.].

[4] I Cor. 13[1 ff.]. Cf. Matt. 7[21].

[5] I Cor. 10[21]. Cf. Matt. 6[24].

[6] *E.g.* Rom. 2[9], Matt. 15[14] (the blind leading the blind) ; Rom. 16[19], Matt. 10[16] (serpents and doves) ; I Cor. 1[22], Mk. 8[11 f.] (seeking a sign) ; I Cor. 7[7], Matt. 19[12] (marriage) ; II Cor. 5[10], Matt. 25[31] (Jesus as Judge) ; Phil. 3[8], Matt. 16[26] (losing and gaining) ; I Thess. 2[15], Matt. 23[31] (killing the prophets); I Thess. 5[6 ff.], Matt. 24[42] (watchfulness).

ment, a collection of Jesus' sayings of which the evangelists themselves made use ; and this is certainly not impossible.[1] But whether the apostle had a written source to draw upon or not, the fact is abundantly clear that stored within his mind was a great multitude of the memorable and decisive words which his Lord, in the days of His flesh, had spoken.

We can go further than this. Apart from direct quotations and indirect reminiscences of particular sayings, Paul's fundamental positions and the whole tone and trend of his religious teaching are a legacy from the historic Jesus. " The distinctively Christian thought of God goes back in the completest possible way to the mind that was in Christ Jesus Himself." [2] At various points in our study we have had occasion to observe Paul's indebtedness. We found, for example, that his doctrine of justification has its roots in certain of Jesus' greatest parables.[3] His teaching on adoption reflects the Master's deep sayings on the Fatherhood of God and the blessedness of the child-heart in religion.[4] His thought of faith is entirely in line with the Gospel conception.[5] His eschatology reproduces many of the leading features of Jesus' pictures of the coming consummation.[6] We need not recapitulate these matters here. But one or two additional points where Paul stands in Jesus' debt call for mention.

Take the apostle's radical attitude to *the law*. It is sometimes maintained that here he was an innovator. But this is not so. For in Jesus' words and deeds the

---

[1] A. Resch, *Agrapha*, 28 f.
[2] J. Baillie, *The Interpretation of Religion*, 435.
[3] See pp. 252 f.　　　　　　　　[4] See pp. 254 f.
[5] See pp. 176 f.　　　　　　　　[6] See p. 263.

decisive break with the law was already foreshadowed.
What do the brief parables about the patched garment
and the new wine mean if not that the doom of legalism
was imminent ? [1] Openly and fearlessly Jesus attacked
the spirit which was exalting the minutiae of tradition
above the living word of God.[2] The new morality which
He taught was too essentially inward to be compatible
with the legalist spirit. His own way of welcoming
sinners involved a clean break with Pharisaism's most
rooted ideas. It might indeed be urged that the passage
where Jesus speaks of coming " not to destroy but to
fulfil " the law points in an opposite direction.[3] But
surely the intention of the words is not to rehabilitate
legalism, but to stress the duty of obedience to God's
revealed will as distinct from the formal observance of a
pettifogging legislation which carried no divine sanction
whatever ; and moreover, the incarnation could be
called a " fulfilling " of the law in the sense of Paul's
statement that " the law was our schoolmaster to bring
us unto Christ." [4] In any case, the Gospels make it
perfectly clear that it was Jesus' collision with the law
which led to His rejection by the leaders of religion and
ultimately to His death. Paul's radical attitude was
thus no innovation. Here again he was following in the
footsteps of the Jesus of history. He was but leading

---

[1] Mark 2[21 f.]   [2] Mark 7[8].   [3] Matt. 5[17 ff.]
[4] Gal. 3[24]. Some scholars regard Matt. 5[18-19] as unauthentic.
A. S. Peake suggests that these verses reflect a later controversy :
they are Jewish-Christian in origin, and Jesus is here made to dis-
avow the Pauline position (art. " Law," in *HDCG*, ii. 15). So also
P. Feine, " Die beiden Verse sind ein Einschub des Evangelisten,
der die Stelle damit für seine eigene Zeit zurechtrückt " (*Theologie
des Neuen Testaments*, 43). E. F. Scott, on the other hand, holds
that " there is no sound reason for questioning their authenticity "
(*The Ethical Teaching of Jesus*, 31). This is confirmed by the parallel
in Luke 16[17].

to its logical and inevitable issue a movement his Master had begun.

Again, take Jesus' teaching on *the kingdom of God*. At first sight, it is perhaps surprising that this conception, so prominent in the Synoptic Gospels, holds no great place in the epistles. But Paul, writing to Gentile Christians, would doubtless feel constrained to translate into other terms an idea whose background and associations were predominantly Jewish. It is noteworthy that where the phrase does occur in the epistles, it is used quite in the spirit of Jesus : there is the familiar double aspect of the kingdom, as a present actuality and a future hope. When Paul writes, " The kingdom of God is not meat and drink ; but righteousness, and peace, and joy in the Holy Ghost," [1] or " God hath translated us into the kingdom of His dear Son," [2] or " The kingdom of God is not in word, but in power," [3] clearly it is the thought of the kingdom as already established on the earth that is in his mind. On the other hand, when he writes, " Flesh and blood cannot inherit the kingdom of God," [4] or " They which do such things shall not inherit the kingdom of God," [5] he is looking beyond the present to the day when the kingdom will break in as a direct act of God. But the substance of Jesus' kingdom-preaching is to be found in Paul even where the term itself does not appear. Whenever the apostle speaks of life as the great correlative of salvation, whenever he dwells on the blessedness of the sons of God, echoes of the Master's proclamation of the kingdom can be heard. Here again his faithfulness to the Jesus of history stands revealed.

Most important of all, however, is the matter of

[1] Rom. 14[17].   [2] Col. 1[13].

[3] I Cor. 4[20].   [4] I Cor. 15[50].   [5] Gal. 5[21].

Paul's *Christology*. It is in regard to this that the charges of innovation and misconstruction have been most confidently affirmed. The apostle's doctrine of Christ, it is said, and Jesus' self-estimate, are radically different : there is no basis in the latter for the former.

What are the facts ? It is a point of first-class importance that there never was any disagreement between the primitive Christian community and Paul on the ground of Christology.[1] This fact has not received the emphasis it deserves. Criticisms of various kinds the apostle to the Gentiles had to meet from his fellow-Christians, and more than once there was a serious clash of opinion ; but the one point on which he seems never to have been challenged was his doctrine of Christ. Leaders of the Jerusalem Church, he tells us, examined him carefully on the Gospel he was preaching.[2] But the central matter—his teaching about Christ —was not called in question. Strange, surely, that the very point at which modern critics grow most vociferous in accusing Paul of innovation was one of the few points at which his contemporary critics had no fault at all to find in him !

The fact is, those who speak as if Paul were the creator of Christology are forgetting that there was a Church and a Gospel and a Christian mission before ever Paul was converted. *Vixere fortes ante Agamemnona multi.* There were men " in Christ before me," says the apostle, regretting his life's lost years.[3] Problems in abundance the story of the earliest Christianity raises : [4]

---

[1] Wernle, *Jesus und Paulus*, 50. [2] Gal. 2[2 ff.]

[3] Rom. 16[7]. Even the Gentile mission had been begun before Paul—a point sometimes overlooked. Von Dobschütz, *Probleme des apostolischen Zeitalters*, 57.

[4] T. R. Glover, *Paul of Tarsus*, 198 : " The hardest of all periods in Church History for the historian to recover and to understand is

but some things are certain. It is certain that the Church from the first preached Christ as Messiah and Lord and Judge.[1] It is certain that the Christians believed that their Lord had poured out His Holy Spirit upon them.[2] It is certain that through Him they were conscious of forgiveness and full salvation.[3] It is certain that they realized His presence in the breaking of bread, and worshipped Him with prayers and hymns in a way that was an implicit confession of His divinity.[4] All this was in the common stock of Christian teaching before Paul had spoken a single word for Christ. There are passages in his epistles where he quotes the very words of primitive creeds and confessions of faith. " I delivered unto you," he tells the Corinthians, " that which I also received,"—and then follows a summary of doctrine which is plainly of early origin.[5] At the opening of the epistle to the Romans, a similar brief statement is found.[6] When Paul uses the phrase " Jesus is Lord," he is quoting what was probably the oldest of Christian creeds : there is reason to suppose that this was the formula used in baptismal confession.[7] No doubt Paul, in the course of long and deep reflection on the mystery of Christ, has gone beyond these comparatively rudimentary positions of the primitive community : he has done this, for example, in his doctrine of pre-existence and of Christ's place as agent in the work of

that short interval, variously estimated between one year and six years, that lies between the Crucifixion and Paul's journey to Damascus."   [1] Acts 2[36], 10[42].

   [2] Acts 2[33]. H. J. Holtzmann, *Neutestamentliche Theologie*, i. 446 : " Die Urchristenheit war eine Inspirationsgemeinde."

   [3] Acts 2[38], 4[12].

   [4] Acts 2[42], 7[59], Col. 3[16]. E. F. Scott believes that in Eph. 5[14] we have a quotation from one of the primitive hymns. *Ephesians*, 231 (*MNTC*).   [5] I Cor. 15[3 ff.]   [6] Rom. 1[3 ff.]

   [7] Rom. 10[9], I Cor. 12[3], Phil. 2[11] ; cf. Acts 2[38], 19[5].

creation.[1] But the circumstance that his Christology stood unchallenged means that nothing in it was felt to be alien to the fundamental tenets of the Church. He was simply making explicit what had been present in germ in the Christian attitude to Jesus from the first. Even pre-existence was less an arbitrary importation than an inference from acknowledged fact.

Now the importance of all this for our present purpose will become evident when it is remembered that behind the Christology of the earliest community (and therefore behind the Christology of Paul) stood the Christology of Jesus Himself. Lake has recently revived the notion that the Jesus of the Gospels never intended to claim for Himself Messianic rights or divine Sonship, and that it was the error of His too enthusiastic followers and apostles which clothed Him with that dignity.[2] All that can be said about this theory is that every page of the Gospels discredits it. Our certainty that Jesus believed Himself to have come forth from the very bosom of God is based on something more fundamental than isolated passages.[3] Such passages, indeed, abound, and their cumulative effect is great. There is the famous declaration, " All things are delivered unto Me of My Father : and no man knoweth the Son, but the Father." [4] There is the prophetic manifesto at the opening of the ministry, clinched by the words, " This day is this scripture fulfilled in your ears." [5] There is the assumption of the power to forgive sins.[6] There is the reply to the

[1] H. R. Mackintosh, *The Person of Jesus Christ*, 42, 74.

[2] *Paul : his Heritage and Legacy*, 43.

[3] The evidence has been admirably summarized by Principal Martin in his Cunningham Lectures, *The Finality of Jesus for Faith*, ch. iii.

[4] Matt. 11^{27}.

[5] Luke 4^{21}, Is. 61^1.

[6] Mark 2^5 ff.

Baptist's question about "One that should come." [1]
There is the demand for men's implicit trust and obedience. [2] There is the claim to be "greater than the temple," "greater than Solomon." [3] There is the story—most autobiographical of all the parables—about the rebel husbandmen, with its central words "I will send My beloved Son." [4] "Surely," says Professor J. A. Robertson, "in Him who thus dares to put upon the lips of God such words about Himself the confidence in His own consciousness of Sonship is complete." [5] But over and above these specific references, the Gospels set before us One whose conscious authority is unparalleled, whose moral perfection is dimmed by no faintest shadow of sin, whose will is God's will, whose very presence is salvation. This is Jesus' own tremendous claim.

Hence it was no perfervid apostolic hyperbole or idolatry which spoke of Jesus at the right hand of God, nor was Paul indulging in unwarranted speculation when he found in Christ the very meaning of the universe. For Jesus was never anything else but central to His own religion. The type of critic who regards Pauline Christology as a flagrant instance of affection outrunning judgment will doubtless always be with us ; but the lack of understanding is in himself and not in Paul. Daring the apostle certainly was in his vision of the ultimate truth, but not too daring. If he saw Jesus enthroned in glory, he was but seeing what Jesus Himself had prophesied. If he dreamed of the wide universe as Christ's possession, he was but envisaging what Christ Himself had claimed.

Our conclusion, therefore, is this. The charge that

---

[1] Matt. 11³ ff.   [2] Mark 8³⁴.   [3] Matt. 12⁶·⁴².
[4] Luke 20⁹ ff.   [5] *The Spiritual Pilgrimage of Jesus*, 185.

Paul changed the character of the original Gospel is baseless. At all points, not least in his Christology, he was true to the mind of Jesus. By the grace of God within him, he was able to draw the overwhelming conclusions to which the life and teaching of Christ had pointed. He was no corrupter, as he has been called, of the faith once delivered to the saints. The very reverse is true. It was Paul, more than any other, who kept the new religion pure and uncontaminated and faithful to its great Original and Object, in days when danger and corruption were threatening it on every side. This, and nothing less, is our debt to the great apostle. His was the loyal mind that preserved Christ's essential Gospel intact for the world ; and his the spiritual genius that has enabled the Holy Catholic Church to realize something of the breadth and length and depth and height of the glory of her own eternal Lord.

III

One of the two questions which faced us at the opening of this chapter—the question of the relation between Paul's Christ-religion and the historic Jesus—has now been answered. We turn to the other : What was the apostle's final estimate of his Redeemer ?

That he recognised Jesus as *the long-promised Messiah* goes without saying. The day of Damascus settled that. The first and fundamental truth which flashed its way into his soul in that tremendous hour was that Jesus was alive. This could only mean that God Himself had set the seal to Jesus' Messianic claim. Jesus was Messiah. Such was the theme of the first Christian sermons Paul preached.[1]

[1] Acts 9[22].

But great and glorious as the conception of Messiah-ship was, it was not really adequate for Paul's purpose. At Damascus he had encountered One clothed in something greater than any outward dignity of office : he had found a personal Saviour. Henceforward, when Paul spoke of " Christ," the official sense of the term was quite submerged beneath the personal. All the local, national, and material ideas which Jewish Messianism had developed so strongly were completely transcended. Blessed in his own soul with so wonderful a redemption, Paul knew instinctively that no racial limits and no traditional categories could hold the Redeemer he had now discovered : His mean-ing, His message, and His mission were universal. Not a new Israel, but a new humanity, was to be His creation. " The first man is of the earth, earthy : the second man is the Lord from heaven." [1] Patriotic Jews whose thoughts of Messiah could not rise beyond One who would restore to God's ancient people their vanished splendours and revivify the dreams that had died were falling infinitely short of the glorious truth. Here was One sent by God to deal with a foe far stronger and more deeply entrenched than the foreign legions that offended His people's nationalism and desecrated the land they loved, One whose campaign was " not against flesh and blood, but against prin-cipalities and powers," [2] against the unseen spirit-forces of the age that deluged the world in sin and all unrighteousness and ruin, against the legions of evil that went marching through the sanctities of the souls of men. Thus the very experience which revealed Jesus to Paul as Israel's Promised One was destined to break through all such categories ; and the very

[1] I Cor. 15⁴⁷.　　　[2] Eph. 6¹².

voice which rang the glad tidings through his heart, "Behold the Messiah," was to cry, almost ere the first echoes had passed, "A greater than Messiah is here."

All this shows once again how radically mistaken is the position adopted by many scholars from Baur to Lake, namely, that everything, or almost everything, in Paul's Christology can be traced back to an inherited pre-Christian Messianic dogma. If Paul and his fellow-Christians had gone to work in this way, simply fitting Jesus into an already existing scheme of things, they would have been implicitly confessing that Christianity to them was no more than a Jewish sect. But while the beginnings of Church history speak of two phenomena, a Jewish as well as a Gentile Christianity, the fact remains that it was *Christianity*, not Judaism. Christian Judaism, as von Dobschütz has done well to point out, would have been a very different entity from Jewish Christianity.[1] To none of the apostles, to Paul least of all, was Jesus a mere *plus*—something to be added on to a traditional dogmatic, and superimposed rather precariously on an edifice already erected. Jesus meant a new creation. Christianity was not a variety of Judaism that had cleverly made room for Jesus : it was a new thing, down to the very foundations.[2] When we find Lake asserting, "There can be little doubt that when Paul said that Jesus was 'the Lord' he was trying to expound his own belief that Jesus was the Hebrew 'Messiah' or 'Anointed One,'"[3] we can only reply that this is precisely what Paul was not doing. Any theory which pictures Paul

---

[1] *Probleme des apostolischen Zeitalters*, 54.

[2] Von Dobschütz, *Probleme*, 53 : "Nicht bloss ein Plus . . . es war tatsächlich doch ein Neues, vom Zentrum aus neu."

[3] *Paul : his Heritage and Legacy*, 122.

constructing his Christology in this artificial and mechanical way scarce needs refuting : it is negatived on every page of the epistles. Not so did those glowing confessions have their birth. They sprang from the experience of a man who had seen Christ face to face, who realized that Christ had done for him something which only the power of God could do, who knew what it meant to be led and guided by the Spirit of Christ every day he lived. -Messiah ? Yes, Jesus was Messiah—not the Messiah of Jewish dogmatic, but the suffering, triumphant, ever-living Messiah of God. " All the promises of God in Him are yea, and in Him Amen." [1] But the Messianic idea, even when redeemed from ancient prejudice, broke down before the glory of the fact. Paul could not rest in it. Here, as at so many other points of his experience, he found himself constrained to " forget the things that were behind," and to keep pressing on to where the wider horizons of God's truth in Christ were beckoning.

His most-loved name for Jesus was not Messiah but *Lord*. We have already seen that the true background for Paul's use of this term is to be sought not in the pagan mystery cults, as Bousset suggested, but in the Septuagint version of the Old Testament.[2] Primitive Christianity on Palestinian soil had learnt to worship Jesus as Lord before the Gentile mission had been inaugurated : the Aramaic liturgical expression " Marana tha " (" Lord, come "), is proof of this.[3] Psalms such as the one hundred and tenth—" The Lord said unto my Lord, Sit thou at my right hand, until I make thine enemies thy footstool "—were

[1] II Cor. 1[20]. [2] See p. 73.
[3] See p. 47.

regularly interpreted by the Church as referring to
Jesus. But Paul's usage of the title Lord went deeper.
Indeed, it would be true to say that for him it had
ceased to be a title. It had become the most sacred
expression of a personal devotion stronger than death.
Love and gratitude and loyalty were in it. The only
way to fathom the word's depths of meaning for the
apostle is to remember that the man who was using
it was conscious of a debt he could never repay. Luke's
account of the conversion most significantly represents
Paul as using this word in the very first sentence he
ever spoke to Jesus—" Who art Thou, Lord ? " [1]—
and it is certain that it was the Damascus experience
and the extraordinary life-revolution springing from
that experience which gave the name its innermost
meaning for Paul for ever afterwards. Everyone who
has experienced a great forgiveness, everyone to whom
the love of Christ has meant all the difference between
victory and defeat, between radiant happiness and
despair, will understand the spirit in which Paul spoke
of himself as Christ's " slave." [2] The ransomed soul
was bound to its Ransomer. No demand that Jesus
could make would be too great. Life's crowning joy
would be to toil unceasingly for the One who had
saved him from death and from something worse than
death. With glad heart Paul acknowledged himself a
bondman to the greatest of all masters. He was the
slave : Jesus was the Lord.

But did this name, as Paul used it, connote divinity ?
It seems impossible to resist that conclusion. In one
of the greatest passages he ever wrote, Paul hailed it as
the " name which is above every name." [3] According
to this passage, it is God Himself who confers it, and

[1] Acts 9⁵.   [2] Rom. 1¹, δοῦλος.   [3] Phil. 2⁹.

it is Jesus in His exalted state who bears it. On the day of Damascus, it was Jesus clothed in glory (δόξα) who had revealed Himself; and from that hour the thought of glory and exaltation was never far away when Paul called Jesus Lord. His place was at the right hand of God. To His authority there were no limits whatever. Before Him all created things would bow. Every voice in the universe would declare, " He is Lord of all."

That Paul held and preached the divinity of Christ becomes still clearer when his adoring language about Jesus' Lordship is taken in conjunction with his use of the name " *Son of God.*" Here again, psalmists and prophets had prepared the way; and Jesus' own filial consciousness, which had expressed itself in words treasured in the Church's memory from the very first, had given the warrant. To Paul, Jesus was Son of God in the sense that through Him the very nature and being of God had been perfectly revealed: He was " the image of the invisible God, the first-born." [1] Moreover, He had done for sinful men what only God could do. This was Paul's own impregnable conviction. None but God could justify; and yet through Jesus he was sure of justification. None but God could reconcile those whom sin had alienated; yet for the chief of sinners one meeting with Jesus had made reconciliation a fact. None but God could legitimately claim the full surrender of a man's soul; and yet Paul found himself constrained and glad to make that surrender in the presence of the cross where Jesus died. What could all this mean if not, in the apostle's own words, that " God was in Christ ? " [2] There are

[1] Col. 1[15]. [2] II Cor. 5[19].

303

passages, too, which suggest that sometimes in Paul's devotional life, in his practice of the presence of God, it was the face of Jesus that filled his vision ; and a man can hardly pray to Jesus without being sure of His divinity.[1] It ought further to be remarked that Paul's mysticism points in the same direction. The fundamental experience of union with Christ, which was the very heart of his religion, has no real parallel in ordinary human relationships : only One whose place was on the side of God and whose nature was divine Spirit could take men into such vital fellowship and unity with Himself. This was the place, and this the nature, which Paul was ascribing to Jesus when he called Him Son of God. Jesus was " declared to be the Son of God with power."[2] " The Son of God was not yea and nay, but in Him was yea."[3] Every occurrence of the name in the epistles is an adoring confession of faith, a confession based ultimately upon direct personal experience. " The life which I now live in the flesh, I live by the faith of the Son of God."[4]

But while Paul spoke thus clearly of the place which Jesus held on the divine side of reality, he could also speak of the Son as *subordinate to the Father*. We pointed out, in dealing with his cardinal conception of union with Christ, that it was never the way of the apostle to thrust God into the background or to stop short of faith's final goal.[5] In uncompromising monotheism he had been reared, and to his dying day a monotheist he remained. The most unequivocal statement of the subordinationist position occurs, of course, in the great picture of the goal to which the whole creation moves : " Then comes the end, when He hands

---

[1] I Cor. 2[1], II Cor. 12[8]. [2] Rom. 1[4]. [3] II Cor. 1[19].
[4] Gal. 2[20]. [5] See pp. 170 ff.

over His royal power to God the Father, after putting down all other rulers, all other authorities and powers. For He must reign until all His foes are put under His feet. . . . And when everything is put under Him, then the Son Himself will be put under Him who put everything under Him, so that God may be everything to everyone." [1] Echoes of the same conception are heard throughout the epistles. The very phrase " the God and Father of our Lord Jesus Christ " envisages a relationship of dependence.[2] In the pictures of Christ as " the first-born of a great brotherhood," [3] and as the Intercessor for men at the throne of God,[4] the same thought reappears. If Jesus has brought salvation, the ultimate ground of salvation is the will of God : it is " of God " that Christ is made our righteousness, and sanctification, and redemption.[5] If Christ came forth in the fulness of the time, it was God who sent Him.[6] If Christ has brought us peace, it is peace with God.[7] Summing up the meaning of the atoning death and resurrection, Paul can say, " It is all the doing of the God who has reconciled me to Himself through Christ." [8] Very clear and emphatic is the statement, " The head of every man is Christ ; and the head of Christ is God." [9] And the great passage which describes the humiliation and exaltation and final majesty of the Son closes with the words, which give the ultimate purpose of it all, " to the glory of God the Father." [10]

Here, then, we have unmistakable evidence that in the thought of Paul Christ is in some way subordinated

[1] I Cor. 15[24 ff.] (Moffatt).
[2] Rom. 15[6], II Cor. 1[3], Col. 1[3], Eph. 3[14].
[3] Rom. 8[29] (Moffatt).   [4] Rom. 8[34].
[5] I Cor. 1[30].   [6] Gal. 4[4].   [7] Rom. 5[1].
[8] II Cor. 5[18] (Moffatt).   [9] I Cor. 11[3].
[10] Phil. 2[11]. See J. H. Michael, *Philippians*, 97 (*MNTC*).

to God. Perhaps such an idea is inherent in the very conception of Sonship. In any case, it is clear that Paul's apprehension by Christ never destroyed nor even imperilled his monotheistic faith. Its reaction was quite different. The resolute monotheism which was the groundwork of all religion was now immeasurably enriched. With Paul, there never was any question of a δεύτερος Θεός : what had happened was that the one and only God now for the first time stood revealed. Eternal love had made itself incarnate, visible, tangible. Creative power had entered redemptively the field of sinful man's experience. In other words, while maintaining his monotheism, and while speaking of the Son as subordinate to the Father both now and in the coming consummation, Paul never conceived of Jesus as being anywhere else than on God's side of the line that separates divine and human.[1] It was by no fantasy of the imagination that he saw Christ occupying a place within the sphere of the Godhead. He knew, by the compelling force of revelation and by the sheer logic of spiritual experience, that no other place was possible. This conviction he has stated in words too plain and decisive to admit of any doubt. " In Him dwelleth all the fulness of the Godhead bodily."[2] " It pleased the Father that in Him should all fulness dwell."[3] Moreover, the juxtaposition of the names in such a greeting as that to the Romans, " Grace to you, and peace, from God our Father, and the Lord Jesus Christ,"[4] itself implies a confession of Christ's divinity.[5] The Church of the Thessalonians is " in God the Father and in the

---

[1] H. R. Mackintosh, *The Person of Jesus Christ*, 72 : " It is certain that he held the deity of Christ."

[2] Col. 2⁹.　　　[3] Col. 1¹⁹.

[4] Rom. 1⁷.

[5] So Sanday and Headlam, *Romans*, 16 (*ICC*).

Lord Jesus Christ." [1] And there is the Trinitarian
benediction, where " the grace of the Lord Jesus Christ "
is correlated to " the love of God, and the communion
of the Holy Ghost." [2] Only " a virtuoso in exegetic
evasion," to use a phrase of Denney's, [3] could explain
away the obvious implication of sayings so striking in
their individual purport, so convincing in their cumulative effect. Paul could never think of God without seeing
the face of Jesus, and he could never commune with
Jesus without feeling the presence of God. The Son
might be subordinate to the Father : yet in the deepest
sense of all, Father and Son were one—and one not only
in mind and will, but in nature and eternal being. Christ
was divine even as God was. He was the fullness of
heaven's wisdom, power, and love, the King of glory,
the everlasting Son of the Father.

Nothing in Paul's estimate of the Redeemer is more
illuminating than the way in which he correlates *Christ
and the Spirit*. He was, indeed, almost bound to take
this step by the very nature of the experience through
which he had passed and of the new life into which he
had entered. The characteristic mark of that new life
was power—power to overcome the world and to live
daily with a wonderful sense of zest and liberty and
moral victory, power to achieve the impossible. Inevitably the life in Christ connected itself with the thought
of the Spirit. For from the very first the Spirit of God
had been associated in men's minds with the gift of
power. This was the idea present in the Hebrew word
" Ruah," which meant literally " breath," or " wind,"
and then came to signify the invisible, mysterious,

[1] I Thess. 1[1].   [2] II Cor. 13[14].
[3] *The Christian Doctrine of Reconciliation*, 80.

superhuman force which sometimes leapt upon men and possessed them at critical moments of life, as in the stories of Gideon, Samson, and Saul.[1] That is to say, the power of the Spirit, as originally conceived, was abnormal in its nature, intermittent in its action, and non-ethical in its manifestation. With the coming of the great prophets, the whole idea was lifted to higher levels ; the moral aspects of the Spirit's working were emphasized ; inspiration now consisted, not in spasmodic miracles and deeds of herculean strength, but in knowledge of the mind and purpose of a righteous God and in complete self-dedication to His will.[2] Yet even so, the Spirit of God remained somewhat aloof and remote from the ordinary life of men in the world. A new orientation was given to the idea by its conjunction with Israel's Messianic hope. The Spirit of the Lord would rest upon the coming Redeemer in a unique and glorious way. His appearing would signalize the dawning of the era of the Spirit. The gift which had been the privilege and prerogative of the few would then be poured out " upon all flesh." [3] This was the great hope which the Church saw fulfilled at Pentecost. In the primitive Christian community there was a tendency at the first—perhaps quite natural under the circumstances —to revert to the cruder conceptions of the Spirit, and to trace His working mainly in such phenomena as speaking with tongues. It was Paul who saved the nascent faith from that dangerous retrogression. Not in any accidental and extraneous phenomena, he insisted, not in any spasmodic emotions or intermittent ecstasies were the real tokens of God's Spirit to be found ; but in the quiet, steady, normal life of faith, in

---

[1] Jud. 6[34], 13[25], 14[6.19] ; I Sam. 19[9].
[2] Is. 61[1] ; Zech. 4[6].   [3] Joel 2[28].

power that worked on moral levels, in the soul's secret
inward assurance of its sonship of God, in love and joy
and peace and patience and a character like that of
Jesus.[1] Schleiermacher's words express Paul's teaching
perfectly : " The fruits of the Spirit are nothing but the
virtues of Christ." [2]

But if old Messianic tradition and recent historic fact
prepared Paul's mind to connect the conceptions of
Christ and the Spirit, his own experience made them
virtually inseparable. In the vision of his conversion, it
was Christ clothed in His " glorious body "—$\tau\grave{o}$ $\sigma\hat{\omega}\mu\alpha$
$\tau\hat{\eta}\varsigma$ $\delta\acute{o}\xi\eta\varsigma$ [3]—His spiritual body, Christ as Spirit, whom
he saw ; and from that moment, his own life had been
flooded with a wonderful spiritual power. Hence he
could define Christ to the Corinthians as " a life-giving
Spirit." [4] The question therefore arises, Are we to go
further than this, and hold that Christ and the Spirit
are identical in the mind and religion of Paul ?

Some have maintained that the words in II Corinthians 3[17] settle the question in the affirmative. " Now
the Lord is that Spirit : and where the Spirit of the
Lord is, there is liberty." [5] It is a difficult verse ; but
when it is taken in close conjunction with what precedes
and follows, its meaning is clear. Lietzmann suggests
that if Paul had left out the middle clauses of his
syllogism and simply said " Now the Lord is liberty,"
he would have conveyed the truth he was aiming at,
while avoiding an unnecessary ambiguity ; and doubtless this is correct.[6] In any case, it would be precarious,

---

[1] Rom. 8[16], Gal. 5[22].   [2] *The Christian Faith*, 576.
[3] Phil. 3[21].   [4] I Cor. 15[45].
[5] In this, says Holtzmann " die ganze paulin. Christologie in nuce
beschlossen liegt " (*Neutestamentliche Theologie*, ii. 90).
[6] *I und II Korinther*, 180 (*HBNT*). Gore, following Hort, proposes an alteration in the text ; but this is unnecessary (*Belief in*

on the basis of this single passage, to argue for a complete identification on Paul's part of Christ and the Spirit. Elsewhere he speaks of the Spirit in relation to Christ in a way which makes it clear that he is referring, not only to the Spirit Christ possesses, but to the Spirit which Christ bestows on believers, the Spirit which in believers witnesses to Christ. " Anyone who does not possess the Spirit of Christ," he warns the Romans, " does not belong to Him." [1] The same idea reappears when he writes to the Philippians about " the supply of the Spirit of Jesus Christ." [2] " God hath sent forth the Spirit of His Son into your hearts," he tells the Galatians.[3] But this is not " identity." In discussing the historic basis of Paul's Christianity, we noticed that the Lord he worshipped still bore the lineaments of the Jesus who had lived and died, the Jesus who in amazing love to men had undertaken and in uttermost self-sacrifice had finished the work of reconciliation which God had given Him to do upon the earth. Certainly it would never have occurred to Paul that this personal Being, this historic Christ, and the Spirit of God were simply to be identified. This is further proved by such phrases as " the Spirit of Him that raised up Jesus from the dead," [4] and " God, who hath given unto us the earnest of the Spirit " ; [5] while the very phrase " the Spirit of Christ," which brings the two names so closely together, " implies an effort to distinguish." [6] At the same time, we cannot but recognize that the ideas have been blended in a remarkable degree. Continually, in Paul's mind, they are acting and reacting upon each

---

Christ, 254). Moffatt's translation, " The Lord means the Spirit," brings out the true sense of the verb.

[1] Rom. 8[9] (Moffatt).   [2] Phil. 1[19].

[3] Gal. 4[6].   [4] Rom. 8[11].   [5] II Cor. 5[5].

[6] E. F. Scott, *The Spirit in the New Testament*, 182.

other. Upon the man who is united with Christ by faith, the Spirit as a divine gift is bestowed ; and the Spirit, in turn, works for the strengthening and intensifying of that union. Only in the light of Christ can the Spirit's true nature be understood ; and only by the Spirit's aid can a man confess Christ's divinity, and say " Jesus is Lord." [1] By the fact of the Spirit, the fellowship of Jesus was made accessible for all believers. On the other hand, as Dr. Wheeler Robinson has well remarked, by the fact of Christ " the Spirit of God was personalized as never before, whilst the holiness of the Spirit was ethicized as never before." " If the Lord gave personality to the Spirit, the Spirit gave ubiquity to the Lord." [2] And always there was the thrilling certainty that the Spirit, as at present experienced, was only the " firstfruits," the " pledge and instalment," the " foretaste " [3] of a coming blessedness, when all believers, freed at last and for ever from the body of humiliation, would bear the very image of Christ, and be clothed in a spiritual body like that of their already glorified Spirit-Lord.

But the passages where Paul's thought climbs to its most stupendous heights and reaches a climax are those in which he speaks of Jesus as *the origin and the goal of all creation*. Men have always found, in the words of Professor R. H. Strachan, that " it is impossible for a Christian who thinks at all to have Christ in his heart and to keep Him out of the universe." [4] To have had a vital and redemptive contact with Jesus is to know,

---

[1] I Cor. 12³.
[2] *The Christian Experience of the Holy Spirit*, 136, 19.
[3] ἀπαρχή, Rom. 8²³ ; ἀρραβών, II Cor. 1²², 5⁵.
[4] *The Historic Jesus in the New Testament*, 72.

beyond doubt or challenge, that it is along the lines of
the pattern of the soul of Jesus that God's world-plan
is built. The man whose own life has suddenly leapt
into meaning beneath the touch of Jesus, who has seen
his own experience transformed from a chaos into a
cosmos by some never-to-be-forgotten Damascus encounter, has a right to claim that he has found the clue
to the riddle of life and destiny. In this sense at least,
Browning's bold words are true, that " the acknowledg-
ment of God in Christ solves all questions in the earth
and out of it." It is a root conviction of Christian
experience that a man who is united to Christ by faith
has not only found a personal Saviour : he has come
into touch with ultimate reality. The veil has been
removed, and he sees into the deep heart of things.
Gazing on the face of Christ, he is made to realize that
everything which is irreconcilable with Christ's Spirit
bears its doom within itself and must ultimately pass
away ; and that everything which shows true kinship
with that Spirit shall survive death and time's cor-
roding influence, and stand for ever. The fact of Christ
is the key to the meaning of the universe ; and Christian
experience will never consent to be robbed of the conviction that the Redeemer who has shown Himself of
absolute and final worth in the experience of the
individual soul must be absolute and final all along the
line of God's creation.

> " That one Face, far from vanish, rather grows,
>   Or decomposes but to recompose,
>   Become my universe that feels and knows."

This is the conviction in which Paul's thought of
Jesus culminates. " There is one Lord Jesus Christ,"
he tells the Corinthians, " by whom are all things, and

we by Him." [1] One of the most explicit statements of this high doctrine occurs in the letter to the Colossians. Jesus, he says, " is the image of the invisible God, the first-born of every creature : for by Him were all things created, that are in heaven, and that are in earth, visible and invisible, whether they be thrones, or dominions, or principalities, or powers : all things were created by Him, and for Him : and He is before all things, and by Him all things consist." [2] The full force of this great passage can be felt only when we remember the situation to which it was addressed. Heresy had reared its head within the Colossian Church. The finality of Jesus was being challenged. The aid of angels and other supernatural powers was being invoked. Man, it was said, was in the grip of cosmical forces and spirit agencies with which Christ by Himself could never cope. The human soul was a weak, helpless thing in a hostile universe. It must form protective alliances. It must call in angelic mediators. It must secure itself by propitiatory gifts and cults and worships. Jesus was insufficient. This was the situation with which Paul had to deal.

No mistake could be greater than to suppose that this is an old story, remote from our modern point of view, and irrelevant to our present problems. The form of the challenge to the faith has changed since the days of Paul : its substance remains the same. Is Jesus God's last word ? Or does His revelation but mark another milestone on the way ? Is there anything in Jesus that can make a man free and victorious in this world of rigid law and scientific necessity ? Or is such freedom a myth ? Does Christianity have anything to say to a man dwarfed into insignificance,

[1] I Cor. 8⁶.   [2] Col. 1¹⁵ ff.

perhaps even terrorized, by the vastness of the material
universe around him ? Take Sir James Jeans' vivid
words on this matter. " We find the universe terrifying because of its vast meaningless distances, terrifying
because of its inconceivably long vistas of time which
dwarf human history to the twinkling of an eye, terrifying because of our extreme loneliness, and because of
the material insignificance of our home in space—a
millionth part of a grain of sand out of all the sea-sand
in the world. But above all else, we find the universe
terrifying because it appears to be indifferent to life
like our own ; emotion, ambition and achievement,
art and religion all seem equally foreign to its plan.
Perhaps indeed we ought to say it appears to be ac-
tively hostile to life like our own." [1] No one can read
words like these without realizing how crucial is the
problem confronting faith in the modern age. And,
in essentials, it is the same problem which the apostle
had to deal with at Colosse, all over again.

How did he deal with it ? He dealt with it by point-
ing to the absolute priority and preeminence of Jesus.
How could the angelic beings supply anything that was
not already present in Christ ? He was above them
all. Indeed, He was the agent in the creation of them
all. And how could the universe have any terrors for
a man or a Church that belonged to Christ ? It was
in Christ that the universe itself cohered and held
together. Christ was " the first-born from the dead." [2]
His resurrection had already proclaimed the doom
of the hostile forces. He had overcome the world.
Satan had fallen like lightning from heaven. To
God's Christ the last word belonged. When Jesus
rose, the new age broke in. A new humanity came

[1] *The Mysterious Universe*, 3.　　　　[2] Col. 1[18].

into being. A new moral and spiritual order was established. The Church, where reconciliation between man and God and between Jew and Gentile was already a realized fact, was a microcosm, a presage of a yet more glorious development where all things— " whether they be things in earth, or things in heaven" [1] —would find their reconciliation in Christ. This was the apostle's answer ; and it still holds good. In every age it has been proved that there is in Christ a power to make men independent of all hostile forces whatever. In Christ, all the goodness and beauty and truth of life are focused. In Christ, all the lines of the divine plans for humanity and for the universe converge. And even while clouds and darkness are around our path, and we can know only in part and see but through a glass darkly, in Christ we can arise and shine, glad that our light is come and that the glory of the Lord is risen upon us.

The Colossian passage quoted above clearly implies a doctrine of Christ's *pre-existence*. From the foundation of the world and before it, the Son had His dwelling with the Father. This thought is present also where Paul uses the expression " God sent forth His Son." [2] When he speaks of Christ sacrificing His riches and becoming poor, " that ye through His poverty might be rich," [3] he is seeing the incarnate life against the background of a pre-temporal glory. The most notable occurrence of this conception is, of course, in the epistle to the Philippians, where Paul says of Christ—" Though He was divine by nature, he did not set store upon equality with God but emptied Himself by taking the nature of a servant." [4] The

---

[1] Col. 1[20].
[2] Gal. 4[4]. Cf. Rom. 8[3].
[3] II Cor. 8[9].
[4] Phil. 2[6 f.] (Moffatt).

incidental way in which these striking words are introduced—in the course of an exhortation to Christian humility and self-negation—indicates that the doctrine of Christ's pre-existence was, for Paul, less an elaborate metaphysical speculation than a self-evident inference from the plain facts of redemption. It has been argued that this whole notion came into Christianity by way of Judaism, that Paul was acquainted with Jewish habits of ascribing pre-existence to such objects of devotion as the Law, the Temple, the Sabbath and the Messiah, and that he simply transferred the category to the new object of his worship, Christ. But indeed it is hardly necessary to search for the origins of the conception in his Jewish heritage and training. For it is clear that as soon as he said " God was in Christ," as soon as he laid hold upon the principle of incarnation, this other idea was bound to follow. Unless the exalted Christ who had met him was simply a deified man (and for such a position there is not a scrap of evidence in Paul—a thoroughly repugnant idea he would have considered it), He must have held from eternity the glory which He now possessed. Bethlehem did not begin the story. Christ had been active in Israel's agelong history,[1] active and creative in the dim mists of the world's dawning day.[2] The human mind may feel itself inadequate to grasp the mystery opening up here before it ; but Paul would have said—and rightly—that the difficulties of the conception were as nothing compared with the difficulty that would have been involved in its denial. To him, in Deissmann's words, pre-existence was " only the result of a simple contemplative inference backwards from the fact of the spiritual glory of the present Christ." [3] And

---

[1] I Cor. 10⁴.   [2] Col. 1¹⁶.   [3] *St. Paul*, 170.

indeed, no man sees Christ correctly who does not see Him *sub specie aeternitatis*. Beneath the rather formidable doctrine of Christ's pre-incarnate life there is a real religious issue at stake. For, as it has been put, " a Christ who is eternal, and a Christ of whom we cannot tell whether He is eternal or not, are positively and profoundly different, and the types of faith they respectively call forth will differ correspondingly both in spiritual horizon and in moral inspiration." [1] Paul was convinced that the love of Christ which had flamed out in history at a definite point of time was really a love to which time was irrelevant. The love which had bled and died on the hill called Calvary, the love which for Stephen had made martyrdom a blaze of glory, the love which across the spiritual midnight of his own soul had cried " Awake, thou that sleepest, and arise from the dead, and Christ shall give thee light," [2]—that love had been the instrument of divine creation, the sustaining principle of the universe, and the dwelling-place of the faithful in all generations. Before the mountains were brought forth, even from everlasting to everlasting, all things were of love ; and love was Christ's, and Christ was God's.

If Paul thus saw in Christ the Alpha of the universe, he also saw in Him its Omega. It is the purpose, he declares, of God's providential ordering and guiding of His creation " that in the dispensation of the fulness of times, He might gather together in one all things in Christ." [3] Well might the Church of apostolic days, knowing the strength of the enemy and seeing its own advent hope receding down the multiplying years, begin to wonder whether the kingdom dream would

---

[1] H. R. Mackintosh, *The Person of Jesus Christ*, 460.
[2] Eph. 5[14].　　　[3] Eph. 1[10].

ever be fulfilled, or whether the new creation of Christ would perish in the desert far from the goal, and chaos and ancient night return. To this question—which is as haunting in the twentieth century as in the first—Paul's answer is clear and definite. The world is not moving on to chaos : it is moving on to Christ. In the person of Jesus lies the key to God's hidden plan with mankind and with the world. No longer is the mystery of things left dark and baffling and unrelieved. Those who ignore or refuse Christ, indeed, cannot share the secret : but to all who have eyes to see, it is an " open secret " now. To them it is given to realize that in the very constitution of the universe there is something which is on the side of the Gospel, and that the ultimate values which give life its meaning all converge on Jesus Christ, like mountain-paths converging as they near the summit. It is from Christ as God's creating and life-giving power that every principle of goodness and every deed of beauty and every word of truth have sprung ; it is in Christ that these things are sustained and have their real existence ; and they are never lost, nor does their influence ever die, for it is to Christ their goal that they move on. The universe may seem a riddle and a chaos ; but the Gospel has put the solving clue into our hand. This is Paul's argument. " So richly," he says, " has God lavished His grace upon us ! He has granted us complete insight and understanding of the open secret of His will, showing us how it was the purpose of His design so to order it in the fulness of the ages that all things in heaven and earth alike should be gathered up in Christ." [1]

This explains the impregnable confidence and the

[1] Eph. 1⁸ ff. (Moffatt).

deathless hope which shine out on every page of the epistles. To despair of the world, if we believe Paul, is simply to despair of Christ. It is to proclaim oneself an atheist. It is to take sides with the forces of Antichrist. For if the redeeming death and resurrection reveal a " love divine, all loves excelling," they reveal also a divine determination which nothing in earth or hell shall prevail to break, and a Christ who is marching from the green hill where He died to the throne of all the world. The faith which has been born of a personal experience on some Damascus road of the spirit cannot stop short of this. It knows that at the name of Jesus every knee shall bow. It knows that creation itself, bound long in affliction and iron, shall yet be reborn and redeemed. It knows that the everlasting gates of the universe shall lift their heads to let the King come in. And then the victory of the love which once agonized and died for reconciliation, the love which even now is interceding, shall be perfect and complete ; and Jesus, seeing of the travail of His soul, shall be satisfied.

I. INDEX OF SUBJECTS

Judgment, 150, 220, 233 ff., 268 ff

Justification, 11, 40, 148, 152 f., 243 ff.

Kenosis, 14

Kingdom of God, 148, 202, 293

Law, 12, 26, 38; what it included, 90; four Jewish attitudes to, 92 ff.; Paul's attitude to, 108 ff.; Paul's attitude compared with that of Jesus, 291 f.

Legalism, 84 ff.

Life, eternal, 192 f., 202

Lordship of Christ, 73 ff., 301 f.

Love of God, 140 f., 238 ff., 250

Love to Christ, 30, 165 f., 185 f.

Merit, 86, 180, 252 f.

Messiah, 9, 46, 120, 134 f., 138 f., 298 ff., 308

Mission-preaching, 5 f., 282 f.

Monotheism, 39

Mystery-religions, 64 ff.

Mysticism, 148 f., 160 ff., 200 f., 304

Nature, 56, 58

"Ordo salutis," 9 f.

Orthodoxy, 13, 215 ff.

Pantheism, 60 f., 166 f.

Parables, 252 f.

Parousia, 270 ff.

Paul, and Paulinism, 2 ff.; as a theologian, 20 ff.; as a Jew, 33 ff.; as a student of O.T., 39 ff.; as a citizen of Tarsus, 48 ff.; and the Stoics, 56 ff.; and the mystery-religions, 64 ff.; his sense of defeat, 96 ff.; his attitude to the law, 108 ff.; his conversion, 81 f., 122 ff.; his relation to the Jesus of history, 120, 273 ff.,

286 ff.; his missionary vocation, 141 ff.; his life "in Christ," 154 ff.; his eschatology, 199 ff., 261 ff.; his Christology, 294 ff., 298 ff.; his teaching on reconciliation, 204 ff.; on the cross, 226 ff.; on justification, 243 ff.

Paulinism, 2 ff.

Pelagianism, 85

Pentecost, 51, 261

Pharisaism, 36 ff., 92, 120, 251, 253, 292

Prayer, 162, 222, 304

Predestination, 15, 143 f.

Pre-existence, 295 f., 315 ff.

Propitiation, 214 ff.

Providence, 229 f., 317 ff.

Punishment, 219 f.

Ransom, 15

Reconciliation, 148 f., 153 f., 204 ff.

Redemption, 85, 116

"Religious-historical" school, 64 f.

Repentance, 95, 222

Representative, 242 f.

Reprobation, 15

Resurrection of believers, 266 ff.

Resurrection of Christ, 125 f., 133 ff., 226 f.

Righteousness, 36, 40, 84, 150, 245 ff.

Rising with Christ, 78, 192 ff.

Sacraments, 5, 78 f.

Sacrifice, 12, 236 ff.

Sanctification, 11, 147, 152 f., 257 f.

Septuagint, 44, 53 f., 55, 73 f., 125

Servant of Jehovah, 229

Shorter Catechism, 106

Sin, origin of, 27, 106; as personal, 104 f.; its seriousness, 106 f.; revealed by the law, 112; interrupts fellowship with God, 205 f.; divine re-

II. INDEX OF AUTHORS

INDEX OF AUTHORS

III. INDEX OF SCRIPTURE REFERENCES